1996

EXCEPTIONAL INDIVIDUALS IN FOCUS

Sixth Edition

James R. Patton
The University of Texas at Austin

Joseph M. Blackbourn
University of Mississippi

Kathleen S. Fad

Merrill, an imprint of Prentice Hall
Englewood Cliffs, New Jersey   Columbus, Ohio

Library of Congress Cataloging-in-Publication Data

Patton, James R.

  Exceptional individuals in focus / James R. Patton, Joseph M. Blackbourn,
Kathleen Fad.—6th ed.
     p. cm
  Rev. ed of: Exceptional children in focus / James R. Patton . . . [et al.]
  Includes bibliographical references in index.
  ISBN 0-13-502352-1
  1. Special education—United States. 2. Handicapped children—Education—
United States. I. Blackbourn, Joseph M. II. Fad, Kathleen. III. Exceptional children
in focus. IV. Title.
  LC3981.P38 1996
  371.9'0973—dc20   95-41896
          CIP

Cover photo: © Lawrence Migdale
Editor: Ann Castel Davis
Developmental Editor: Carol A. Sykes
Production Editor: Mary M. Irvin
Photo Editor: Anne Vega
Design Coordinator: Jill Bonar
Text Designer: DMC & Company
Cover Designer: Frankenberry Design
Production Manager: Laura Messerly
Electronic Text Management: Marilyn Wilson Phelps, Matthew Williams, Karen L. Bretz,
Tracey Ward

This book was set in ITC Bookman by Prentice Hall, Inc. and was printed and bound by
The Book Press. The cover was printed by Phoenix Color Corp.

 © 1996 by Prentice-Hall, Inc.
A Simon & Schuster Company
Englewood Cliffs, New Jersey 07632

Earlier editions, entitled *Exceptional Children in Focus*, © 1991 by Macmillan Publishing Company and © 1987, 1983, 1979, 1974 by Merrill Publishing Company.

Photo credits: pp. 2, 86, 212, 238, 282 by Anne Vega/Merrill/Prentice Hall; pp. 22, 48,
by Andy Brunk/Merrill/Prentice Hall; pp. 70, 108, 194, by Todd Yarrington, Merrill/Pren-
tice Hall; p. 130 by Barbara Schwartz/Merrill/Prentice Hall; pp. 158, 258, 302 by Scott
Cunningham/Merrill Prentice Hall.

Printed in the United States of America
10 9 8 7 6 5 4 3 2 1

ISBN: 0-13-502352-1

Prentice-Hall International (UK) Limited, *London*
Prentice-Hall of Australia Pty. Limited, *Sydney*
Prentice-Hall of Canada, Inc., *Toronto*
Prentice-Hall Hispanoamericana, S. A., *Mexico*
Prentice-Hall of India Private Limited, *New Delhi*
Prentice-Hall of Japan, Inc., *Tokyo*
Simon & Schuster Asia Pte. Ltd., *Singapore*
Editora Prentice-Hall do Brasil, Ltda., *Rio de Janeiro*

To our children, in whom we take great pride,
  Kimi,
    Audra, Alyssa, Lucian, Victoria,
    Mary, Tom

Preface

People who work with exceptional individuals sometimes convey the impression that life is always serious and tragic. Stressing the sorrows that arise for individuals with disabilities, these people tend to overlook the joys and rewards in the fields of human services and education. Moreover, professors in teacher training institutions so often preoccupy themselves with statistical data and basic facts that they neglect to give students a "feel" for exceptional people and what it is like to work with them. Thus, the unknowing may get the erroneous impression that working in these fields will be dry and tedious, or even worse, full of sadness.

We have found that working with exceptional children, youth, and adults is exciting, engaging, and uniquely rewarding. Despite occasional "down" moments, it is a world of joy and delightful communication. When working with exceptional persons, one's perspective becomes very important. We can mourn because a rosebush has thorns or rejoice because a thornbush has roses. Those who cannot see the joy and humor in life's struggles will soon find that the thorns drain their enthusiasm and strength to endure the difficult periods.

Shortly after undertaking the writing of this book, we looked up from our professional journals full of confusing definitions, elaborate theories, conflicting results, and current controversies. We suddenly realized we had fallen into the same trap as many others in attempting to teach students about exceptional individuals. We had blindly missed the essence of our field. Our preoccupation with academic analysis had distracted us from viewing the emotional side of our work. We had forgotten the joy of watching a child with a physical disability take her first steps, an adolescent with mental retardation get his first job, or a child with a behavior disorder bring his temper under control. We had even forgotten about the bad times—our disappointment when an elementary student with a learning disability returned from summer vacation having lost much that he had worked so hard to learn; our agony when we held down a self-destructive child with emotional disturbance; and our anxiety as we told desperate parents about the lack of local adult services for their daughter who was about to finish school.

If we, as professionals in special education and human services, do not project the joys as well as the pains of working with exceptional people, we are not projecting reality. If students enroll in an introductory course about exceptional people and they only learn how many times a child with Down syndrome rocks during lunchtime, the frequency of thumb sucks of a student with a severe disability, or the number of head bangs exhibited by a child with serious emotional disturbance, then it is no wonder that individuals with disabilities are thought to be odd. And it is no wonder that those of us working with people with disabilities are also considered a little crazy. It is imperative that we stress that exceptional individuals are just like the rest of us and should be included in ongoing events of everyday life—whether that be in a school setting, the workplace, or community.

Our message is simple: The fields of human services and education are exciting and vibrantly alive. Rather than permitting dry academic commentary, nit-picking detail, and only sorrowful emotional experiences to dominate introductions to exceptionality, basic courses should impart a flavor of the personal joy of dealing with exceptional people.

However, we are worried about misinformation and misconceptions concerning exceptional individuals. Please note that we consider exceptionality to apply to people whose physical traits, mental characteristics, psychological abilities, and/or observable behaviors are significantly different from the majority of any given population. This deviation can be in either direction and includes giftedness. Our concern derives from the fact that the misinformation and misconceptions can have a profound effect on the attitudes of the general public and therefore influence interpersonal relations and public policy.

With these ideas in mind, we have pushed aside traditional academic format and customary formalities in an attempt to provide you with a light, enjoyable reading experience. You need not take copious notes or scrutinize the print; just sit back, gather some basic information, and share with us the joys of working with exceptional people.

Acknowledgments

We are extremely grateful to our colleagues who have been part of the "Focus" family since the first edition and whose contributions have made this book so very special. Former co-authors include: Jim Payne, Jim Kauffman, Gweneth Brown, Richard DeMott, and Ruth Ann Payne. We are particularly thankful to Jim Payne (teacher, scholar, writer, entertainer, consultant . . . car salesman) for being instrumental in getting this family project going from the beginning.

We also want to thank Dr. Virgil S. Ward, who gave us helpful comments regarding giftedness, and Ed Polloway and Dave Smith, who shared some of their experiences with us. We are very appreciative to those reviewers who validated the goals we set for this edition: Margaret A. Cooper, West Georgia College; Jack Hourcade, Boise State University; Charles Hughes, Penn State; and Natalie Kees, Colorado State University. We are also very fortunate to be working with some wonderful folks at Prentice Hall/Merrill Education. We appreciate the support, assistance, and patience (as usual) that Ann Davis, Carol Sykes, and Pat Grogg showed us during the development of this book. We also want to thank Marie Maes for her copyediting skills and Mary Irvin for her production expertise.

J. R. P.
J. M. B.
K. S. F.

Contents

Chapter 5
Mental Retardation   87

Chapter 6
Autism, Pervasive Developmental Disorders, and Other Severe Disabilities   109

Chapter 9
Hearing Impairment   177

Chapter 10
Communication Disorders   195

1
INTRODUCTION TO EXCEPTIONALITY

A citizen advocate captured the essence of the paradox that many individuals with disabilities struggle against on a daily basis:

> It seems funny and ironic . . . that most people spend an exorbitant amount of time trying to distinguish themselves as unique and different while all that a person with a disability wants is to be just like everyone else.

The other day the little 4-year-old girl from next door came over and watched me rake leaves. For over 30 minutes she watched and then, out of the blue, said, "My daddy has a glass eye."

Well, how do you respond to that? Since I didn't know what to say or do, I just kept on raking the leaves and said, "Oh."

She continued, "Yeah, he really does, but I don't understand it. He can't see any better with it in than he can with it out."

Most people would agree that there's humor in the innocence of that 4-year-old's statement. It's funny to me, it's probably funny to you, and it was certainly funny to my one-eyed neighbor. Thank goodness we can occasionally share a laugh about a circumstance which involves an unfortunate condition.

DEFINITIONAL PERSPECTIVE

The title of this book, as well as the table of contents, indicate that we will be examining certain types of exceptionality. In so doing, two problems arise: first, what exactly makes one exceptional; and second, how does one select only a few topics from a potential vast array of choices? This chapter is designed to answer these two questions as well as provide a backdrop for approaching all of the other chapters in the book.

As the citizen advocate's statement suggests, individuals who are different in some way often have to struggle to be treated like others. This is not to say that persons who are exceptional in some way do not want to have an individuality of their own. The message is that for too long difference has meant different treatment rather than acceptance and inclusion. What is desirable is a scenario where we can celebrate difference in a context of acceptance and support.

Nature of Exceptionality

A generally accepted international, federal, provincial, or state definition of exceptionality does not exist. The notion of exceptionality suggests something that is noticeably different. Sometimes, the term is misinterpreted to mean above average only, as reflected in the Dear Abby letter in Figure 1.1. In addition to reprimanding the letter writer, Abby's response addresses the narrow definition of exceptionality that is often associated with the term *exceptionality*.

The concept of exceptionality that is used in this book includes the ideas expressed in the Dear Abby response and adds some additional features that pertain to the conditions covered in the chapters that follow.

> Exceptionality refers to individuals, including children, youth, and adults, whose behavior and/or features deviate from the norm, either above or below, to such an extent that special needs are present and certain services and/or supports may be warranted.

Although this perspective provides a guide for understanding exceptionality, it also has some inherent problems. First, how much deviation is needed to make one exceptional? This is an obvious problem with a condition like behavior disorders. Second, how does one determine what the norm is in a society where normal is hard to define? Norms are influenced significantly by factors such as culture and context. Third, must one require services to be considered exceptional? It is very possible for a person to have special needs but not require services or supports or only require such interventions for a limited

Figure 1.1

Dear Abby

Reader Takes Exception To Use of 'Exceptional'

By Abigail Van Buren

DEAR ABBY: You recently published a letter from the mother of a Mongoloid child in which she refers to him as "exceptional" and "special." I must thank you for printing such letters, since they always give me a good laugh.

Imagine having the gall to use words describing excellence, superiority and noteworthiness in reference to people with mental and physical deficiencies.

I can hardly wait for a SWAT team to discover that their "special weapons" are slingshots, or to hear of the shock of a teacher who has been refused tenure as a result of his or her "exceptional" work in the field of education. —WILLIAM G. ANDERSON JR.

DEAR MR. ANDERSON: My Webster's New Collegiate Dictionary defines "exceptional" as "forming an exception: rare." Also "better than average" and "BELOW average."

And "special" is defined as "that which is distinguished by some unusual quality; being other than usual; unique."

I am always pleased when a reader "gets a good laugh" from something in my column, but the letter I published about the Down Syndrome (please, not "Mongoloid") child was not meant to be amusing. Furthermore, what gives you a good laugh strikes me as being FUNNY—meaning "different from the ordinary." And more than a little cruel.

Source: Taken from the DEAR ABBY column by Abigail Van Buren. © UNIVERSAL PRESS SYNDICATE. Reprinted with permission. All rights reserved.

amount of time. These are legitimate concerns, and unfortunately, they do not lead to easy solutions. However, if the above definition can be considered a general guide that does not lead immediately to eligibility criteria, then it can serve as a global way of considering those individuals who fit the concept of exceptionality.

Terminology

This section on terminology addresses three major topics. First, an attempt to clarify the difference between the terms *disability* and *handicap* is undertaken. Second, a discussion of "person first" language is presented. Lastly, a primer on frequently used abbreviations and acronyms is provided.

A considerable amount of confusion and misapplication continues regarding the use of the terms *disability* and *handicap*. Currently, the term *disability* is the preferred terminology, and most professional and advocacy groups support its usage. However, the use of the term *handicap* is still prevalent in the popular media (e.g., headlines using the term *handicap*), professional literature (e.g., visual handicap), and public policies (e.g., signage for handicapped parking).

The two terms do have different meanings. Using Govig's (1982) fundamental ideas, the two concepts can be distinguished in the following way. *Disability* is a general term that describes any temporary or long-term reduction of a person's activity or ability as a result of an acute or chronic condition. *Handicap* refers to the additional negative burden placed by society on an individual through barriers affecting areas such as access, transportation, and attitude. Ramsey (in Orlansky & Heward, 1981) provides a good example of how this plays out in reality.

> Take a man who has been a carpenter for twenty years. He's skilled. He belongs to a union. One day on the job, he hacks off several fingers on his right hand. At that point, he has a disability, because everyone else has ten fingers and he doesn't. Now he probably would still be able to do carpentry work. He may have to do it a little bit different from before. It becomes a handicapping condition when, let's say, the labor union to which he belongs says, "Hey, man, we can't keep you on any more because the insurance will not cover you, and you are a risk. We feel like you can't do the work any more, because you don't have all ten fingers." At that point in time, his disability has become a handicapping condition (p. 166).

It is now convention when referring to individuals with disabilities to use person first language. This stylistic convention stresses that, for an individual with a disability, attention should be directed first to the person him- or herself and second to the disabling condition. Therefore, the phrase "adult with a learning disability" is preferred over "learning disabled adult." As can be seen in the latter expression, emphasis is on the condition rather than the person. It should be noted that even knowledgeable people will lapse back into the older convention from time to time, and the older phrasing will appear in materials that were published before a few years ago. Nevertheless, person first language should be used at all times in all current contexts.

The field of human services, including special education, rehabilitation, and social work, is prone to use shortcuts regarding commonly used terms, resulting in a plethora of abbreviations and acronyms that only insiders might recognize. To assist the person new to the field, a list of abbreviations and acronyms is provided in Table 1.1. This particular list is not exhaustive but does include many of the most frequently used expressions.

Table 1.1
Commonly Used Abbreviations

Abbrev	Meaning	Abbrev	Meaning
AAMR	American Association on Mental Retardation	IFSP	individual family service plan
		IHP	individualized habilitation plan
ADA	Americans with Disabilities Act	ITP	individual transition plan
ADHD	attention deficit/hyperactivity disorder	IWRP	individualized written rehabilitation plan
ASL	American Sign Language	LD	learning disability
BD	behavior disorder	LDA	Learning Disabilities Association
CBA	curriculum-based assessment		
CBM	cognitive behavior modification	LEA	local education agency
CCTV	closed-circuit television	LEP	limited English proficiency
CEC	Council for Exceptional Children	LRE	least restrictive environment
		MR	mental retardation
CIC	clean intermittent catheterization	NTD	neural tube defect
		O&M	orientation & mobility
CMV	cytomegalovirus	OSERS	Office of Special Education and Rehabilitative Services
CNS	central nervous system		
CVS	chorion villus sampling	OT	occupational therapist
DD	developmental disability	PHI	physical & health impairments
DSM	Diagnostic and Statistical Manual of Mental Disorders	PL	public law
		PT	physical therapist
ED	emotional disturbance	REI	regular education initiative
EHA	Education of the Handicapped Act	RID	Registry of Interpreters of the Deaf
ELP	estimated learning potential	SEA	state education agency
EMR	educable mentally retarded	SES	socioeconomic status
ESL	English as a Second Language	SLP	speech/language pathologist
FAE	fetal alcohol effect	SPED	special education
FAPE	free, appropriate public education	TAT	teacher assistance team
		TBI	traumatic brain injury
FTT	failure to thrive	TDD	telecommunication device for the deaf
HI	hearing impairment		
Hz	Hertz	TMR	trainable mentally retarded
ICF/MR	intermediate care facilities for individuals with mental retardation	VH	visual handicap
		VI	visual impairment
IDEA	Individuals with Disabilities Education Act	WISC	Wechsler Intelligence Scale for Children
IEP	individual education program		

Categorical Distinctions

A discussion about the merits or problems of identifying individuals as having some type of exceptionality continues. Without question, strong arguments for and against labeling can be made. Nevertheless, most systems in operation today that involve individuals who are exceptional rely on the use of different categories of disability or superior abilities.

A number of sources can be consulted for a taxonomy of disabilities or giftedness. Disabling conditions and their resulting nomenclature used in schools are based on federal or state statutes. The terminology used to describe these conditions in adult settings may change, depending on locale and agency involvement. Various ways to subcategorize giftedness are discussed in Chapter 11. A way to organize the types of exceptionality discussed in this book is based on the areas of functioning that are the primary areas affected (see Figure 1.2). One must not overlook the fact that a person may have secondary problems in other areas as well and that some individuals (e.g., those with autism) have needs of such scope that they cut across all areas of functioning.

It is also noteworthy to point out that each area of exceptionality covered in this book represents a heterogeneous group of individuals.

Figure 1.2
Categorical Distinctions by Area of Functioning

Areas of Functioning			
Learning	**Socio-emotional**	**Communication**	**Physical** (Motor, Vision, Health)
mental retardation	emotional/behavior disorders	communication disorders	orthopedic/physical impairments
learning disabilities	socially maladjusted	hearing impairments	health impairments
attention deficit/ hyperactivity disorder			traumatic brain injury
			visual impairments
←	autism, pervasive developmental disorders		→
←	gifted		→

Within any of the categorical areas, much variation exists. With this in mind, caution must be exercised in discussing characteristics of a general nature; that is, one must not overgeneralize a set of characteristics to everyone within a given category.

Disability Statistics

Quantifying the extent of exceptionality is not an easy task. In discussing the number of individuals with various types of exceptionality, we must examine two different data sources: school-based data and adult data.

School-age statistics. The most complete source of data on students with disabilities is the *Annual Report of Congress* published by the Department of Education. The 16th Annual Report published in 1994 provided the following statistics on students ages 6 to 21 identified as needing special and/or related services for the school year 1992–93.

Specific learning disabilities	2,369,385
Speech or language impairments	1,000,154
Mental retardation	533,715
Serious emotional disturbance	402,668
Multiple disabilities	103,215
Other health impairments	66,054
Hearing impairments	60,896
Orthopedic impairments	52,921
Visual impairments	23,811
Autism	15,527
Traumatic brain injury	3,903
Deaf-blindness	1,425
TOTAL	4,633,674

When the ages 0 to 5 group of children with special needs is added to this figure, the number of children and youth served is 5,170,242. This figure represents approximately 6.4% of the population of all children and youth in this age group.

Adult statistics. Although the school-based figures are subject to error for a variety of reasons (e.g., interstate variation for determining eligibility), it is even more difficult to determine the number of adults who are disabled. As Scotch (1990) admonishes, "It is clear to most of us within the disability research community that there is a serious need for more and better data about people with disabilities in the United States."

As discussed in Chapter 14, approximately 49 million Americans have a disability. (Table 14.2 provides a more detailed analysis of the reported numbers.) In 1994, Lou Harris and associates conducted a study for the National Organization on Disability to look more closely at the level of participation of adults with disabilities, focusing on changes since 1986 and on the comparison to those who are not disabled. Highlights of findings include:

- Jobless rate of persons with disabilities did not improve—it remained at 66%.

- Persons with disabilities are better educated now and more likely to graduate than before but are twice as likely to have no diploma than those who are not disabled.

- More individuals with disabilities are college educated although it is still low—16%.

- Household income of persons with disabilities is still a problem—59% have annual incomes of $25,000 or less.

- Disability profile of respondents:

Physical disabilities	54%
Health impairments	26%
Sensory impairments	8%
Mental disability	7%
Unspecified	5%

- Of the respondents, 53% indicated that the onset of their disability occurred after the age of 39.

A number of conclusions can be drawn from the data from the Lou Harris survey and the school-based data. First, it is obvious that the adult data reflect the reality that as people get older, they acquire any number of physical and/or heath conditions that require services or supports. Second, the data do not represent an upward extension of the school-identified population. It is safe to say that many individuals with learning disabilities or emotional/behavior disorders are not being picked up in the adult studies of disability. Third, the disability statistics for adults must be examined with caution given the nature of disability in adulthood. In other words, some conditions that lead to recognition during school become more difficult to detect in adulthood settings, even though their impact on a person's life may be significant. It might be suggested that the categorical distortions between the school data and adult data are very much a function of the nature of adult services that determine eligibility as well as the ways the data are collected.

Disablism (Handicapism)

Many groups of people in our society are treated differently by the community at large as a result of being perceived in a less than favorable way. All of the categories of exceptionality covered in this book are vulnerable to devalued treatment. A concept that provides a framework for measuring mistreatment is *disablism*. The original term, *handicapism*, promoted by Bogdan and Biklen (1977) is revised in light of current preferred usage. Similar to racism, sexism, and ageism, disablism results in mistaken beliefs (stereotyping); irrational, preconceived opinions (prejudice); and ill-treatment (discrimination) on the part of individuals or society. Bogdan and Biklen defined handicapism as "a set of assumptions and practices that promote the differential and unequal treatment of people because of apparent or assumed physical, mental, or behavioral differences" (1977, p. 59). The following is an example of how disablism works:

Stereotyping:	viewing adults with mental retardation as childlike.
Prejudice:	leading to the belief that they are incapable of being responsible for their own behaviors.
Discrimination:	resulting in these adults being denied library cards or similar privileges.

Disablism can be manifested in many different ways. On a personal level, it can be displayed in avoidance behavior on the part of the person who is not disabled or by telling tasteless jokes that target people with disabilities. On a societal level, disablism can be seen in regulatory policies and practices such as in the example cited above. It can also be seen in the way individuals who are exceptional are portrayed in the media. From poster children to characters in motion pictures, ample evidence of disablist images abounds.

The portrayal of individuals who are exceptional in motion pictures is voluminous. As a matter of fact, 14 motion pictures that have won academy awards for best picture, best actor, or best actress have included characters who were disabled (Safran, personal communication, 1995). The portrayals have ranged from disablist (e.g., *Dr. Strangelove*) to inaccurate (e.g., *Charley*) to extremely realistic and well done (e.g., *My Left Foot*). Table 1.2 contains a list of many motion pictures that have characters who are exceptional or that address issues related to exceptionality.

BACKGROUND INFORMATION

Changes in Service Delivery

The last few years have brought the most recent wave of service delivery to individuals who are disabled. The three types of service delivery discussed in this section are depicted in Figure 1.3. The first definable approach involved the use of facilities as the primary venue for providing services. Characterized by institutional placements, sheltered employment, separate schools, and totally segregated classes, the thrust was to remove the person or student and take him or her to where centralized services were located.

This first wave, although still much in existence in some parts of the United States and many parts of the world, evolved into a services-based orientation. In this model, individuals might be pulled from the mainstream of society or general education, but an effort to integrate these students was present. This approach to service delivery could be seen in deinstitutionalization, transitional sheltered workshops, resource rooms, and self-contained classes in the neighborhood schools.

The most recent wave is characterized as supports-based. This approach advocates inclusion in the community and at school, accompanied by requisite supports to maintain the individual in these environments. Terms like *supported employment, supported living,* and *inclusive education* are commonly heard these days. The difference

Figure 1.3
Paradigm Shifts in
Service Delivery

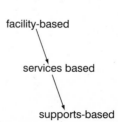

Table 1.2
Motion Pictures With Characters Who Are Disabled or Gifted

Title	Identifier	Title	Identifier
Awakenings	BD	Of Mice and Men	MR
Bedlam	MR	One Flew Over the	
Being There	MR	Cuckoo's Nest	BD
Benny and Joon	BD	Ordinary People	BD
Best Boy	MR	Other Side of the Mountain	PHI
Bill	MR	Patch of Blue, A	VI
Blackboard Jungle	At Risk	Philadelphia	PHI
Born on the Fourth of July	PHI	Places in the Heart	VI
Butterflies Are Free	VI	Rainman	Autism
Camille Claudel	BD	Regarding Henry	TBI
Charley	MR	Rudy	LD
Children of a Lesser God	HI	Scent of a Woman	VI
Coming Home	PHI	See No Evil, Hear No Evil	VI
Deliverance	MR	Sneakers	VI
Dr. Strangelove	PHI	Stand and Deliver	At Risk
Dream Team	BD	Sting, The	PHI
Edward Scissorhands	PHI	Sybil	BD
Elephant Man, The	PHI	Tim	MR
Fisher King	BD	Tin Man	HI
Forest Gump	MR	To Kill a Mockingbird	MR
Gaby: A True Story	PHI (P)	To Sir with Love	At Risk
Hand that Rocks		Wait Until Dark	VI
the Cradle, The	MR	Whatever Happened	
Heart is a Lonely Hunter, The	HI	to Baby Jane	PHI
I Never Promised You		Young Frankenstein	PHI
a Rose Garden	BD	Zelly and Me	BD
If You Could See What I Hear	VI		
King of Hearts	BD		
La Strada	MR		
Last Picture Show, The	MR	**KEY**	
Little Man Tate	G	behavior disorder	BD
Lorenzo's Oil	PHI	gifted	G
Man Without a Face, The	PHI	hearing impairment	HI
Mash	VI, HI	learning disability	LD
Miracle Worker, The	VI, HI	mental retardation	MR
Moby Dick	PHI	physical or health impairment	PHI
My Left Foot	PHI	visual imparment	VI

between physical integration associated with a services-based paradigm and inclusion, which is being promoted now, is that the latter concept implies a degree of acceptance and sense of community. It also underscores the notions of self-determination and empowerment, which are discussed later in this chapter.

Legislative Mandates

Legislation has played a major role in guaranteeing the rights and addressing the needs of individuals who are exceptional. Many pieces of legislation have contributed to the outcomes noted above, including the Developmental Disabilities Assistance and Bill of Rights Act of 1990 (PL 101–496), the Carl D. Perkins Vocational and Applied Technology Education Act of 1990 (PL 101–392), and Jacob K. Javits Gifted and Talented Students Act of 1988 (PL 100–297). Three federal laws stand out and arguably have had the greatest impact: Individuals With Disabilities Education Act (IDEA), Section 504 of the Vocational Rehabilitation Act, and Americans With Disabilities Act (ADA). These three laws are discussed below and highlighted for comparison purposes in Table 1.3 on page 16.

Individuals With Disabilities Education Act (IDEA) (PL 101– 476).   IDEA is the most recent reauthorization of the original Education of All Handicapped Children's Act (EHA), signed into law in 1975 as PL 94–142. Since 1975, this law has been reauthorized three times (1983, 1986, 1990), with each set of amendments having significant effects on the education of students with disabilities. When EHA was reauthorized in 1990, the name of the law changed to its current title. Furthermore, two additional disabling conditions (autism and traumatic brain injury) were added to the list of categories.

The major provision of IDEA is that all students ages 3 to 21 with disabilities are entitled to a free, appropriate public education in the least restrictive environment. Incentives exist for serving young children ages 0 to 2, and all states are providing such services. Key features of IDEA, along with a short description of what they mean, are listed in Table 1.4 on page 18.

Section 504 of the Vocational Rehabilitation Act (PL 93–112).   In 1973, amendments to the Vocational Rehabilitation Act were enacted. This law was most recently amended as the Rehabilitation Act Amendments of 1992 (PL 102–569). Section 504 of this act became the "bill of rights for people with disabilities" by ensuring that individuals with disabilities could not be discriminated against, particularly in the areas of education and employment. The significance of this legislation continues to this day. (Chapter 4 on Attention Deficit/Hyperactivity Disorder examines the importance of the law for obtaining needed accommodations in school settings.)

Americans With Disabilities Act (ADA) (PL 101–336).   Considered to be the most important piece of civil rights legislation to be enacted since the Civil Rights Act of 1964, ADA provides similar protections for and opportunities to individuals with disabilities. The scope of the law extends to both public and private settings, and affects employment, public services, transportation, public accommodations (e.g., restaurants), and telecommunications. Although some concern has arisen regarding how much of an impact this law has made on the lives of persons with disabilities, its intent is well founded, and its potential for making a difference is tremendous.

RECURRENT THEMES

Certain themes are woven throughout this book. They represent prevailing trends that are noticeable in the field of human exceptionality today. It is our opinion that these topics should guide our thinking as we begin to look more closely at the specific categorical areas that follow.

Inclusion

The intent of inclusion, as discussed previously, is for individuals who are different to be welcomed, accepted, and encouraged to participate as equal members of the group—whether the setting be at school or in the community. The following are some inclusionary practices:

School-based:
1. Educating students with disabilities in general education classrooms.
2. Creating opportunities for students with disabilities to make friends with students who are not disabled.
3. Allowing students with disabilities to participate in all facets of school life.
4. Providing needed supports to students so they can be successful in general education settings.
5. Teaching general education students about disabilities and individual differences.
6. Emphasizing that differences enrich us all.

Community-based:
1. Creating opportunities for adults who are disabled to participate with those who are not disabled.

Table 1.3
Comparison of IDEA, Section 504, and ADA

	The IDEA	Section 504	The ADA
Mission	To provide a free, appropriate public education (FAPE) in the least restrictive environment.	To provide persons with disabilities, to the maximum extent possible, the opportunity to be fully integrated into mainstream American life.	To provide all persons with disabilities broader coverage than Section 504 in all aspects of discrimination law.
Scope	Applies to public schools.	Applies to any program or activity that is receiving federal financial assistance.	Applies to public or private employment, transportation, accommodations, and telecommunications, regardless of whether federal funding is received.
Coverage	Only those who are educationally disabled, in that they require special education services, ages 3–21 years.	All qualified persons with disabilities, regardless of whether special education services are required in public elementary, secondary, or postsecondary settings.	All qualified persons with disabilities, and qualified nondisabled persons related to or associated with a person with a disability.
Disability Defined	A listing of disabilities is provided in the act, including specific learning disabilities.	No listing of disabilities provided, but inclusionary criteria of any physical or mental impairment that substantially limits one or more life activities, having a record of such an impairment, or being retarded as having an impairment.	No listing of disabilities provided. Same criteria as found in Section 504. HIV status and contagious and noncontagious diseases recently included.

Table 1.3 continued

	The IDEA	Section 504	The ADA
Identification Process	Responsibility of school district to identify through "Child Find" and evaluate at no expense to parent or individual.	Responsibility of individual with the disability to self-identify and to provide documentation. Cost of the evaluation must be assumed by the individual, not the institution.	Same as Section 504.
Service Delivery	Special education services and auxiliary aids must be mandated by Child Study Team and stipulated by the Individual Education Program.	Services, auxiliary aids, and academic adjustments may be provided in the general education setting. Arranged for by the special education coordinator or disabled student services provider.	Services, auxiliary aids, and accommodations arranged for by the ADA coordinator. Requires that accommodations do not pose an "undue hardship" to employers.
Funding	Federal funds are conditional to compliance with IDEA regulations.	No authorization for funding attached to this civil rights statute.	Same Section 504.
Enforcement Agency	Office of Special Education and Rehabilitative Services in U.S. Department of Education.	The Office for Civil Rights (OCR) in the U.S. Department of Education.	Primarily the U.S. Department of Justice, in conjunction with the Equal Employment Opportunity Commission and Federal Communications Commission. May overlap with OCR.
Remedies	Reimbursement by district of school-related expenses is available to parents of children with disabilities to ensure a FAPE.	A private individual may sue a recipient of federal financial assistance to ensure compliance with Section 504.	Same as Section 504 with monetary damages up to $50,000 for the first violation. Attorney fees and litigation expenses are also recoverable.

Source: Adapted with permission from the *Section 504 Compliance Handbook.* © Thompson Publishing Group (800)677-3789.

Table 1.4
Key Components of IDEA

Provisions	Description
Free appropriate public education	The primary requirement of PL 94–142 is the provision of a free, appropriate public education to all school-age children with disabilities.
Lease restrictive environment	Children are educated with nondisabled children as much as possible.
Individualized education program	All children served in special education must have an individualized education program (IEP).
Due process rights	Disabled children and their parents must be involved in decisions about special education.
Due process hearing	Parents and schools can request an impartial hearing if there is a conflict over special education services.
Nondiscriminatory assessment	Students must be given a comprehensive assessment that is nondiscriminatory in nature.
Related services	Schools must provide related services, such as physical therapy, counseling, and transportation, if needed.

Source: Smith, et al. Used by permission.

2. Educating the public about disabilities and individual differences and providing opportunities for interaction.
3. Encouraging friendships between adults with disabilities and others who are not disabled.
4. Welcoming and supporting newly hired workers who are disabled.
5. Ensuring that adults with disabilities are involved in age-appropriate activities.

Empowerment

Many professionals and parents realize that it is in the best interests of those with disabilities to be better prepared to make decisions about their own lives. Concerted efforts have been made to teach skills related to self-determination, thus empowering these persons to be more in control of their lives.

According to Wehmeyer (1993), self-determination refers to "the attitudes and abilities necessary to act as the primary causal agent in one's life, and to make choices and decisions regarding one's quality of life free from undue external influence or interference" (p. 6). In this definition, attitudes correspond to the personal beliefs and perceptions one has of oneself as well as the degree of control one has in a given environment. Abilities relate to the skills and proficiencies that are needed to be able to act as the causal agent in one's life.

In addition to having the self-confidence and skills to make decisions about one's life, it is equally important to have options from which to choose. The following excerpt from a position paper on self-determination developed by Arc of Texas (1995) illustrates this point:

> Integral to the notion of self-determination and choice is the necessity of having options. If there is only one option presented, there is no real choice. Choice requires personally meaningful options, access to information about the choices, and the skills and experiences to make responsible decisions.

Lifespan Perspective

The field of human exceptionality has been somewhat forced to expand its focus beyond the issues of childhood and adolescence. The vast number of individuals who are disabled, as suggested previously, creates a great need to look at disability from a lifespan perspective. Even for those disability areas that do not have large identifiable groups in adulthood, increased professional interest can be detected.

The main motivation of studying exceptionality across the lifespan is that disability in most cases does not disappear with the onset of young adulthood. There is ample evidence indicating that the incidence of many disabilities is a function of age, particularly middle age and older. Furthermore, attention to the many normative and nonnormative events in a person's life and their effect on functioning has intensified, as more researchers are studying the life experiences of people throughout adulthood.

It is important to stress that the issues of adulthood are vastly different from those of childhood. With this in mind, it is understandable that models of intervention used with children and youth are typically not appropriate for adults. If one studies adults with disabilities, then one must be sensitive to the complexities of adulthood.

Multicultural Considerations

In a pluralistic society where linguistic and cultural diversity is the norm, it is critically important that exceptionality always be considered in the context of a person's language and culture. From an educational perspective, school personnel must be sensitive to a student's values and background. Such an understanding should guide assessment, curriculum, management, and instruction.

Without question, it is often very difficult to determine the needs of a student whose language is not English and whose culture differs from what is expected at school. Because the issues associated with cultural diversity and disability are so important, we have dedicated an entire chapter to this topic (see Chapter 12).

Multidisciplinary Nature of Exceptionality

Given the range of needs that are demonstrated by individuals who are exceptional, many different professionals may be involved in working with such individuals. These professions include the following:

1. Medicine and Allied Health: neonatologists, pediatricians, neurologists, geneticists, psychiatrists, pharmacists, physical therapists, occupational therapists, speech/language pathologists, audiologists, and school nurses.
2. Psychology: school psychologists, clinical psychologists, psychometrists, child mental health specialists, and art and music therapists.
3. Social Work: school social workers, medical social workers, and case managers.
4. Education/Training: general educators, special educators, vocational educators, transition specialists, school counselors, employment specialists, vocational rehabilitation counselors, and recreation therapists.

With such an array of professionals potentially involved in the day-to-day lives of persons with exceptional needs, it is essential that collaborative working relationships develop.

Family Considerations

The impact of a disability on a family is tremendous—physically, emotionally, and financially. Family involvement has changed over the years
from passive roles to being encouraged to participate much more
actively. From IDEA's emphasis on parent participation in their child's
programs to the reality that parents may be the only case manager for
their adult child, a need to get families involved has emerged.

A change can also be noticed in that professionals are now focusing on families rather than on parents only. The needs of siblings and
extended family members have been identified as critical elements of
working with families. Much like the individual, families may need
varying levels and durations of support in coping with a member of
their family who is disabled.

FINAL THOUGHTS

As indicated in the preface to this book, our approach to human
exceptionality is a personal one. This is evidenced by the many
vignettes that begin each of the following chapters. By sharing these
personal stories that we or our closest colleagues have experienced, we
want to give the reader a "feel" for people who are exceptional and
what it is like to work with them.

References

Arc of Texas (1995). *Self determination*. Position paper, Austin: Author.

Bogdan, R., & Biklen, D. (1977). Handicapism. *Social Policy, 7*(5), 59–63.

Harris, L. & Associates (1994). *National Organization on Disability/Harris Survey of Americans with Disability*. New York.

Orlansky, M. D., & Heward, W. L. (1981). *Voices: Interviews with handicapped people*. Englewood Cliffs, NJ: Merrill/Prentice Hall.

Wehmeyer, M. (1993). Self-determination as an educational outcome. *Impact, 6*(4), 16–17, 26.

ONE

LEARNING AND BEHAVIORAL DISORDERS

2

LEARNING DISABILITIES

Anna was in the sixth grade. She was a good student in most respects. She tried hard and did acceptable work in most areas. She was easy to get along with and related well to her peers, but she just couldn't spell.

Most sixth-grade classes love art projects and mine was no exception. I had acquired a kiln and some clay discarded by another school in the district, and we were having a really great time making all kinds of things. Anna brought me a beautiful slab pot that she had just finished. It was about 2 inches high and 6 inches in diameter, and I commented on its nice form and proportion in addition to the quality of construction. Obviously elated, Anna said that she was going to label her bowl so that everyone would know what it was (she didn't like having it called a "pot") and hurried off to do the job. About 20 minutes later she was back with her bowl. In perfectly formed, 2-inch letters, she had written on the side of her treasure, BOWEL.

I worked with Josh for 8 months on penmanship. I felt he was really making progress. His writing was more legible, he reversed fewer letters, and he could now mark within the lines. On the last day of the school year, a small box was left anonymously on my desk. Inside was a small figurine of an owl with the following note:

25

Now that I think about it, it really wasn't bad when you realize that at the beginning of the year, he couldn't even hold a pencil.

Eddie could count and add. If you showed him 3 dots plus 5 dots, he would say 8. However, when presented with any numeral, he experienced difficulty identifying it. After 1 year, I was exhausted and frustrated with the entire process of teaching him the identification of numbers. As he arrived for the first day of school for the second year, he dropped by my resource room and asked, "Am I going to learn the names of my numbers this year?"

I responded, "I sure hope so."

He quickly replied, "Don't worry about it, there is always another year."

Dr. Fonerden:

I wish to explain to you a strange mental weakness, to which I have all my life been a victim. At the age of seven or eight, I could read quite well, but shut the book and I could not spell the smallest words. My aunt who instructed me, beleeveing that it was obstinacy on my part, turn me over to my grandfather, and he having punished me severely gave me a collum of words to commit by a certain time; but alas, when the time had expired, I could not spell the first word, which was urn. Hour after hour and day after day was I compeled to study over this word; but let me shut the book for ten minutes and I could not spell it right, except by chance, and to my utter mortification a little collored boy was called up to spell it for me, he having lurned it from hearing it repeated to me so often. At last to such an extent was I persicuted on account of this word that I detur-mined to run away . . . Now this peculiarity of my youth sticks by me still. When I went to sea, I toodk a dictionary, with the determi-nation never to return home until I had lurned to spell; but it was no use. If I had kept my resolve I should never have returned. The hours of study I have wasted in endeavoring to become a good speller would have given me a profession. For that which I read, if it excite any interest, becomes stamped upon my memory indelibly, with this single exception, that which I wonce lurne I never forget. When I left school I wrote a very good hand, but spoilt it in endeavoring so to disguise the letters, that they might pass for what they should be, instead of what they were. I had occasion very recently, to direct a letter to my sister, but could not do so untill I had looked over many books to find the name Rachal, which I could not spell. I have been puzzled to distinguish between the agative too and preposition to, and between the article the and the pronoun thee. Were I to write this over from memory a great majority of the words would be spelled differently.

. . . The chief difficulty that I have to contend with is this; that when I write the most familiar words, and then ask myself are they spelt right, some juggling friend whispers in my ear many ways of spelling them, and I became lost in a maze of doubt and conjecture. To no other than yourself would I make this humuliating confession; and only to you in the faint hope that you may suggest a remedy. If you can, all that you have done to develope my mind, and to strengthen my character, will be as nothing in comparison.

Yours, truly[1]

Patrick Milton Wills frowned as he closed the file folders containing the information presented at the eligibility meeting for Edwin and J. C. Fifteen years ago, when he first became director of special education for the Marion County Schools, he had anticipated that his job would become easier as the years rolled by. Instead, it seemed to him that the decisions he faced were getting tougher all the time. True, the decisions about Edwin and J. C. were not his alone. He was only one member of the eligibility committee that was to decide whether these students qualified as handicapped under PL 94–142, and therefore, were eligible for special education. But that didn't make it any easier for him to decide how he felt about these boys' education. "Fact is," he thought to himself, "I have my hunches about them both. But if I were cross-examined in court, I'd have an awfully hard time defending any decision on either of them with hard facts and figures that make sense."

Mr. Wills let his mind drift back to the state's adoption of the LD definition under which Edwin and J. C. were being considered for special education. After seemingly interminable wrangling among state officials and LD experts, the state education department decided that the proposed federal formula for defining LD was too complicated and unreliable. Learning disability, the state decided, meant a difference of 20 or more points between WISC-R Full-Scale IQ and standard scores for the Woodcock-Johnson achievement test

---

[1]From *American Journal of Insanity* (pp. 61–63), author unknown, 1850.

in written language or mathematics, or the Peabody Individual Achievement Test in math or reading. Seemed simple enough, he thought at the time. He remembered how the superintendent had slapped him on the back and said, "Well, P. M., I think we've finally got us a definition that'll cut out a lot of this needless haggling about who belongs in our LD classes."

Only it hadn't proved to be so simple. Take Edwin, for example. He was a third grader with a WISC-R Full-Scale IQ of 74. His W-J standard scores were lower than his IQ, 19 points in written language and 17 in mathematics. He didn't quite qualify for LD services under the definition, but he was certainly having lots of trouble in school. His teacher was at his wit's end to know what to do with Edwin. He was a constant behavior problem, according to the teacher—nearly always out of his seat, taunting and teasing his classmates, bullying smaller children on the playground, making life miserable for everyone. This was not a teacher whose class was generally disorderly or who had difficulty managing and teaching most children. Obviously, Edwin was not a bright child, though he didn't quite qualify as mentally retarded. And he was having more academic difficulty than one would expect based on his IQ. A lot more difficulty, in fact. His parents were extremely concerned and wanted him placed in one of the county's self-contained LD classes. But the classes were already filled. Besides, nearly 4% of the county's students were already identified as LD, many of them with test score discrepancies smaller than Edwin's.

Then there was the case of J. C., a bright and talented sixth grader. J. C. had a Full-Scale WISC-R score of 129. Here was a highly motivated, well-adjusted boy who was well-liked by his peers, well-liked by his teachers, and well-read on nearly every topic. But he had only third grade math skills. On all achievement tests, he scored about two standard deviations above the mean in written language; but his math scores were consistently 40 or more standard points below his IQ. He seemed not to care; his peers seemed not to notice; his parents were convinced that the problem was simply poor teaching and strongly resisted the notion of his being identified as LD. They gave permission for J. C.'s formal evaluation for special education only with great reluctance. And, to make matters worse, P. M. Wills knew that J. C.'s math instruction had been, for the past three years, anything but exemplary. "Perhaps," he thought, "J. C. does not belong in an LD program even though he does technically fit the definition. I think his problems could quickly be resolved by a skilled tutor. And if he were my son, I don't think I'd want him in special education either."

P. M. Wills sighed. "Where are all those nice, neat cases I was taught about in graduate school?" he asked himself.[2]

DEFINITION AND PREVALENCE

The idea that some people have specific disabilities in learning is not new. The term *learning disability,* however, is only a little over 25 years old. Besides being the most recently labeled, learning disability (LD) is certainly the most controversial and least understood special education category. Ironically, nearly everyone has heard the term *learning disability*—and most people who talk about LD use the term *as if* they understand it. Recent estimates indicate that perhaps 1,000 people *per day* in the United States alone are newly and officially classified as learning disabled (Reeve & Kauffman, 1988). And LD is now by far the largest category of special education in terms of the number of children and amount of money involved. Yet the definition of learning disability is still being debated. As one leading scholar and his colleagues put it, "though even the most illiterate student of education is likely to know the term, even the most literate scholar is likely to have difficulty explaining exactly what a learning disability is" (Hallahan, Kauffman, & Lloyd, 1985, p. 2).

Why do we have so much difficulty defining a problem that is so widely recognized and deciding the precise meaning of such a popularly applied label? Probably we find the definition difficult because the *idea* of a learning disability is pretty straightforward but application of the concept to real people is extremely complex. The same is likely true for the difficulty we have in trying to decide how many children have a learning disability: The abstract formula is a neat gadget, but it doesn't work very well in the real world of schools and children. As Hallahan et al. (1985) explain:

> Learning disability is easy to define as an abstraction. When we
> consider flesh and blood children, however, our abstract definition
> that seemed so adequate, or even elegant, on paper becomes a
> house of cards. The moment we try to apply our neatly written cri-
> teria to an actual child, our definition collapses around us, a casu-

---

[2]From *Introduction to Learning Disabilities* (pp. 293–294) by D. P. Hallahan, J. M. Kauffman, and J. W. Lloyd, 1985, Englewood Cliffs, NJ: Prentice-Hall. Copyright 1985 by Prentice-Hall. Reprinted by permission.

alty of the child's living, breathing individuality. Naturally, if we have difficulty deciding that any given child fits our definition, then we have little basis for stating how many children are LD. Our estimation of the prevalence of learning disability often is based on a statistical probability that, like our definition, is attractive in the abstract but unworkable in practice (pp. 292–293).

In the abstract, experts estimate that 1% to 3% of the school-aged population (ages 6 to 17) has a learning disability. In the real world of classrooms of the late 1980s and early 1990s, about 4.4% of the United States school population has been identified as learning disabled (U.S. Department of Education, 1989). Meanwhile, controversy about definition continues. The current federal definition of LD, which is included in PL 94–142 and its subsequent amendments, reads as follows:

Specific learning disability means a disorder of one or more of the basic psychological processes involved in understanding or in using language, spoken or written, which may manifest itself in an imperfect ability to listen, think, speak, read, write, spell, or do arithmetic calculations. The term includes such conditions as perceptual handicaps, brain injury, minimal brain damage, dyslexia, and developmental aphasia. The term does not include children who have learning problems which are primarily the result of visual, hearing, or motor handicaps, of mental retardation, or environmental, cultural, or economic disadvantage (U.S. Office of Education, 1977, p. 42478).

Although language and academics remain major areas of concern related to defining learning disabilities (Mercer, King-Sears, & Mercer, 1990), most children with learning disabilities, in essence, have been defined by exclusion. They are not emotionally disturbed, culturally disadvantaged, retarded, visibly crippled (although the term *invisibly crippled* has been used), deaf, or blind. They simply do not learn some specific, basic developmental and academic tasks as most children do. And nobody knows why for sure. Although this continues to be the situation in most cases reported by Mercer et al. (1990), the authors also report that there is a growing consistency among and between the states as to the factors critical to defining learning disabilities. This line of thinking, however, precludes the possibility of a person with learning disabilities being multiply handicapped. Hammill, Leigh, McNutt, and Larsen (1981) offer a good example of why this interpretation is not accurate. "Take for example a blind 14-year-old child who lost spoken language as a consequence of a brain tumor. This would be a clear-cut case of a multiply handicapped LD child" (p. 338).

Because learning disabilities are a relatively new area of study, service, and research, definitions must be considered in an experimental, developmental stage. Other attempts at definition have been offered as well. Hallahan and Kauffman (1977) suggested that much more specificity is needed in labeling each person's particular problem, for example, "specific learning disability in remembering the spelling of words" (p. 29).

Of particular note to anyone interested in learning disabilities is the emergence of other definitions. Representatives from major professional and parent organizations forming the National Joint Committee on Learning Disabilities[3] (NJCLD) were motivated by displeasure with the definition used in PL 94–142, and as a result, approved the following definition in 1981 (Hammill et al., 1981):

> *Learning disabilities* is a generic term that refers to a heterogeneous group of disorders manifested by significant difficulties in the acquisition and use of listening, speaking, reading, writing, or mathematical abilities. These disorders are intrinsic to the individual and presumed to be due to central nervous system dysfunction. Even though a learning disability may occur concomitantly with other handicapping conditions (e.g., sensory impairment, mental retardation, social and emotional disturbance) or environmental influences (e.g., cultural differences, insufficient/inappropriate instruction, psychogenic factors), it is not the direct result of those conditions or influences (p. 336).

The NJCLD recently modified the 1981 definition, adding new content as well as changing some of the wording.[4] This revised definition was accepted by this organization in January 1990 and reads as follows:

> *Learning disabilities* is a general term that refers to a heterogeneous group of disorders manifested by significant difficulties in

---

[3]The National Joint Committee on Learning Disabilities represents the following organizations: American Speech-Language-Hearing Association (ASHA); Association on Handicapped Student Service Programs in Postsecondary Education (AHSSPPE); Council for Learning Disabilities (CLD); Division for Children with Communication Disorders (DCCD), Council for Exceptional Children; Division for Learning Disabilities (DLD), Council for Exceptional Children; International Reading Association (IRA); Learning Disabilities Association (LDA)—formerly the Association for Children and Adults With Learning Disabilities; National Association of School Psychologists (NASP); and the Orton Dyslexia Society (ODS).

[4]Position paper of the NJCLD, 1990. A copy of the paper can be obtained from any of the member organizations.

the acquisition and use of listening, speaking, reading, writing, reasoning, or mathematical abilities. These disorders are intrinsic to
the individual, presumed to be due to central nervous system dysfunction, and may occur across the life span. Problems in self-regulatory behaviors, social perception, and social interaction may exist
with learning disabilities but do not by themselves constitute a
learning disability. Although learning disabilities may occur con-
comitantly with other handicapping conditions (e.g., sensory
impairment, mental retardation, serious emotional disturbance) or
with extrinsic influences (such as cultural differences, insufficient
or inappropriate instruction), they are not the result of those conditions or influences.

ETIOLOGY

As mentioned previously, learning disabilities have traditionally been
defined by exclusion. Consequently, it has been denied that children
became learning disabled because of mental retardation, emotional
disturbance, visual or hearing impairment, crippling conditions, or
environmental disadvantage (lack of appropriate stimulation or opportunity to learn). What is left? As the argument goes, if the child is not
learning and the lack of achievement cannot be explained in any other
way, there must be something wrong in the child's head—there must
be brain dysfunction.

As will be mentioned in the discussion of the etiologies of other
exceptionalities, brain damage can result from a very large number of
factors. But knowing that brains *can be* injured by many factors does
not prove that a given child's brain *has been* injured. It is also
extremely difficult to provide conclusive evidence that a learning disability is the direct result of brain injury, even if it is known that the
brain has been damaged. Consequently, it is safe to say only that brain
injury is a suspected etiological factor in many cases of learning disability.

By most definitions, children with serious emotional disturbance
are excluded from the learning disabled population; however, there is
little doubt that emotional factors are involved in learning disabilities.
Children with mild emotional disturbance and children with learning
disabilities do exhibit many similar characteristics, but it is not clear
whether emotional disturbance is an etiological factor in or a consequence of a learning disability (Hallahan et al., 1985; Kauffman,
1985).

There is a third possible etiological factor in learning disabilities
that special educators are only now beginning to face squarely:
instructionally related problems such as inadequate teaching (Wallace

& Kauffman, 1986). Although it would be ridiculous to suggest that *all* children with learning disabilities have been poorly taught, it seems likely that in a significant number of cases the problem is as much one of providing appropriate instruction as of finding the child's disability. This line of thought places a lot of responsibility on the teacher, but that is where it should be. If a child is not learning, it may be concluded that the teacher has not found an effective way of teaching. The malady may be as much in the teacher's lack of instructional prowess as in the child's lack of ability to perform (see Engelmann & Carnine, 1982).

LEARNING DISABLED OR LEARNING DYSLABELED?

Given the ambiguities and controversy surrounding the definition of learning disabilities, it is not surprising that there are arguments about what the children in question should be called. Concern for the label to be attached to those who have only recently been recognized as a distinct group of handicapped individuals is heightened by the realization that other special education labels seem to have a deleterious effect on children. It is no secret that *retarded* can be a bad name, and it does not take a Rhodes scholar to recognize that *emotionally disturbed, autistic, stutterer, crippled, hyperactive,* or any other special term used to describe a handicapped individual can likewise become an epithet designed to hurt or degrade the person. Many of the people who were instrumental in developing the "new" field of learning disabilities in the 1960s were also determined to avoid stigmatizing still another group of children. In a frantic effort to foil the pernicious influence of labels known to carry negative connotations, these people thought up a wide variety of new ones, all of them used at some time or other, to refer to essentially the same type of child or condition. Moreover, many of the terms used to describe individuals who experience difficulty in learning-related endeavors reflect a given professional orientation or affiliation. A sample of such terms follows:

Attentional Deficit Disorder	Learning Impaired
Atypical Child	Minimal Brain Dysfunction
Brain Damaged	Minimal Cerebral Dysfunction
Brain Injured	Organic Brain Syndrome
Choreiform Child	Performance Deviation
Developmental Aphasia	Performance Disabled
Developmentally Imbalanced	Performance Handicapped

Driven Child	Problem Learner
Dyslexia	Problem Reader
Dyssychronous Child	Psycholinguistic Disability
Educationally Handicapped	Psychoneurological Disorder
Educationally Maladjusted	Psychoneurological Learning Disability
Hyperactive Behavior Disorder	Reading Disability
Hyperkinetic Child	Remedial Education Case
Interjacent Child	Special Learning Disability
Invisibly Crippled Child	Specific Learning Disability
Language Disordered	Strauss Syndrome
Learning Disabled	Underachiever
Learning Disordered	

Predictably, as soon as people found out what these labels really meant, the names became noxious. Of course, what is derogatory in a name is the social role, quality, deviancy, or conformity it suggests. In our society the imagery conjured up by *any* label for a handicapping condition tends to be stigmatizing, not because of the label itself, but because of our archaic attitudes toward handicaps. The stigma of being exceptional will not go away, no matter what the label, until a handicap is no longer the reason for pity, mourning, disgust, humor, segregation, or reverence. When we can laugh, cry, teach, learn, struggle, and enjoy life with persons who have handicaps as we do with other individuals who share our human limitations, there will be no pain in labels (see Burbach, 1981).

But stigma is not the only problem with labeling. We need to classify people in order to avoid total confusion and miscommunication. The real issues in labeling are: Labeled according to what criteria? Labeled by whom? and Labeled for what purpose? When labels are based on objective and relevant criteria, are applied by responsible professionals, and are used to communicate essential information about an individual, they can even be helpful to the individuals involved.

Numerous factors are known to influence how a child is perceived and categorized including (1) the social role and cultural context of children's behavior, (2) the fads and predispositions of labelers, (3) the legislation and legal rules regarding exceptional children, and (4) the awareness or unawareness of environmental cues for children's behavior on the part of diagnosticians. Some of these factors inevitably contribute to "dyslabelia."

Social and Cultural Contexts

Social and cultural contexts vary from location to location and change over time. In our country, attitudes toward the behavior of children in school have changed dramatically over the last century. Gnagey (1968) reports that S. L. Pressey found a list of misbehaviors and recommended punishments published in North Carolina in 1848. Among them were:

Playing cards at school (10 lashes)

Swearing at school (8 lashes)

Drinking liquor at school (8 lashes)

Telling lies (7 lashes)

Boys and girls playing together (4 lashes)

Quarreling (4 lashes)

Wearing long fingernails (2 lashes)

Blotting one's copybook (2 lashes)

Neglecting to bow when going home (2 lashes)

Today, many Americans would be more likely to recommend lashes for playing too many video games or for a student's *insistence* on bowing when going home. The important thing to remember is that whether or not a child is considered disturbed, retarded, learning disabled, speech handicapped, gifted, and so forth, depends to a significant degree on when, where, and with whom the individual lives and works (i.e., on the demands and expectations of the environment). A case in point is that most mildly retarded children are not considered retarded until they enter school and are not thought of as retarded by most people after they leave the school environment.

Learning disabilities tend to be "invisible handicaps." In essence, because students with learning disabilities do not have any severe or obvious physical or mental abnormalities, the expectations of teachers, administrators, parents, employers, and even other students are consistent with those expectations for the average student. The failure of students with learning disabilities to meet the expectations of others in their various "life environments" (i.e., school, work, etc.) often results in perceptions of laziness, lack of motivation, disinterest, and even rebelliousness. Such perceptions on the part of teachers and administrators can lead to a limiting or absence of effective classroom intervention or accommodation. Social dysfunction, as a major problem for students with learning disabilities (Baum, Duffelmeyer, & Geeland, 1988), and the efficacy of teaching social skills to this population (Blackbourn, 1989) are well documented.

Ellis (1991) suggests a model of the negative effect of poor class-room skills (related to social interaction) on the perception of teachers and other students (see Figure 2.1). He also outlines a model of the possible positive outcomes available to students with learning disabilities if they are prepared to interact effectively with the material, the teacher, and the students in regular classrooms (see Figure 2.2). These models, developed by Dr. Ellis, explain the dynamics of the classroom and how they impact the social/academic status of the student with learning disabilities.

Figure 2.1
Negative Effect of Poor Classroom Skills

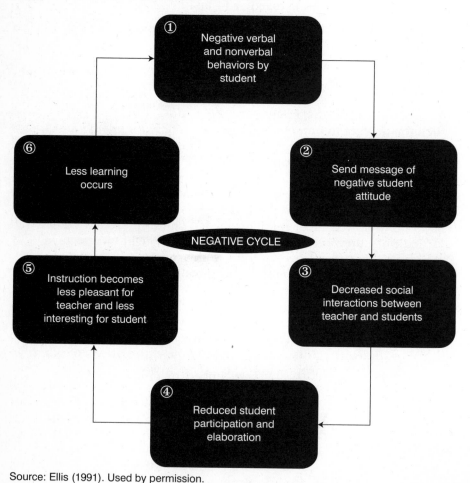

Source: Ellis (1991). Used by permission.

Figure 2.2
Positive Cycle

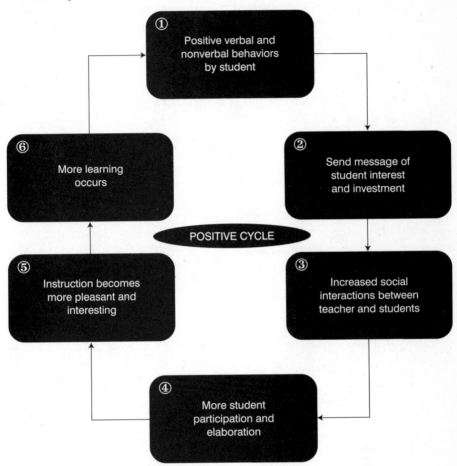

Source: Ellis (1991). Used by permission.

Fads and Predispositions

Like clothes and furniture, labels for exceptional children become fashionable and go out of style. People who label children—physicians, psychologists, educators—are influenced by "in" terms. A child may receive a certain label because it "sounds right" or because it is more acceptable to parents than another term that seems to be more denigrating. White and Charry (1966) studied approximately 3,000 referrals to school psychologists. They found a significant relationship between the child's socioeconomic level and IQ and the label given. Children low in IQ and socioeconomic level more often were labeled *culturally disadvantaged* or *educationally inadequate*, while children high in IQ and socioeconomic level were more often labeled *brain injured* or *emotionally disturbed*. It seemed clear to these investigators that the labelers had definite biases or expectations that influenced how they chose to interpret and label children's behavior.

Legislation and Legal Rules

It is not a complete distortion of reality to say that legislation and school codes sometimes "make" children exceptional. It is obvious to most of us which children need help, but what to call them is a problem. Now, if a state legislature decides that money and services will be available for *educationally handicapped* children, then *educationally handicapped* children will be identified and served in the schools of that state, regardless of the fact that in another state they would be labeled *learning disabled, maladjusted,* or *Type 600*. For example, for a number of years the state of Illinois decided that "maladjusted children . . . means children between the ages of 5 and 21 years who, because of social and emotional problems, are unable to make constructive use of their school experience and require the provisions of special services designed to promote their educational growth and development" (The School Code of Illinois, 14–1, par. 2). Children who in most states would be considered *learning disabled* were considered, in Illinois, to be *maladjusted* because "social problems" was interpreted as "serious educational maladjustment resulting from extreme discrepancy between ability and school achievement associated with such factors as perceptual impairment, severe learning disorders, and neurological disorders" (Article VII, Rule 7.01b). One is tempted to speculate that if funds were provided for "sinful" children, wickedness would abound among our youngsters.

Environmental Cues

No one likes to take the blame for children's educational deficiencies—not parents, and certainly not teachers who are always tempted to look outside the classroom for the reasons for the child's lack of success. The mind, the intelligence, the culture, the emotions, the family, the brain—certainly, somehow, somewhere, teachers hope to find the locus of the problem and avoid having the buck stop with them. How often have children been labeled *mentally retarded, learning disabled,* or *emotionally disturbed* primarily because teachers did not recognize their own ineptitude? It is clear that many times teachers inadvertently reinforce the very behavior they want to stop (Smith, 1984; Wallace &

Kauffman, 1986) or simply do not know how to teach effectively (Engelmann & Carnine, 1982).

Furthermore, we want to emphasize the point that labels themselves do not add any information to our store of knowledge, offer any explanation of what is observed, or provide new insights. Labels are only succinct ways of communicating a concept or set of expectations. There is danger in thinking that once a problem is classified or labeled, a solution has been found and appropriate intervention will automatically follow. There is also danger in using labels as explanations for behavior, a type of circular reasoning known as reification:

> "Why isn't this child, who appears to be of normal intelligence, learning to read?"
> "Well, because he has a learning disability."
> "But how do you know that he is learning disabled?"
> "Because he appears to have normal intelligence but he isn't learning to read."

The danger in reification or in labeling for its own sake is that sloppy thinking will prevent children from being helped. Exceptional children have suffered too many indignities and have waited too long for effective education for us to play word games.

CURRENT DEVELOPMENTS

Within the last few years, a number of important events have occurred that have influenced the field of learning disabilities. Services to students with learning disabilities have expanded to include children at a preschool level as well as college students. Although there is still a paucity of information about the corresponding services for adults with learning disabilities, some attention is beginning to be directed in this area (Patton & Polloway, 1982).

The sophistication of various organizations concerned with learning disabilities has also been witnessed. The Learning Disabilities Association of America (LDAA) has continued to be concerned with the problems faced by LD citizens. The Council for Learning Disabilities (CLD), the Division for Learning Disabilities (DLD) of the Council for Exceptional Children, and the Orton Dyslexia Society (ODS) also have continued to be professionally involved with encouraging research, sharing information, and furthering the development of the field. In addition, in various locations throughout the nation, other organizations are forming. These groups, however, differ from those previously mentioned in that they are composed of adults with learning disabilities (e.g., groups such as Time Out to Enjoy).

A current controversy in the field of learning disabilities involves the inclusion movement. The basic premise of this movement is that many students who are served in pull-out programs (i.e., resource settings) for part of the day could be better educated in the regular classroom. Inclusion involves the merger of special education and regular education and requires that regular educators assume primary responsibility for the education of all students, including those with disabilities or special needs.

Implementation of inclusionary practices would require the following: (1) extensive in-service and preservice training for regular educators in special education competencies; (2) collaboration and shared responsibility between regular and special educators; and (3) a restructuring of regular education settings to accommodate the needs of all children.

Opponents of inclusion cite lack of research support, erroneous assumptions as the basis of the program, and the potentiality for failure of the program and an associated negative impact on integration/mainstreaming efforts as reasons to maintain the current service delivery models. Proponents of inclusion point to the inappropriateness of all pull-out (resource room) programs for children with mild handicaps (Will, 1986), the mandate to educate children with handicaps in the least restrictive environment, and the increased number of "at-risk" students served by the public schools as major components in their rationale. Regardless of one's perspective related to inclusion, the program seems to be taking root (Baum & Duffelmeyer, 1990; Smith, Polloway, Patton, & Dowdy, 1995).

There also have been some major research efforts focusing on individuals with learning disabilities. In 1977, the federal government funded five major research projects specifically focusing on students with learning disabilities. The five institutes were located at the University of Illinois at Chicago Circle, the University of Kansas, the University of Minnesota, the University of Virginia, and Columbia Teachers College in New York. All of these LD institutes developed multifaceted research programs, the results of which are having a major impact on the field of learning disabilities (Kneedler & Hallahan, 1983). By no means do we want to imply that the only notable research is emanating from these sources. On the contrary, many other significant research efforts have been conducted by various research groups and other individuals as well.

Two of the most prominent have been the Learning Strategies Approach (Alley & Deshler, 1979) and the Learning Styles Approach (Dunn, 1990). While both approaches have gained a good deal of acceptance, they differ significantly in the theory and means employed in intervening with learning disabled students. Also, several special education professionals question the legitimacy of the Learning Styles Approach (Kavale & Forness, 1987; 1990) (see Figure 2.3).

The Learning Strategies Approach focuses on teaching the student with learning disabilities specific ways to process information. The goals of the Learning Strategies Approach are to (1) provide learning disabled students with those skills necessary to function in the regular classroom and (2) facilitate generalization of these skills to "normal" academic settings. Strategies that focus on test taking, paraphrasing, sentence writing, and social interaction are all included in the Learning Strategies Approach.

The Learning Styles Approach focuses on modifying instruction according to an individual student's learning style. In this approach, the teacher assesses the student to determine how he or she learns

Figure 2.3
A Comparison of the Learning Styles and Learning Strategies Approaches to Instruction

	Learning Styles	Learning Strategies
Goal	Create classroom environments that are responsive to the specific learning needs of students.	Provide the students with critical skills necessary to process classroom content.
Responsibility for academic success	The teacher.	The student.
Advantages	1. Puts the student at the center of the instructional process. 2. Focus on individualization of intervention. 3. Ties weaker modalities into the instructional process to develop student proficiency in these areas.	1. Strong, longitudinal research base. 2. Focuses on generalization of the skills acquired to a variety of environments. 3. Can facilitate transition from class to class and/or school to school. 4. Ties content and strategies together in the instructional setting.
Disadvantages	1. May inhibit effective transition due to a lack of consistency between teachers and/or schools. 2. Theoretical underpinning and research-base controversial.	1. Requires linguistic ability appropriate to a 9-year-old. 2. Requires intensive, long-term intervention to teach specific strategies.

best and then modifies materials, methods, and the classroom environment to meet the student's needs. The primary goal of the Learning Styles Approach is to make the classroom environment more responsive to the learning disabled student's needs.

Both the learning styles and learning strategies approaches to instruction have given support to the inclusion movement for students with learning disabilities. This movement, which is an outgrowth of the mainstreaming movement of the 1970s and the regular education initiative of the 1980s, contends that students with disabilities can learn most effectively in regular classroom settings with their age-appropriate peers. For the inclusion movement to succeed, teachers must possess the necessary skills to create a facilitative classroom environment and provide effective instruction to students with disabilities. Indeed, the American Federation of Teachers has recently adopted a position in opposition to inclusive education due to the lack of preparedness among regular teachers to effectively manage and teach students with disabilities. The learning strategies and learning styles approaches to instruction could offer the regular classroom teacher viable alternative means for accomplishing the goals of the inclusive education movement.

At the present time, professionals and nonprofessionals alike are tackling some major questions confronting the field. Some of these issues are:

How are services best delivered to students with learning disabilities?

Which model of intervention (remedial, compensatory, vocational, functional skills, or learning strategy) is most appropriate for students with learning disabilities?

How should persons with learning disabilities be identified?

Are various intervention techniques and therapies (e.g., pharmacological, dietary, and megavitamin) effective or warranted?

How do students with learning disabilities process information?

What impact and implication does the competency movement have on students with learning disabilities?

How should we prepare professionals to work with students who possess learning disabilities?

Attempts to ameliorate the confusion and indefiniteness of the concept of learning disabilities and efforts to research the nature of this handicapping condition must be encouraged, supported, and continued. Yet we must always be mindful of the specific individuals toward whom such endeavors are directed. The problems that they face daily can have profound social, academic, and vocational repercussions. Let us not fail to realize a learning disability is not something that a person merely outgrows.

SUGGESTIONS FOR WORKING WITH CHILDREN WITH LEARNING DISABILITIES

1. Always remember the major purpose or objective of the child's effort. It's easy to lose sight of the relative unimportance of some of the things we expect from nonhandicapped children. For example, if the goal is to have the child write a composition, don't be obsessive about neatness and spelling; rather focus on the expression and flow of ideas.

2. Be sure you don't expect the child to perform beyond his or her capacity. A child cannot be expected to perform tasks *just because he or she is intellectually bright.* Some individuals have specific learning problems even though they are generally bright. Expect the child to try and make a little improvement in the area where you're offering instruction.

3. Realize that working in the area of disability is frustrating. Remember that some things are very hard for you to do, and you probably have found successful ways of avoiding them. When you are pushed to do things you find very difficult (e.g., singing, swimming, reading, math, or whatever), you probably tend to become emotional about it rather quickly. It shouldn't surprise you if the child responds in the same way.

4. Try another way. See if you can find a different method of teaching the skill, one that might be simpler or easier for the child. Or try to substitute a slightly different skill for the one that seems so difficult to learn. For example, if the child has great difficulty in writing things by hand, try letting her or him type or use a word processor.

5. Be sure the environment is conducive to learning and successful performance. Give clear instructions. Comment positively on the child's efforts. Eliminate distractions by working in a quiet, uncluttered place.

6. Try to figure out what strategies the child is using to learn or perform. If he or she doesn't appear to be using a strategy or is using one that is ineffective, try to think through and teach the child a new and more effective approach to the task. For example, the child may not be aware that there are common strate-

gies that people use to try to remember things, like saying things to themselves and making associations between what they can and are trying to remember.

✦ PONDER THESE

1. *If you were in Patrick Milton Wills' shoes, how would you handle the cases of Edwin and J. C.? (See the vignette at the beginning of this chapter.)*

> When teaching the
>
> l _ _ _ _ _ _ _ d _ _ _ _ _ _ _
>
> Behavior is often mislabeled
>
> When a kid doesn't learn
>
> To his b _ _ _ n people turn
>
> And that's why we say he's dys _ _ _ _ _ _ _.

2. *Professionals in the field of assessment and special education often have difficulty deciding whether a student is learning disabled or merely low achieving as a result of any number of environmental, economic, or cultural reasons. What would be the advantages and disadvantages of using a term like* educationally handicapped *to describe all students who are having learning-related problems in school?*

3. *Federal and some state governments are considering putting a "cap" on the LD category—passing laws or regulations that would prohibit school districts from receiving funding for services to more than a certain percentage of students placed in LD programs. For example, a district might receive special education funding for LD programs for no more than 2% of its enrollment. Debate the merits of such a cap.*

INFORMATION/RESOURCES

1. The Center on Learning
   3061 Dole Center
   University of Kansas
   Lawrence, Kansas 66045

2. Center for the Study of Learning and Teaching Styles
   St. John's University
   Jamaica, New York

3. The Slingerland Institute
   One Bellevue Center
   411 108th Avenue N.E.
   Bellevue, Washington 98004

4. Council for Learning Disabilities
   P.O. Box 40303
   Overland Park, Kansas 66204

References

Alley, G. R., & Deshler, D. (1979). *Teaching the learning disabled adolescent: Strategies and methods.* Denver: Love.

Baum, D. D., & Duffelmeyer, F. (1990). The regular education initiative: Is it developing roots? *National Forum of Special Education Journal, 2,* 4–11.

Baum, D. D., Duffelmeyer, F., & Geeland, M. (1988). An investigation of the prevalence of social dysfunction among learning disabled students. *Journal of Learning Disabilities, 21,* 380–381.

Blackbourn, J. M. (1989). Acquisition and generalization of social skills in elementary-age children with learning disabilities. *Journal of Learning Disabilities, 22,* 28–34.

Burbach, H. J. (1981). The labeling process: A sociological analysis. In J. M. Kauffman & D. P. Hallahan (Eds.), *Handbook of special education* (pp. 361–377). Englewood Cliffs, NJ: Merrill/Prentice-Hall.

Dunn, R. (1990). Bias over substance: A critical analysis of Kavale & Forness' report on modality based instruction. *Exceptional Children, 56,* 352–356.

Ellis, E. (1991). SLANT: A Starter Strategy for Class Participation. Laurence, KS: EDGE Enterprises, Inc.

Engelmann, S., & Carnine, D. (1982). *Theory of instruction: Principles and applications.* New York: Irvington.

Gnagey, W. J. (1968). *The psychology of discipline in the classroom.* Englewood Cliffs, NJ: Merrill/Prentice Hall.

Hallahan, D. P., & Kauffman, J. M. (1977). Categories, labels, behavioral characteristics: ED, LD, and EMR reconsidered. *Journal of Special Education, 11,* 139–149.

Hallahan, D. P., Kauffman, J. M., & Lloyd, J. W. (1985). *Introduction to learning disabilities.* Englewood Cliffs, NJ: Merrill/Prentice-Hall.

Hammill, D. D., Leigh, J. E., McNutt, G., & Larsen, S. C. (1981). A new definition of learning disabilities. *Learning Disability Quarterly, 4,* 336–342.

Kauffman, J. M. (1985). *Characteristics of children's behavior disorders* (3rd ed.). Englewood Cliffs, NJ: Merrill/Prentice Hall.

Kavale, K. A., & Forness, S. R. (1987). Substance over style: Assessing the efficacy of modality testing and teaching. *Exceptional Children, 54,* 228–239.

Kavale, K. A., & Forness, S. R. (1990). Substance over style: A rejoinder to Dunn's animadversions. *Exceptional Children, 56,* 357–361.

Kneedler, R. D., & Hallahan, D. P. (Eds.). (1983). Research in learning disabilities: Summaries of the institutes. *Exceptional Education Quarterly, 4*(1).

Mercer, C. D., King-Sears, P., & Mercer, A. R. (1990). Learning disabilities definitions and criteria used by state education departments. *Learning Disabilities Quarterly, 13*(2), 141–152.

Patton, J. R., & Polloway, E. A. (1982). The learning disabled: The adult years. *Topics in Learning and Learning Disabilities, 2*(3), 79–88.

Reeve, R. E., & Kauffman, J. M. (1988). Learning disabilities. In V. B. Van Hasselt, P. S. Strain, & M. Hersen (Eds.), *Handbook of developmental and physical disabilities,* (pp. 316–335). New York: Plenum.

Smith, D. D. (1984). *Effective discipline.* Austin, TX: Pro-Ed.

Smith, T. E. C., Polloway, E. A., Patton, J. R., & Dowdy, C. A. (1995). *Teaching children with special needs in inclusive settings.* Boston: Allyn & Bacon.

U.S. Department of Education (1989). *Eleventh annual report to Congress on the implementation of the Education of the Handicapped Act.* Washington, DC: Author.

U.S. Office of Education (1977). *Education of all handicapped children: Implementation of Part B of the Education of the Handicapped Act. Federal Register, 42,* 42474–42518.

Wallace, G., & Kauffman, J. M. (1986). *Teaching students with learning and behavior problems* (3rd ed.). Englewood Cliffs, NJ: Merrill/Prentice Hall.

White, M. A., & Charry, J. (Eds.). (1966). *School disorder, intelligence, and social class.* New York: Teachers College Press.

Will, M. (1986). *Educating students with learning problems: A shared responsibility.* Washington, DC: U.S. Department of Education.

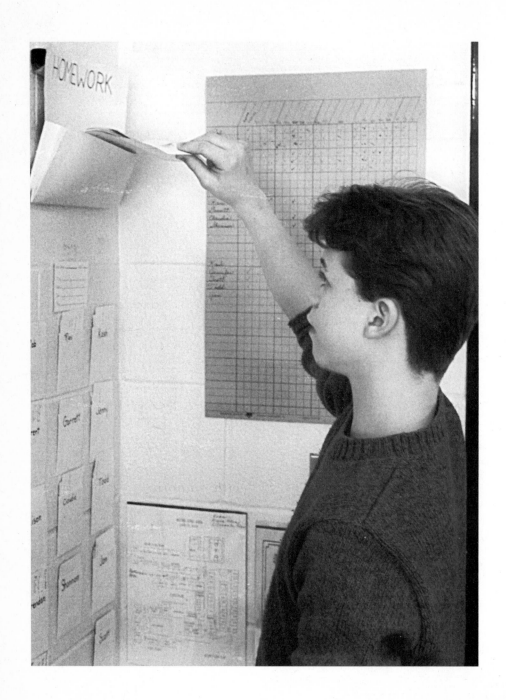

3

EMOTIONAL/BEHAVIOR DISORDERS

Wesley is 16 years old and has been labeled emotionally disturbed since he was 6 years old. That year, when he was in first grade, he attacked his elementary school principal and tried to kill him. During the next several years, he progressed from a regular class to a resource room to a self-contained class to a class on a separate campus, where he goes to school now. Wesley is very bright (his measured IQ is about 135), but he often refuses to complete assignments. He dresses in baggy pants and black t-shirts, has long hair and tattoos, and looks bored with the world. At his last ARD meeting, we were working with him to set some social/behavioral goals. Since he's always had problems with authority figures and frequently threatens or curses them, we thought it would be a good idea to write a goal addressing the skill of speaking respectfully to adults, including teachers and principals. We were in the middle of a discussion of why it's important not to curse at your boss, a policeman, or your school principal when his father interrupted us. Wesley's dad commented, "Of course I want Wesley to get along with people. But if somebody gets in his face, then they should expect Wesley to get right back in their face, and sometimes that might mean he cusses someone out. That's what I would do, and that's what I've taught my son to do. He's not going to take any *$#^ from anybody." It was one of the first times I remember that a room full of educators had nothing to say.

In all of my years of teaching, James was one of my favorite students. James lived with his mother. His father had been charged with the sexual abuse of James's sister. Their dad would force his daughter to have sex with him and make home videos, which he would force James to watch. Whenever anything went wrong, James got blamed and punished for it. He was a very quiet boy, thin and shy, but very kind and loving. After James's father got arrested, he was dishonorably discharged from the Air Force and forbidden to come near James's home. Because James was so quiet and so reluctant to ask for help, we had to keep a close eye on things. The last month of school, the child protective workers came to see me. We had noticed that James had been very tired in school and having a hard time getting his work done. As it turned out, James's mother had rented out his room to a stranger. James had nowhere to sleep or do his homework except in the living room. He did his best to sleep while his mother and her friends watched TV and socialized. When the social worker told his mom that she needed to give James his room back, she couldn't understand why. She said that she needed the money and that James should be willing to help out.

John was almost 14. Academically, he was at a low second grade level. He had been expelled from a special public school class for children with brain damage because he threatened the teacher and other children and had actually beaten another child with a chain. He was on the waiting list to be admitted to the state mental hospital, but he was to be enrolled in my public school class for children with emotional disturbance because there was nowhere else for him to go. When his mother brought him to school the first day, he refused to get out of the car. She coaxed and pleaded, but he refused to budge. She got the principal, and he coaxed and pleaded, but John would not talk to him. John's mother and the principal came to me. I went out to the car and coaxed and pleaded, but he would not even look at me. Now what? We decided that we would tell him it was time to come in and that he was going to come into the building now. He could choose the way he was going to come in—he could walk or we would carry him. Once he had come in and looked over the classroom, he would have another choice—to stay or to go home—and the decision would be his alone. We told him, but he did not appear to listen, and he did not budge. We pulled him out of the car, and he stood up and walked into the building. Five minutes later we were showing him the classroom; he was smiling and talking and decided to stay. John tested me out in several other ways, and I was beginning to wonder if I was getting anywhere with him. About a month later a new boy entered the class and began the usual testing. Did I mean what I said and would I level appropriate consequences for behavior? At a beautifully timed moment, John went over to the new boy and said, "Look, you might as well do what Mr. Phillips tells you to, because it's for your own good. Besides, he means what he says, and if you don't do it, you'll only be hurting yourself."

It's hard to know who is emotionally disturbed and who isn't. When I was in high school, the valedictorian of our class of 412 students was always a little different. Sarah had few friends and never seemed to fit in with any of the normal high school social groups. She seemed to learn things without effort and so much more quickly than the rest of us could that we were in awe of her. After I went to college, I didn't hear much about Sarah, except that she still lived with her parents, never dated, and had few, if any, friends. In the fall of my junior year in college, I opened the newspaper and saw her picture. She had gone to the park near our high school and shot herself in the head. Nowadays, the teen suicide rate is so high that most people pay attention when teenagers are withdrawn and depressed and watch for signs of suicide. I wish that someone had paid some attention to Sarah. I figured that she was one of those people who could have discovered a cure for cancer or composed a symphony or written a Pulitzer prize winning novel. Instead, she was dead at age 19.

DEFINITION AND PREVALENCE

Emotional disturbance and *behavioral disorders* are two of a confusing array of terms used to describe children who have difficulty relating to others or behaving acceptably. While the federal law governing special education describes this category of students as seriously emotionally disturbed, an increasing number of professionals and many state regulations describe similar students as behaviorally disordered. The terminology for this category of special education is in transition, and this chapter will use *emotionally disturbed* and *behaviorally disordered* (ED/BD) interchangeably.

Definition

Descriptions and definitions of students who are ED/BD are confusing because of the overlap with other disciplines, especially psychiatry and psychology. Psychiatrists and psychologists usually refer to descriptors and categories in the *Diagnostic and Statistical Manual of Mental Disorders* (4th ed.) (DSM-IV) (American Psychiatric Association, 1994). Educators have had to write their own definitions to fit children's behavior in school. Essentially, teachers have defined children with ED/BD as those who behave in harmful or inappropriate ways that cause them academic and social problems. The current federal definition was based on one written by Bower (1959, 1982) and defines students who are seriously emotionally disturbed as follows:

> The term means a condition exhibiting one or more of the following characteristics over a long period of time and to a marked degree, which adversely affects educational performance: (a) an inability to learn that cannot be explained by intellectual, sensory, or health factors; (b) an inability to build or maintain satisfactory interpersonal relationships with peers and teachers; (c) inappropriate types of behavior or feelings under normal circumstances; (d) a general pervasive mood of unhappiness or depression; or (e) a tendency to develop physical symptoms or fears associated with personal or school problems (Education of All Handicapped Children Act of 1975 [PL 94–142]; Individuals With Disabilities Education Act, 1990 [PL 101–476]).

Unfortunately, the federal definition has several clauses that are vague and confusing. Sometimes it is of little help in deciding who is and who is not disturbed (Kauffman, 1993). Its flaws seem to allow many children with ED/BD to go unserved, while perhaps overidentifying students who fit certain patterns of acting out behavior.

The definition is also difficult to specify because it excludes students who are socially maladjusted, unless they are also emotionally disturbed. The exclusion of social maladjustment from the category of emotional disturbance is a significant concern because the difference between social maladjustment and emotional disturbance is not clear. Many professionals would agree with Nelson, Rutherford, Center, and Walker (1991), who pointed out that one of the major factors affecting the abilities of policy makers and researchers to clarify this issue is the lack of a generally accepted definition of social maladjustment. In other words, the definition excludes a group of students without defining who they are. A socially maladjusted child will often exhibit some of the characteristics that are used to define emotional disturbance, and it is difficult to know how to differentiate the two disorders.

As this book goes to press, there is a proposal for a new definition of emotional disturbance that is being considered. It suggests that the category be called Emotional or Behavioral Disorder (EBD). The proposed definition qualifies the condition so that transient, expected responses to stressors are excluded and allows for an EBD label along with other disabilities. The new definition would also emphasize a two-step diagnostic process similar to that used in the learning disability and mental retardation categories. It includes ethnic and cultural considerations, suggests some clinical diagnoses that could perhaps create eligibility if concomitant with learning problems, and does not require the distinctions between social and emotional maladjustment.

Identification of Emotional/Behavioral Problems

Algozzine, Patton, and Serna (in press) point out that the behavior of students in and of itself is not a problem. The effects of the behavior for students identified as ED/BD are the source of concern. While all children behave inappropriately *sometimes,* children with ED/BD exhibit behavior that goes to an extreme: They are too aggressive or too withdrawn, too loud or too quiet, too euphoric or too depressed. Furthermore, they exhibit these extreme behaviors over a long period of time, not just for a short while. In addition, they tend to exhibit behaviors in strange contexts—there is often nothing wrong with what they are doing, only with when and where they are doing it. In short, children with ED/BD *behave in ways their teachers consider undesirable or inappropriate, and their behavior differs from that of normal children along three crucial dimensions:* (1) *severity*—the extremes to which their behavior goes; (2) *chronicity*—the period of time over which they exhibit inappropriate behavior; and (3) *context*—the time and place they do certain things.

For over 20 years the federal estimate of the prevalence of serious emotional disturbance among school-aged children and youth was about 2%. Nowadays, estimates of the prevalence of ED/BD vary from less than 1% to more than 25% of the student population, depending on the individual state. Nationally, in the 1991–92 school year, less than 1% of public school students, or about 8.9% of all special education students, were served in the ED/BD category. Since 1976–77, the number of students in the ED category has grown by almost 120,000 or 46% (U.S. Department of Education, 1993).

Still, many authorities in the field believe that realistically, as many as 12% to 18% of students under the age of 18 are mentally ill. A report by the Associated Press in 1989 indicated that children with emotional problems are significantly under identified and under served. Those students who are served in the ED category are just a small part of an ever growing population of children in America who have emotional and behavioral problems ("Problems found," 1990). The fact that less than half the number of children *conservatively* estimated to fall into this category are receiving services means that children with ED/BD are one of the most neglected, underserved groups of children in American schools today.

It is not difficult to guess why estimates of the prevalence of ED/BD vary so greatly and why so few of the estimated number of eligible children receive special education. When you have a very vague, jumbled, and subjective definition, it is next to impossible to make an accurate count of the number of children who fit it. If there is a lot of room for argument about whether or not a child qualifies under the label of ED/BD, then the school officials responsible for special education may have difficulty identifying and serving many children (Kauffman, 1993). Because of money and personnel constraints, school officials may feel that they must overlook students who are arguably not disabled. The question of prevalence of ED/BD sometimes seems in practice to be less "How many children with ED/BD are there?" than "How many children with ED/BD can we afford?"

ETIOLOGY

The causes of erratic, disturbing, debilitating human behavior have always been a puzzle. All that is clear is that such behavior stems from a complex interaction of many factors. These factors have long been known, but the exact role of each has never been fully understood.

The devil made him do it has always been one of the explanations for aberrant and disturbing behavior. The idea that God and the devil battle for control of the mind and body has been with us for centuries. It is not uncommon, even today, to hear spiritual explanations of and cures for troublesome behavior. Although we no longer burn people at the stake or leave them in the wilderness to die when their behavior is significantly different from that of their peer group, many people still believe that demonic or divine powers control behavior.

Something just snapped in his head is another popular explanation of deviant behavior. Some individuals with severe psychopathology, such as schizophrenia and autism, may also have abnormal levels of specific biochemicals (hallucinogens and neurotransmitters); however, not all individuals with those disorders demonstrate such abnormal biochemistry (Algozzine et al., in press). Nutrition may also play a role in behavior problems. The *quantity* of a person's intake of food, as in malnutrition, can cause some behavioral disorders. Likewise, the *quality* of a person's food input can also affect behavior. Vitamin deficiencies and food allergies have been suggested as causes for some behavioral disorders, especially some variations of hyperactivity and attention deficit disorder. Central nervous system dysfunction and brain injuries may also be related to aberrant behavior. Yet, in the vast majority of cases, even those involving severe disorders, there is no clear evidence of a specific biological etiology. The search for medical explanations and cures remains, to this day, mostly a matter of speculation.

It runs in the family, the genetic or hereditary explanation, is in operation for some psychological disorders. For example, an individual's chances of developing schizophrenia are much higher if he or she has parents with schizophrenia. Other types of severe disorders such as psychoses are also found more often among close blood relatives. However, some disorders may result from child-rearing practices as well as from genetic factors. Obtaining family histories and seeking genetic counseling are some of the ways that families can investigate these relationships. The search for genetic contributions to the development of disordered behavior, like the search for other biological causes, is still going on.

He has a sick mind is often the ultimate explanation of those who approach behavior from a psychoanalytic perspective. Algozzine et al., (in press) explain that in this view, emotional development, just like physical development " . . . is viewed as progressing through stages of development from immaturity and psychological dependency toward emotional maturity and independence." Childhood behavior disorders are thought to be the result of exaggerations in normal developmental stages, and deviant behavior is considered as symptomatic of underlying disturbances in development caused by failure to resolve important conflicts. To put it simplistically, emotional disorders result from early experiences that later cause anxiety, stress, or other unresolved emotions. There is not a great deal of scientific evidence for this point of view, but it is deeply and pervasively entrenched in our culture.

He just can't seem to find himself suggests that a person does not know or understand his own feelings or perceptions, or has not developed an adequate self-concept. Deviant behavior supposedly arises because the person has not learned introspection, self-awareness arenas, self-regard, sensitivity, and the like. The role of one's feelings and lack of self-awareness *as a cause* of emotional or behavioral disorders has not been demonstrated in any scientific manner.

He never learned how to get along implies that deviant patterns of behavior are learned and that appropriate behavior can be taught. A body of scientific evidence indicates that this may be correct, particularly for mild disorders; however, there is not conclusive evidence that *all* emotional problems (especially those that are more serious) are learned behaviors. Behavioral theory is especially important to educators because they are in the business of teaching children new patterns of behavior. When behaviors are considered to be the result of prior learning, then the learning environment can be arranged and teaching strategies can be used that will increase desirable behaviors or decrease undesirable ones. Students' problems are solvable (Algozzine et al., in press).

The disturbing versus disturbed question represents an ecological perspective on behavioral disorders. Ecological theorists believe that deviant behavior depends as much on where and with whom a child interacts as it does on the type of interactions of the individual. According to Algozzine et al. (in press), the ecological perspective is that "deviance, disturbance, and behavior problems are as much a function of reactions to behavior as they are the behavior in and of itself. Emotional disturbance is behavior that is poorly fitted to circumstances and setting." Even though ecological theorists agree that deviance is a misfit between a person's behavior and the expectations of the immediate environment, they do not necessarily agree on the source of the problem.

Most likely, behavioral disorders and emotional disturbance result from the interaction of many factors, including a genetic predisposition, a biophysical basis, family and societal factors, expectations of school and community, and stresses that may trigger or precipitate behavior problems. We do know that there are certain factors that predispose children to greater long-term risk for emotional and behavioral problems. Today's society is often a dangerous place for children.

Garwood and Sheehan (1989) summarized the conditions that are most likely to put infants and children at great risk for emotional as well as physical problems: poverty, single and teenage parent families, low birth weights, congenital anomalies, Fetal Alcohol Syndrome, Failure to Thrive, abuse and neglect, poor nutrition, and environmental poisons. In addition, risk factors like homelessness, substance abuse, and violence may give mental health a challenge. It sometimes seems that environmental conditions in some children's lives make it impossible *not* to have emotional or behavioral problems.

CLASSIFICATION SYSTEMS/CHARACTERISTICS

Classification of children with ED/BD has not been very meaningful for special educators. The traditional psychiatric categories have been of almost no value whatsoever in teaching. Some systems of classification

(Achenbach & Edelbrock, 1983; Quay, 1979) have identified children as primarily (a) aggressive, rude, attention-seeking, and hyperactive; (b) anxious, hypersensitive, fearful, and withdrawn; or (c) delinquent, truant, or antisocial (according to middle-class standards). The simplest and most productive classification system for *educators* has traditionally involved two categories: mild or moderate and severe. Though this distinction is not included in the definition (the title of the category is Seriously Emotionally Disturbed), it is one way to practically differentiate children based on the type and scope of educational intervention they require. Students who have mild or moderate problems can usually be taught in regular public school classes if the teacher gets some advice and consultation in behavior management; or they can be taught in resource rooms, where the child spends only part of the day with a specially trained teacher. Occasionally, these children (who are often labeled *neurotic, personality disordered,* or *behavior disordered*) must be taught in segregated special classes, but they are ordinarily returned to a regular class in 2 years or less. Children with severe problems, often classified as psychotic, frequently must be educated in special classes in public schools or sometimes in special schools or in institutions. Some children with severe ED/BD may never enter the educational mainstream.

Because the law requires that students be served in the least restrictive environment possible, it is important to consider the advantages and disadvantages of various placements before making a decision. Table 3.1 represents some of the advantages and disadvantages of various placement options for students with ED/BD.

CONCEPTUAL MODELS OF INSTRUCTION AND TREATMENT

There are different conceptual models—sets of assumptions about what the problem is, how it came about, and what can be done about it—that can be adopted in working with children with ED/BD (Gallagher, 1988). In fact, there are so many different models, each having proponents who claim their ideas are best and the advocates of other models are ignorant or malicious, that the field is confusing for a beginning student. We will try to guide you through this array of models.

You should keep three things in mind. First, there are many ways to group models that conceptually "slice" the field. Ours is not the only way to do it; other sources may give descriptions of more or fewer models or use different terminology. Second, relatively few professionals let themselves become the prisoners of a single model even though they think one model is better. Most thoughtful people realize that each model has its limitations and that it is an attempt to impose a useful

Table 3.1
Advantages and Disadvantages of More Restrictive and Less Restrictive Placements for Students With Serious Emotional Disturbance

Advantages	Disadvantages
Less Restrictive Placements	
• Regular Classrooms (with or without support)	
• Resource Rooms	
1. Prevents the regular educator from giving up on the child and turning to "experts"	1. Expense and time required to train regular educators to work with students and special educators and special educators to work as consultants to regular educators.
2. Permits students to model appropriate behavior of their peers; increased interaction	2. Problems with classroom management and discipline
3. Possibly less expensive	3. Lack of consistent expectations for the students
4. May be able to serve more students	4. Time and materials required for individualization
5. Students do not experience problems with reintegration	5. Fear and frustration of teachers
6. Students follow regular curriculum	
More Restrictive Placements	
• Hospitals	
• Residential Facilities	
• Separate Campuses	
• Separate Classes	
1. Flexibility to provide different curricula and different goals	1. Student's opportunities for peer interactions are limited, especially when student is not at neighborhood school with peers from his neighborhood
2. Progress can be more closely monitored	2. Travel time for students can be excessive
3. Accountability of program is more clearly defined	3. No possible modeling of appropriate peers; no opportunities for socialization with nondisabled peers
4. Intervention can be more consistent	4. Difficulties with reintegration back into regular school or class
5. Student follows only one set of guidelines and expectations	
6. Teacher's time goes to instruction only, not consultation	
7. One team for consistent discipline	

Source: From "Placement" by K. S. Fad, in press. In B. Algozzine, J. Patton, and L. Serna (Eds.), *Childhood behavior disorders*. Austin, TX: Pro-Ed.

order on information and events, but that it is not a full and complete description of reality. Third, you can get into trouble by being mindlessly eclectic. Many students and some professionals try to take the position that they see merit in *every* conceptual model. And because they want to maintain a friendly neutrality on all issues, they fail to make necessary judgments on the basis of research evidence or common sense. Our contention is that if you are going to help children with ED/BD most effectively, you have to have your feet on the ground *and* be guided by the findings of research.

Psychoanalytic Model

The psychoanalytic model, based on the ideas of Freud and other psychoanalysts, has its biggest appeal for psychotherapists and social workers. Educators who respond to this model tend to advocate a permissive classroom in which the child can "work through" or express his underlying problems freely. A premium is placed on two things: (1) an accepting attitude of the teacher toward the child's feelings and (2) an understanding of the unconscious motivation of the child's behavior. There are several problems in relying on the psychoanalytic model.

First, there is very little empirical research showing that it works. You may find anecdotal reports of successes or cases reporting favorable results, but few of these reports are based on scientific research. In most of them, the effects of "treatment" are not clearly and reliably measured or demonstrated. Second, this model does not focus on improving the student's actual behavior. It is very difficult for teachers to focus on *internal* changes in students when the students' behaviors are disruptive, aggressive, antisocial, or dangerous. The third limitation of the psychoanalytic model is that the process of psychoanalysis is very time consuming, and its time lines are not always realistic. Waiting months or even years for the change process endorsed by this model may be impractical and frustrating.

Psychoeducational Model

Psychoeducation is not well defined, even by the people who are identified with it. Implying a combination of psychological and educational concepts, this model includes psychoanalytic ideas about unconscious motivation and puts a premium on the teacher-pupil relationship. There is a concern for "surface behavior" (what children *do*) and for academic progress, primarily achieved by talking to children and getting them to achieve insight into their own problems. This model offers most of its teaching through projects and creative arts. Although we think the psychoeducational approach is far more sensible than the psychoanalytic model, it still suffers from the same flaw—little or no supporting data from empirical research. However, it does represent some commonsense approaches to talking to children about their behavior, including the *life-space interview,* developed by Long. Another strategy that has its roots in the psychoeducational model is cognitive behavioral modification training, which is supported by scientific research data.

Humanistic Model

Nonauthoritarian, self-directed, self-evaluative, affective, open, personal—these words are often used to describe the humanistic model. This model grew out of humanistic psychology and the development of open schools, alternative schools, and other nontraditional practices of the late 1960s and early 1970s. These approaches represent an attempt to give more attention to the affective side of education and to get children more involved in their own education. Humanistic educators made important contributions to society by highlighting how it feels to learn, succeed, fail, be a pupil, be a teacher—in other words, how it feels to be human. Unfortunately, the proponents of this model seem too often satisfied with merely developing a nontraditional educational setting and have not always documented its effectiveness in helping children improve their academic learning and behavior.

Ecological Model

Many concepts of the ecological model were adapted from research in biological ecology and ecological psychology. Every child is enmeshed in a complex social system. Consequently, one has to consider the entire social system, not just the child in isolation. Educators should be concerned with the child in the classroom, the family, the neighborhood, and all other arenas of the social environment. The value we see in this model is not in the specific tactics it offers for teaching or managing behavior, but in its overall approach or strategy for dealing with the child's problems. For example, one might use behavior modification tactics for teaching and managing the child, but use an ecological strategy that involves the child's family and community. The ecological view seems very sensible to many educators and is also supported by some research.

Behavioral Model

The behavioral model includes these fundamental ideas: (1) behavior can be observed and directly and reliably measured; (2) behavioral excesses and deficits *are* the problem, not underlying or unconscious feelings; and (3) behavior is a function of its consequences and can be modified by changing the consequences. If children's behavior is learned, then the problem with children with ED/BD must be that they have learned the wrong behaviors. The solution is to teach them new, more appropriate ones. In classrooms operated according to a behavioral model, specific behavioral goals are achieved by using specific teaching and management techniques. Also, a careful daily measurement of behavior is designed to tell the teacher to what extent the techniques are leading to an achievement of the goals.

The behavioral model seems to be the most valuable model for teachers for two reasons: (1) it is supported by more scientific research than any of the others; and (2) it is compatible with certain sensible, research-supported aspects of other models. One can talk meaningfully with children about their behavior (psychoeducational), care about their feelings and individuality (humanistic), deal with all aspects of their social environment (ecological), and still be a good behaviorist. *But without the behavioral model as a basis, the components of the other models are relatively much less significant or useful.*

Because children with ED/BD come to the attention of teachers, parents, peers, and others as a result of their behavioral excesses and deficiencies, many professionals remain firmly committed to working with students' observable behaviors. Kauffman's 1986 challenge to educators is still pertinent:

> Not to define precisely and measure these behavioral excesses and deficiencies, then, is a fundamental error: It is akin to the malpractice of a nurse who decides not to measure vital signs (heart rate, respiration rate, temperature, and blood pressure), perhaps arguing that he/she is too busy, that subjective estimates of vital signs are quite adequate, that vital signs are only superficial estimates of the patient's health, or that the vital signs do not signify the nature of the underlying pathology. The teaching profession is dedicated to the task of changing behavior demonstrably for the better. What can one say, then, of educational practice that does not include reliable and forthright measurement of the behavior change induced by the teacher's methodology? I believe simply this: *It is indefensible* (pp. 339–340).

ISSUES IN THE EDUCATION OF CHILDREN WITH ED/BD

One of the foremost challenges to both regular and special educators today is how to best serve the growing numbers of students with emotional and behavioral problems. For a long time, their treatment was the domain of psychotherapists, usually psychiatrists (medical doctors with training in psychiatry), psychoanalysts (psychiatrists with a special training in psychoanalysis), or clinical psychologists (nonphysicians with advanced graduate training in psychology). Fortunately, most psychotherapists now readily admit that teachers are also equipped to offer significant assistance to these students. Despite the best efforts of mental health professionals and educators, the outlook for students with emotional and behavioral problems is bleak. Some of the problems for students in this category are detailed in the following:

- Students with emotional and behavioral problems seem to be significantly under identified and under served. The Council for Children with Behavioral Disorders (CCBD) estimates that less than half of the eligible students in this category are receiving services.

- Students with emotional and behavioral problems are the worst of all 12 special education categories on several key indicators: *days absent per year, grade-point average, drop-out rate,* and *productive involvement after high school.* They are also very likely to be involved in criminal activity after leaving school (U.S. Department of Education, 1993).

- The placement information for students with emotional and behavioral problems demonstrates a pattern of very restrictive placements. More than 54% of students in this category are in separate classes, separate schools, or residential or homebound placements.

- The "social maladjustment" issue is a serious concern. CCBD believes that this exclusionary clause denies services to students with underlying emotional disorders such as depression or anxiety because those students often demonstrate serious acting out behaviors and are discipline problems.

- The educational services provided for students with emotional problems often do not meet their needs. Epstein, Foley, and Cullinan (1992) surveyed teachers about their ED/BD students. Their survey indicated that teachers often have no systematic, well-thought-out, justifiable program for these students, relying instead on a hodgepodge of features that may or may not be effective.

- One of the biggest problems for professionals who deal with students who are emotionally disturbed/behaviorally disordered is prevention. We have not really done a very good job with early identification and prevention of problems *before* they get serious. Recently, several studies have investigated the factors that put students at greatest risk for serious problems. Not surprisingly, these factors, which are presented in Table 3.2, have a lot to do with students' families. Because the number of students with serious emotional disturbance (SED) is increasing, there will likely be an ever increasing need for communities to attend to some of these risk factors while children are still young and before they develop serious behavioral problems.

INCLUSION OF STUDENTS WITH EMOTIONAL/BEHAVIORAL PROBLEMS

There is increased pressure today to include all students with disabilities in regular education environments. However, since students with ED/BD often display challenging and/or disruptive behaviors, regular educators may be reluctant to include them in regular education situations. In addition, their educational needs, which often include a structured environment and instruction emphasizing social competencies, cannot always be met in regular education. In the spring of 1993, the Executive Committee of the CCBD met and discussed the group's position on "full inclusion." The resulting CCBD position on inclusion of students with emotional and behavioral disorders is stated below:

> Consistent with IDEA, CCBD supports a full continuum of mental health and special education services for children and youth with emotional and behavioral disorders. We believe that educational decisions depend on individual students' needs. Consequently, in contrast to those individuals and groups who advocate for full inclusion, CCBD does **not** support the notion that all special education students, including those students with emotional and behavioral disorders, are always best served in general education classrooms (Position Statement on Full Inclusion, 1993).

The requirements of the law are clear: A full continuum of services must be available and decisions about students' programs must be made on an individual basis.

SUGGESTIONS FOR WORKING WITH STUDENTS WITH ED/BD

1. Children with ED/BD are masters at making their problems yours. Make sure you don't let yourself get caught up in their

Table 3.2
Factors That Put Students At Risk for Serious Emotional or Behavioral Problems

Percent of Sample	
	Family/Setting Risk Factors
52.4%	Family income below poverty level
52.4%	Divorce between natural parents
30.0%	Three or more siblings
11.5%	Adopted
16.3%	Parent psychiatric hospitalization
18.7%	Parent convicted of felony (current or previous)
14.2%	Siblings institutionalized (current or previous)
17.2%	Siblings in foster care
37.8%	History of family mental illness
58.1%	History of family violence
48.1%	History of family chemical dependence
11.2%	Family unavailable for aftercare
40.3%	Negative peer influence
	Child Risk Factors
59.6%	Previous psychiatric hospitalization
40.3%	Physically abused (reported)
36.3%	Sexually abused (reported)
15.7%	Chronic runaway (greater than 3 prior attempts)
20.6%	Suicide attempt(s)
29.0%	Chronic school truancy
69.6%	Below grade-level school achievement
8.7%	Drug/alcohol dependency
36.3%	Frequent suspension/expulsion
18.1%	Other handicapping conditions (e.g., physical, sensory)
	Child Dangerousness
4.8%	Sexually abusive (adjudicated)
1.8%	Previous felony conviction
65.1%	Dangerous to others (history of aggression/violence)
41.8%	Dangerous to self (self-injurious)
20.6%	Fire-setting

Source: From *Integrating Services for Children and Youth With Emotional and Behavioral Disorders* (p. 6) by C. M. Nelson and C. A. Pearson, 1991, Reston, VA: The Council for Exceptional Children. Reprinted by permission.

"pathology." For example, such children may try to drag you into senseless arguments or make you feel that their problems with following classroom rules are your fault. You must emotionally distance yourself from interactions with children to be able to tell their difficulties from yours.

2. Children should know what you expect from them. Children with ED/BD especially need to know what is and is not OK. Don't keep them guessing.

3. When you make a rule or give an instruction, make it stick. By this we mean think through the rule or instruction before you give it, tell the child the consequences of meeting or not meeting your expectation, and be consistent in applying the consequences. Before you tell the child what to do, you must consider whether doing it is appropriate and important, whether the consequences are reasonable and desirable, and whether or not you can follow through with the consequences.

4. Don't expect love and attention in return. If all that children with ED/BD needed was someone to love them, we could cure most of them next year (maybe even this year!). If you want to help them, you must be willing to extend love, affection, and *structure*—appropriate rules, clear expectations, and consistent consequences—without the expectation that you'll receive respect, love, or gratitude in return.

5. Don't demand perfection or steady progress; do expect gradual improvement. Remember that we all have our quirks and our bad days. Life for most children with ED/BD is especially rocky. The goal is to help them get their behavior smoothed out enough to live happily and independently in the mainstream of society. The goal can't be reached overnight, and it leaves a lot of room for imperfection by most people's standards.

6. Try very hard to work with the families of ED/BD students. Communication is very important. Behavior change will come more quickly when parents and teachers are consistent in their expectations and with their consequences. When in doubt, communicate!

◆ *PONDER THESE*

1. *Study the following behaviors. According to your interpretation of the definition, which behaviors indicate*

emotional disturbance or a behavioral disorder? Under what conditions, if any, would you consider the behaviors normal? Rank order them from most serious to least serious.

- Interrupting conversations
- Banging head against the wall
- Screaming
- Killing another person
- Refusing to work
- Eating paper
- Swearing
- Saying, "I'm no good. I hate myself. I wish I were dead."
- Sleeping in class
- Setting fire to the bathroom

2. *Consider the following scenario, and then describe ways you could respond to the situation:*

    Elmer has a pair of scissors. He is making deep scratches on the wall of the classroom. You tell him to stop, but he pays no attention. You go to him and take hold of his arm and matter-of-factly say, "No, Elmer, you can't do that." He flies at you, tries to scratch you with the scissors, and screams, "Let me go, you *$!" You loosen your grip on Elmer, and he runs out of the room. You follow, but lose sight of him as he rounds the corner at the end of the hall. You suspect that he has gone into the boys' rest room. As you enter the rest room, you see Elmer perched on top of the stall partition. He has taken off one shoe and is about to throw it at you. As you approach him he shouts, "Get away from me. You can't make me come down. I'll kill you, you *$!. I'll break my leg, and then my dad will sue you. You come any closer and I'll knock your teeth out."

3. *Children with ED/BD have a way of forcing other people to make decisions for them or about their behavior. Much of the controversy in the field concerns the child's right to make his own decisions versus the teacher's responsibility to make decisions for the child. For each of the following problems, specify the decisions you would be willing to make for a child and those you believe should be left to him:*

- The student is not coming to class on time.
- The student refuses to read.
- The student hits others.
- The student makes loud animal noises in class.
- The student takes things that are not his.
- The student does not bathe and smells so bad no one will sit by him.

References

Achenbach, T. M., & Edelbrock, C. S. (1983). Taxonomic issues in child psychopathology. In T. H. Ollendick & M. Hersen (Eds.), *Handbook of child psychopathology* (pp. 65–93). New York: Plenum.

Algozzine, B., Patton, J., & Serna, L. (in press). *Childhood behavior disorders.* Austin, TX: Pro-Ed.

American Psychiatric Association. (1994). *Diagnostic and statistical manual of mental disorders* (4th ed.). Washington, DC: Author.

Bower, E. M. (1959). The emotionally handicapped child and the school. *Exceptional Children, 26,* 6–11.

Bower, E. M. (1982). Defining emotional disturbance: Public policy and research. *Psychology in the Schools, 19,* 55–60.

Epstein, J. H., Foley, R. M., & Cullinan, D. (1992). National survey of educational programs for adolescents with serious emotional disturbance. *Behavioral Disorders, 17*(3), 202–210.

Gallagher, P. A. (1988). *Teaching students with behavioral disorders. Techniques and activities for classroom instruction.* Denver, CO: Love Publishing Company.

Garwood, S. G., & Sheehan, R. (1989). *Designing a comprehensive early intervention system: The challenge of Public Law 99–457.* Austin, TX: Pro-Ed.

Kauffman, J. M. (1986). Educating children with behavior disorders. In R. J. Morris & B. Blatt (Eds.), *Special education: Research and trends* (pp. 249–271). New York: Pergamon.

Kauffman, J. M. (1993). *Characteristics of emotional and behavioral disorders of children and youth* (5th ed.). Englewood Cliffs, NJ: Merrill/Prentice Hall.

Nelson, C. M., Rutherford, R. B., Center, D. B., & Walker, H. M. (1991). Do public schools have an obligation to serve troubled children and youth? *Exceptional Children, 57*(5), 406–415.

Position statement on full inclusion. (1993, August). *CCBD Newsletter,* p. 1.

Problems found in 1 to 5 children. (1990, December 9). *Washington Post,* p. A27.

Quay, H. C. (1979). Classification. In H. C. Quay & J. S. Werry (Eds.), *Psychopathological disorders of childhood* (2nd ed.), (pp. 1–42). New York: Wiley.

U.S. Department of Education. (1993). *To assure the free appropriate public education of all children with disabilities. Fifteenth annual report to Congress on the implementation of the Individuals With Disabilities Education Act.* Washington, DC: Author.

4

ATTENTION DEFICIT/ HYPERACTIVITY DISORDER

Sam, a very bright fourth grader, was found to have Attention Deficit/Hyperactivity Disorder (ADHD). He had an extremely difficult time paying attention to what was going on in the classroom. In a previous school, his resulting frustration with not being able to follow a discussion or teacher presentation led to some strange and inappropriate behaviors. These behaviors had become so extreme (e.g., getting on the floor and barking like a dog—his creativity allowed him to imitate a variety of breeds) that he was considered emotionally disturbed.

A number of months after he had been diagnosed as ADHD and had been on Ritalin, he approached his teacher and asked if he could stop taking the medication because he did not like the way it made him feel. Although it was not the teacher's call nor were his attention problems and hyperactivity completely under control, the teacher did contact Sam's mother and physician to discuss an idea she had. The teacher was comfortable in trying a behavioral program with Sam in the absence of any pharmacological intervention. She felt that Sam had demonstrated the incentive necessary to make such a system work.

This chapter has been adapted from *Attention Deficit Hyperactivity Disorder in the Classroom: A Practical Guide for Teachers* by C. A. Dowdy, J. R. Patton, T. E. C. Smith, and E. A. Polloway, in press, Austin: Pro-Ed. Adapted by permission.

71

The intervention was based on cueing Sam when his behavior was getting "out of control." When Sam started losing it, the teacher would briefly stop what she was doing, get his attention, and say "Sam, you need to get in control." She would also fingerspell the letters i and c as a paired association for "in control." Sam's response was typically an immediate attempt to get his behavior under his own control because he knew that otherwise he would have to get back on medication.

The goal of the program was self-control. The verbal reminder was faded out, so the teacher—never breaking her instructional stride—would simply fingerspell the letters i and c whenever necessary. Over the course of a few weeks, Sam was able to control his inattentive behaviors at levels comparable to his classmates. He never had to take medication for his attentional problems again.

With his ability to control his own behaviors successfully, he was able to engage his schooling in ways he had not been able to do previously. He graduated from high school with honors and went on to attend one of the most prestigious institutions in the United States, majoring in engineering. There is no question that, even after he was able to self-regulate his behaviors, he still had his share of educational mishaps. However, his education journey turned out to be quite different from what was predicted by observers during his dog days of elementary school.

Attention deficit/hyperactivity disorder (ADHD) is one of the most intriguing, beguiling, and complicated topics in the field of education. It is also recognized as one of the most common childhood disorders. This condition has had a fascinating history and remains controversial today, mainly because professional perspectives and personal opinions vary greatly regarding the nature and treatment of ADHD. Nevertheless, the last few years have witnessed an increased awareness of and activity regarding this disorder.

DEFINITIONAL PERSPECTIVE

Attention deficit/hyperactivity disorder is an invisible developmental disability that affects a significant number of individuals. As a developmental disability, it can be identified in childhood, continue into adulthood, result in significant problems in many functional life activities, and require certain services. For students, functional limitations will be reflected in difficulty with an assortment of school-related activities, both academic and nonacademic. ADHD is a hidden disability because there are no specific physical characteristics associated with the condition; it is only through behavioral manifestations that it becomes recognizable.

Various terms have been used throughout the 50 years that the concept has been reported in the literature (Lerner & Lerner, 1991). Fundamentally, however, the condition has referred to problems in attention, impulsivity, and hyperactivity. The predominance of any one of these features at a given period of time is a function of the professional thinking at that time.

Currently, the term *attention deficit/hyperactivity disorder* is being used most frequently in the United States. This terminology is used in the fourth edition of the *Diagnostic and Statistical Manual of Mental Disorders* (DSM-IV), published in 1994—the most frequently cited reference on this condition. From a global perspective, the World Health Organization's tenth edition of the *International Classification of Diseases* (ICD-10), published in 1992, is typically used and promotes the term *hyperkinetic disorders* to describe conditions related to problems in attention and hyperactivity.

Diagnostic Criteria

According to the *Diagnostic and Statistical Manual of Mental Disorders* (DSM-IV), ADHD is classified as a disruptive disorder characterized by persistent patterns and inappropriate degrees of inattention and/or hyperactivity-impulsivity. These principal features distinguish ADHD from other disruptive disorders such as conduct order (i.e., physical fighting) and oppositional defiant behavior (i.e., recurrent pattern of disobedience).

The major criteria contained in DSM-IV are likely to guide diagnostic practice in the near future. The final criteria evolved from extensive committee work and changed throughout the process of revision. According to DSM-IV, ADHD can be one of four types that are based on two sets of symptoms. The diagnostic criteria are presented in Table 4.1.

Based on the criteria listed in Table 4.1, four types of ADHD are possible. The DSM-IV codes for these four are listed in brackets.

- Attention-deficit/hyperactivity disorder, combined type (if criteria A1 and A2 are met for the past 6 months) [314.01]
- Attention-deficit/hyperactivity disorder, predominantly inattentive type (if criterion A1 is met but criterion A2 is not met for the last 6 months) [314.00]
- Attention-deficit/hyperactivity disorder, predominantly hyperactive-impulsive type (if criterion A2 is met but criterion A1 is not met for the last 6 months) [314.01]

Table 4.1

DSM-IV Diagnostic Criteria for Attention-Deficit/Hyperactivity Disorder

A. Either (1) or (2):

    (1) six (or more) of the following symptoms of **inattention** have persisted for at least 6 months to a degree that is maladaptive and inconsistent with developmental level:

        Inattention

        (a) often fails to give close attention to details or makes careless mistakes in schoolwork, work, or other activities

        (b) often has difficulty sustaining attention in tasks or play activities

        (c) often does not seem to listen when spoken to directly

        (d) often does not follow through on instructions and fails to finish schoolwork, chores, or duties in the workplace (not due to oppositional behavior or failure to understand instructions)

        (e) often has difficulty organizing tasks and activities

        (f) often avoids, dislikes, or is reluctant to engage in tasks that require sustained mental effort (such as schoolwork or homework)

        (g) often loses things necessary for tasks or activities (e.g., toys, school assignments, pencils, books, or tools)

        (h) is often easily distracted by extraneous stimuli

        (i) is often forgetful in daily activities

    (2) six (or more) of the following symptoms of **hyperactivity-impulsivity** have persisted for at least 6 months to a degree that is maladaptive and inconsistent with developmental level:

        Hyperactivity

        (a) often fidgets with hands or feet or squirms in seat

        (b) often leaves seat in classroom or in other situations in which remaining seated is expected

        (c) often runs about or climbs excessively in situations in which it is inappropriate (in adolescents or adults, may be limited to subjective feelings or restlessness)

        (d) often has difficulty playing or engaging in leisure activities quietly

        (e) is often "on the go" or often acts as if "driven by a motor"

        (f) often talks excessively

        Impulsivity

        (g) often blurts out answers before questions have been completed

        (h) often has difficulty awaiting turn

        (i) often interrupts or intrudes on others (e.g., butts into conversations or games)

Table 4.1
continued

B. Some hyperactive-impulsive or inattentive symptoms that caused impairment were present before age 7 years.

C. Some impairment from the symptoms is present in two or more settings (e.g., at school [or work] and at home).

D. There must be clear evidence of clinically significant impairment in social, academic or occupational functioning.

E. The symptoms do not occur exclusively during the course of a pervasive developmental disorder, schizophrenia, or other psychotic disorder and are not better accounted for by another mental disorder (e.g., mood disorder, anxiety disorder, dissociative disorder, or a personality disorder).

Code based on type:

314.01   Attention-Deficit/Hyperactivity Disorder, Combined Type: if both Criteria A1 and A2 are met for the past 6 months

314.00   Attention-Deficit/Hyperactivity Disorder, Predominantly Inattentive Type: if Criterion A1 is met but Criterion A2 is not met for the past 6 months

314.01   Attention-Deficit/Hyperactivity Disorder, Predominantly Hyperactive-Impulsive Type: if Criterion A2 is met but Criterion A1 is not met for the past 6 months

Coding note: For individuals (especially adolescents and adults) who currently have symptoms that no longer meet full criteria, "In Partial Remission" should be specified.

314.9   Attention-Deficit/Hyperactivity Disorder Not Otherwise Specified: This category is for disorders with prominent symptoms of inattention or hyperactivity-impulsivity that do not meet criteria for Attention-Deficit/Hyperactivity Disorder.

Source: From *Diagnostic and Statistical Manual of Mental Disorders* (4th ed., pp. 83–85) by the American Psychiatric Association, 1994, Washington, DC: Author. Reprinted by permission.

- Attention-deficit/hyperactivity disorder not otherwise specified (for disorders with prominent symptoms of inattention or hyperactivity-impulsivity that do not meet criteria for ADHD) [314.09]

Teachers should be familiar with the symptoms that are associated with the criteria listed in Table 4.1 and with the different types of ADHD. Since the diagnosis of ADHD typically occurs in noneducational settings by psychologists or medical personnel, students so identified will bring with them a dossier of information about their condition that most likely will be based on DSM-IV criteria.

Prevalence of ADHD

Estimates of the existence of attention deficit/hyperactivity disorder in the school-age population range from conservative figures under 2% to liberal ones of 30%. These extreme variations in prevalence rates reflect the lack of an exact definition and problems in identification. Nevertheless, even more conservative estimates suggest that a substantial number of individuals may have this condition.

LEGAL BASES FOR SERVICE DELIVERY AND PROTECTION

Individuals With Disabilities Act (IDEA) (PL 101–476)

Attention deficit/hyperactivity disorder is recognized as a disability under IDEA. However, it was not added as a separate disability category in the 1990 reauthorization of this law. Some people are pleased that ADHD has finally been recognized under IDEA; others are very disappointed that it did not become a distinct category of disability.

In 1991, the U.S. Department of Education issued a Policy Memorandum that indicated that students with attention deficit disorder (the terminology used by DOE) who need special education and/or related services can qualify for such services under existing categories. Students whose primary disability is ADHD are eligible under the category Other Health Impaired (OHI). This category includes all chronic and acute conditions that result in limited alertness and that adversely affect educational performance. To date, there is little evidence to suggest that the OHI categorical designation is being utilized for students identified as ADHD (Reid, Maag, Vasa, & Wright, 1994).

Students whose primary disability is not ADHD, although they display the symptoms highlighted in Table 4.1, may be likely to qualify under other categories. For instance, Reid et al. (1994), in their school-based study of students with ADHD who were receiving special education services, found that nearly 52% were identified as behaviorally disordered, 29% were identified as learning disabled, and 9% were identified as mentally retarded.

Prior to the U.S. Department of Education's (1991) Policy Memorandum, many professionals in the field of learning disabilities assumed that students with attention deficit/hyperactivity disorders who were experiencing significant problems in school were meeting eligibility requirements for learning disabilities and therefore receiving services. In reality, however, only approximately 50% of those students with ADHD were qualifying for special educational services. The often heated discussion preceding the reauthorization of IDEA in 1990,

which focused on whether ADHD should be a separate disability category, drew attention to this underserved group of students.

Over the last few years, many professionals have come to realize
that there was a sizable number of students with ADHD who were
floundering in school and not qualifying for services that might be beneficial to them. As a result, changes in policy and thinking have
occurred. Unfortunately, policy and thinking do not always result in
best practice.

Section 504 of the Vocational Rehabilitation Act (PL 93–112)

In the past, some students, albeit not many, have qualified for services
under Section 504 of the Vocational Rehabilitation Act. The intent of
the law as it applies to schools is to provide general or special education and related aids and services that are designed to meet individual
educational needs of persons with disabilities as adequately as the
needs of those who are not disabled. This is not a "special education"
law but a civil rights law that covers the entire educational system.

Section 504 includes a larger group of persons who are disabled
and differs in some respects from IDEA. This law protects all students
who have disabilities, defined as any physical or mental impairment
that substantially limits one or more major life activities. Since one of
the stated life activities is learning, it becomes obvious that it also
applies to schools. If a school has reason to believe that a student has
a disability as defined under Section 504, the school must evaluate the
student. If it is determined that the student is disabled under this law,
then the school must develop and implement a plan for the delivery of
services that are needed (Council of Administrators of Special Education, 1992). However, a written individual education program (IEP) is
not required.

If a student with ADHD cannot qualify for services under IDEA, it
might be possible to do so under Section 504. However, many of the
substantive and procedural components found in IDEA are either different or missing. Nevertheless, Section 504 provides another avenue
for accommodating the needs of students with ADHD. Figure 4.1 provides a flow chart of how both IDEA and Section 504 function relative
to a possible diagnosis of ADHD.

CAUSES OF ADHD

Like the causes of other developmental disabilities of students, the
precise etiology of ADHD typically is not known or cannot be specified.

Figure 4.1
IDEA/504 Flow Chart

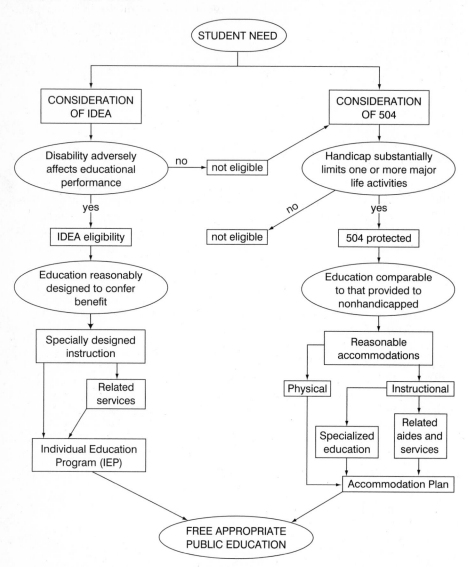

Source: From *Student Access: A Resource Guide for Educators: Section 504 of the Rehabilitation Act of 1973* by the Council for Administrators of Special Education, 1992, Reston, VA: Author. Reprinted by permission.

However, most professionals agree that it is a neurologically based condition. Whether the exact causes are neuroanatomical (i.e., brain structure), neurochemical (i.e., chemical imbalance), neurophysiological (i.e., brain function), or some combination of these is still being investigated. As a result, neurological evidence for explaining ADHD is not yet available (Riccio, Hynd, Cohen, & Gonzalez, 1993).

Some data exist to suggest that genetics may play a role in ADHD. Studies have shown a familial association of various features associated with it. Parents and siblings of children with this disorder have higher rates than would be expected. Certain neurological conditions may be transmitted genetically that predispose an individual to attention and hyperactive problems.

GENERAL FEATURES OF ADHD

Placement Realities

Most students with ADHD are in general education classrooms and do not need to be removed from these settings. However, certain accommodations may need to be made to address their needs. Reid et al. (1994) found that the great majority of students with ADHD who were receiving special education services were in general education most, or all, of their school day.

That most students are in general education suggests that classroom teachers need to understand this condition and know how to deal with it. Special educators must be prepared to collaborate with general educators in this venture and know how to modify curriculum, instruction, and assignments. Special education teachers also need to be competent managers of behavior and adept at teaching students how to manage their own behavior.

Classroom Manifestations

The specific characteristics of ADHD that manifest themselves in the classroom can vary greatly. Recognizing them and knowing how to accommodate them are the challenges that confront teachers. A general sense of what behavior might arise in classroom settings is available from examining the DSM-IV criteria. Behaviors that might be associated with ADHD and manifested in classroom settings can be grouped into the following categories: attention/concentration, reasoning/information processing, memory, executive functions (e.g., planning/organizing actions), social/emotional areas, communication, and academic performance.

Most of the suggested ways for accommodating each presenting behavior are relatively minor modifications and can be accomplished easily. However, the payoff for taking the time to make these accommodations is well worth the effort. Specific techniques for addressing various classroom manifestations of ADHD can be found in other sources (Dowdy et al., in press; Reiff, 1993).

A classroom behavior that is often misinterpreted by teachers is a lack of confidence. As Goldstein and Goldstein (1990) point out, what is often seen as purposeful noncompliance is actually better viewed as a lack of competence. In other words, many students with ADHD will seem to defy teacher directives when in fact they really are not able to react in a competent way. The misinterpretation of a lack of confidence and the likely punishment that follows it create problems for students who are really not trying to defy their teachers. For this reason, it is important that teachers are aware of this phenomenon and able to distinguish between the two behaviors.

Attainment/Outcome Data

As mentioned previously, ADHD may endure into adulthood. Two scenarios are possible: (1) The characteristics associated with one's condition continue to be problematic for the individual; (2) the residual effects of previous problems associated with ADHD linger. Either scenario can have a profound effect on the adult outcomes of individuals with ADHD.

Much of what is known about the adult status of individuals with ADHD comes from follow-up studies that have been conducted. The literature on adults with ADHD reveals that a significant portion of those who have it will have difficulty dealing with the demands of adulthood. As Goldstein and Goldstein (1990) state, "The years of ADHD problems certainly take their toll on adult outcomes" (p. 25). They also note that successful adult adjustment is determined by the following general variables: intelligence, socioeconomic status, socialization, activity level, ability to delay rewards, aggression, and family mental health.

SCHOOL-BASED MODEL OF INTERVENTION

Even though it has been established that ADHD is not just a childhood condition, it is also true that most intervention efforts, when they are implemented, occur in school settings. This is not to suggest that adult issues are not as important, because various facets of ADHD can affect significantly the lives of adults.

A school-based approach to addressing the needs of students with ADHD must be comprehensive to assure appropriateness. A model of educational intervention that covers a full range of target areas is depicted in Figure 4.2. This model is built on four fundamental intervention areas: environmental management, instructional accommodations, student-regulated strategies, and medical management. It also contains two mediating variables (identification and placement/programmatic considerations) that influence how the four major areas are invoked. The model also has two supportive features (counseling and collaboration) that enhance the overall quality of intervention services. A brief explanation of the four major intervention areas is provided.

Environmental Management

Environmental management relates closely to the concept of classroom management, which can be defined as "all teacher-directed activities that support the efficient operations of the classroom that lead to the establishment of optimal conditions or learning and order" (Smith, Polloway, Patton, & Dowdy, 1995, p. 350). Changes to the classroom setting and implementation of behavior management systems are examples of environmental management.

Classroom or environmental management is made up of seven dimensions, all of which should be considered when addressing the needs of students with ADHD. The following are various management dimensions and select examples that relate to students with ADHD:

1. Psychosocial: student, teacher, peer, family factors
2. Physical: arrangement of classroom, seating, assistive technology
3. Instructional: scheduling, transitions, grouping, lesson planning, homework
4. Procedural: classroom rules and procedures

Figure 4.2
Model of Educational Intervention

Source: From *Attention Deficit Hyperactivity Disorder in the Classroom: A Practical Guide for Teachers* by C. A. Dowdy, J. R. Patton, T. E. C. Smith, and E. A. Polloway, in press, Austin: Pro-Ed. Reprinted by permission.

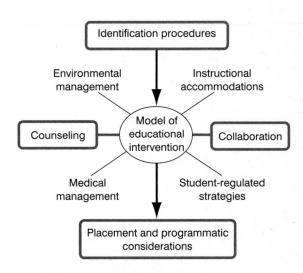

5. Behavior: creating and increasing desirable behaviors, decreasing undesirable behaviors, generalizing and maintaining behaviors

6. Personnel: teaching assistance, peer tutors, volunteers

7. Time: work environment of teacher, instructional applications

A working understanding and proper application of behavior management principles are extremely important. Emphasis should be on the use of positive reinforcement and movement toward a system where students self-regulate their behaviors.

Instructional Accommodations

Students with ADHD may benefit greatly from certain accommodations that are made to their instructional programs. Such accommodations can involve curriculum, materials, instructional processes, and the products students produce as a result of instruction. Examples of accommodations that may be appropriate for students with ADHD include:

1. Curriculum: life, study, and social skills instruction

2. Material: use of a variety of media, advanced organizers, multi-level materials, graphic aids, highlighting

3. Process: active involvement in the lesson; use of demonstration/guided practice/independent practice paradigm; clearly stated directions; cooperative learning situations; adaptations regarding speed, accuracy, and amount of assigned work

4. Products: alternative final products, portfolios, testing accommodations, grading considerations

Student-Regulated Strategies

These strategies, though initially taught by the teacher, can be viewed as interventions that are intended to be implemented independently by the students. Characteristically, students with ADHD display certain behaviors (e.g., various attentional problems) for which self-regulatory interventions (e.g., self-monitoring) are appropriate and warranted. These strategies offer the promise of enhancing the educational development of students with ADHD by:

• Increasing their selective attention/focus
• Modifying their impulsive responding

- Providing them with verbal mediators to assist in academic and social problem-solving situations
- Teaching them effective self-instructional statements to enable them to "talk through" tasks and problems
- Providing strategies that may lead to improvement in peer relations and the development of prosocial behaviors (Rooney, 1995)

Medical Management

Although school personnel are not involved in the prescription of medication for students with ADHD, they do play an important role in its usage. Monitoring students who are on medication is probably the most critical aspect of being part of the treatment team. It is essential that school personnel communicate with parents and physicians regarding the effects of the medications that a student is taking.

The most commonly used medication is methylphenidate (the brand name is Ritalin), which is a mild stimulant. Studies have indicated that 84% to 93% of medical professionals who prescribe medication for children with ADHD select this drug. Another medication used with children with ADHD is premoline (the brand name is Cylert).

The medications prescribed to address the behaviors associated with ADHD have a number of possible outcomes, which range from positive to negative. Some of the desirable outcomes of using medication with students who have ADHD are increased attention, improved academic performance, and increased appropriate behaviors. Some of the negative outcomes include weight loss, irritability, behavior swings, nausea, organ damage, and dizziness. All involved with the treatment program must be alert to all of these factors and willing to make adjustments as necessary.

FINAL THOUGHTS

Attention deficit/hyperactivity disorder is a condition that has been discussed for some time now, but it still remains illusive. ADHD continues to mystify the profession, families, and those who have it. From a school perspective, students with ADHD present a real challenge, as they have problems that are at the heart of the process. From an adult perspective, these same characteristics, plus the baggage that comes with living with these problems for many years, can have a significant effect on major life functions. For these reasons, we must take this condition seriously and strive to do the following:

- Create accommodative environments in which persons with ADHD can thrive.
- Teach self-regulatory behaviors that create independence.
- Provide appropriate supports, as needed.
- Link individuals with requisite services.

SUGGESTIONS FOR WORKING WITH PERSONS WITH ADHD

1. Consider the physical arrangements in which the person will be, whether it be a classroom or the workplace.
2. Present both verbal and nonverbal information in a clear and organized fashion.
3. Understand that certain behaviors should not be interpreted as noncompliance.
4. Allow individuals who are hyperactive to have opportunities to be active.
5. Refrain from using a behaviorial intervention system that is largely dominated by the use of negative reinforcement (e.g., threats).
6. Teach individuals to manage their own behaviors.
7. Be an active member of the person's intervention team.
8. Prevent potential problems by considering them ahead of time and instituting appropriate accommodations.
9. Monitor the outcomes of a prescribed medication closely, and report this information regularly to parents and the treating physician.
10. Help individuals gain a realistic understanding of their strengths and limitations.

✦ *PONDER THESE*

1. *Consider the cross-cultural implications of ADHD. Are the criteria established in DSM-IV valid in other parts of the world?*
2. *Are there television personalities—either actors or characters portrayed by actors—whose behaviors suggest a possible ADHD label?*

3. *Explain why students with ADHD continue to be under-identified and underserved in schools today.*

4. *How might the following areas of adult functioning be affected for someone with ADHD?*

- *Interpersonal relationships*
- *Personal responsibility*
- *Personal financial management*
- *Job seeking*
- *Leisure pursuits*

References

Dowdy, C. A., Patton, J. R., Smith, T. E. C., & Polloway, E. A. (in press). *Attention deficit hyperactivity disorder in the classroom: A practical guide for teachers.* Austin: Pro-Ed.

Goldstein S., & Goldstein, M. (1990). *Managing attention disorders in children.* New York: Wiley.

Lerner, J. W., & Lerner, S. R. (1991). Attention deficit disorder: Issues and questions. *Focus on Exceptional Children, 24*(3), 1–17.

Reid, R., Maag, J. W., Vasa, S. F., & Wright, G. (1994). Who are the children with attention deficit-hyperactivity disorder? A school-based survey. *Journal of Special Education, 28*, 117–137.

Reiff, S. F. (1993). *How to reach and teach ADD/ADHD children.* West Nyack, NY: Center for Applied Research in Education.

Riccio, C. A., Hynd, G. W., Cohen, M. J., & Gonzalez, J. J. (1993). Neurological basis of attention deficit hyperactivity disorder. *Exceptional Children, 60*, 118–124.

Rooney, K. J. (1995). Classroom interventions for students with attention deficit disorders. *Focus on Exceptional Children, 26*(4), 1–16.

Smith, T. E. C., Polloway, E. A., Patton, J. R., & Dowdy, C. A. (1995). *Teaching students with special needs in inclusive settings.* Boston: Allyn & Bacon.

5

MENTAL RETARDATION

Harvey is an enthusiastic, polite child who entered a new school district in the fifth grade. The previous year, Harvey had been tested, found to have a measured IQ of 57, and placed in a self-contained class for students with mental retardation. When Harvey entered his new school, he did not know his alphabet and could count only to twenty. He was assigned to an inclusion class that has a regular education teacher all day and a special education teacher for half a day. In this class abilities and labels range from talented and gifted to mentally retarded. The two teachers share teaching and tutoring responsibilities for all of the students. Because Harvey was so limited in his academic skills in language arts and math, he was assigned additional tutoring on a daily basis. The language arts tutoring focused on acquisition of basic English skills—letter identification, letter sounds, and basic words. During the first 6 weeks, his teachers decided that Harvey's oral comprehension was at grade level, so they modified their science and social studies materials to include a generous amount of oral instruction and group work. Harvey was able to join in group projects for presentation before the entire class. Before long, Harvey began to shine. The other students began to benefit from Harvey's easy going way of responding to difficulties and his impeccable manners. They also became more sensitive to the reality that although some people may have intellectual limitations, they all have something to offer others.

One day in language arts tutoring, Harvey exclaimed in a rush of words, "I got it! I got it! Mr. Wayne, I got it! Do you want to hear?" Harvey proceeded to read all of the words in a sentence, then all of the sentences in a short story. Harvey was reading and understanding what he read for the first time in his life!

Never limit what someone can do on the basis of tests. Expose all children to the wonders of learning. They may surprise themselves and delight you![1]

I worked with Allen every day for 6 months, teaching him how to garnish sandwiches in a high-volume restaurant. He learned very slowly, but he was fun and interesting to work with. We always joked with one another. Not even I would ever have guessed that he had a tested IQ of 52. By about the sixth month, Allen was doing his job without my assistance, except during the rush periods. Over the next 3 months, Allen became very skillful and could garnish at an impressive rate—except during the very busy times when it was sometimes too hectic, even for me. Slowly, day by day, pressure began to build. One night when tempers were short at cleanup time, Allen started yelling, "Don't touch me! Push, push, push, that's all you do. Don't come close to me. I hate this place! I hate hamburgers! I hate salads! I hate mustard!" With this outcry, he flung the mustard container against the kitchen wall and ran out the back door. Impulsively, I took off after him. Finally, I caught him down by the incinerator in the back lot. He yelled, his voice shaking and hands trembling, "You'd better leave me alone!" Fearing that he might run in front of a car, I stepped closer to reach him. He pulled a kitchen knife about 10 inches long from his pocket and said, "Don't come near me, I hate you. Take another step and I'll kill you!" Then he dropped the knife to the ground, fell to his knees, and wept. He pulled me close to him, held my legs, and murmured, "I'm sorry. I love you. I'm sorry." Before the night was over, we had talked it out and completed our cleanup duties together. That was over 5 years ago. Today, he is still garnishing sandwiches at the same high-volume restaurant, and we are still the closest of friends.

[1]This story was contributed by Lynne Lewis, MSW and LPC, Lockhart Independent School District, Lockhart, Texas.

Bobby was diagnosed as having mild mental retardation when he was in the second grade. His parents had been surprised at the diagnosis, but agreed to special education placement. Bobby seemed like a normal child. He played with the other children in the neighborhood, he had no speech or physical problems, and his interests/activities were age-appropriate. Bobby spent the next 9 years in special education classrooms. When he reached the age of 16, he immediately quit school. Bobby went to work for a local discount store that was part of a national chain. At night Bobby worked on his GED (general education development) high school equivalency diploma, which he finished in 4 years. As time went on, Bobby advanced in his career, married, and had three children. At 26 years of age—10 years after quitting school—Bobby became manager of his own discount store in the chain. His six figure salary was far superior to that of most persons labeled mildly mentally retarded.

Most people are aware of the Special Olympics, although some people may not realize that there is more to it than just track and field events. Other sports (e.g., skiing, soccer, and basketball) are also part of this program. Nevertheless, this story concerns the track and field competition. For months, a friend of mine, a teacher of students with moderate mental retardation, had been preparing them for the district-level meet. They practiced every day. As every track runner knows, "getting out of the blocks" is a critical part of any running event. This teacher consistently worked on this aspect with her students. She would yell, "Get on your mark, get set, GO." After months of training, her students were ready. The district meet approached. They were "psyched"—they wanted to do well so they could go to the state meet. Although they had entered a number of different events, they were most excited about the running. The truth of truths—athlete versus athlete—had arrived. The officials lined up the runners in their appropriate positions. The adrenaline was flowing. The excitement was building to a climax. The official starter asked if the runners were ready. They or their sponsors indicated that they were. The starter then began the countdown: "Get on your mark, get set . . ." "BLAM!" The race had begun! Unfortunately, the participants from my friend's class were still at the starting line, startled by the loud sounds that had just thundered from the starter's gun to be sure, but still waiting anxiously for him to say, "GO!"

Almost 20 years ago, long before the current inclusion move-ment, I worked part time as a one-on-one tutor/assistant. The stu-dent I worked with, Nancy, was 11 years old and had Down syn-drome. She was born when her parents were in their mid-forties. Both were well-educated professionals and were strong advocates for their daughter. Instead of spending her whole school day in a self-contained class, which was common at the time, Nancy was in some regular education classes and a resource room on a regular elementary campus. Nancy's parents were always on the lookout for something that would improve her functioning level. The year I worked with her, she had already been through patterning training in Philadelphia and was in the process of taking megadoses of vita-mins.

Nancy's parents were also very concerned about her social interactions. Every Halloween, they had a big party and invited all the kids from their neighborhood, as well as teachers. However, whenever it was time to eat, Nancy would disappear. Even though they wanted Nancy to be a part of school and community peer groups, her parents were embarrassed by her table manners and wouldn't let her eat with any of her friends—they set up a table for her in a separate room.

DEFINITION

Special education textbooks typically devote a considerable amount of space to discussions of the *definitions* of mental retardation, both from a historical and a functional perspective. One reason for such lengthy considerations may be that although the concept of a normal distribution of intelligence and abilities has long been accepted, soci-ety's view of what constitutes *normal* functioning continues to change over time. (In any population, there are a very small number of indi-viduals with extraordinarily high or low abilities and a large number of individuals with average abilities.) As a culture, our views on disabili-ties and the role of people with disabilities in society has certainly undergone dramatic adjustment during the past decade. The way that we view individuals with mental retardation is shaped by many vari-ables in our culture, including our current (1) values, (2) willingness to tolerate and appreciate diversity, (3) requirements for conformity, (4) expectations for achievement, and (5) definition of *normal*.

A series of definitions of mental retardation have been used over the years. Public Law 94–142, now the IDEA, refers to mental retarda-tion in basically the same terms as the 1983 definition by Grossman:

"significantly subaverage general intellectual functioning resulting in or associated with concurrent impairments in adaptive behavior and manifested during the development period" (p. 11). *Subaverage intellectual functioning* refers to a score on an intelligence test that is approximately 2 or more standard deviations below the mean. *Adaptive behavior* refers to one's ability to cope with the demands of daily life and is manifested in such things as sensorimotor, communication, self-help, socialization, academic, and vocational skills. The *development period* consists of the time span between conception and the nineteenth birthday.

For many years prior to the Grossman definition, emphasis was placed solely on an intelligence test score for classifying a person as mentally retarded. If children scored in the retarded range on an IQ test, they were classified as mentally retarded even if they functioned adequately in the community, at school, on the job, or with peers. They were placed in special classes for students with mental retardation simply because they scored in the retarded range on standardized tests and had trouble with academic learning. Many of these children were able to get along well in their community and with their peers. After leaving school, they functioned successfully in their jobs, and in some cases have married and raised fine families (see the vignette about Bobby at the beginning of this chapter).

For these individuals, being labeled mentally retarded served no constructive purpose. If consideration had been given to adaptive behavior, they would not have met the criteria nor been labeled as mentally retarded. It is important to emphasize that in determining eligibility for educational services, the definition of mental retardation assigns equal weight to both the intellectual functioning and the adaptive behavior dimensions. In other words, to be classified as mentally retarded, a person must show deficits in both areas. For individuals who have left school after experiencing academic difficulties, yet who can get along well on a job in the community, the label of mental retardation would no longer apply (Beirne-Smith, Patton, & Ittenbach, 1994).

Although the IDEA definition is operative in the *federal* law, many states have their own definitions of mental retardation. For years, a new definition has been considered, discussed, and finally proposed. In 1992, the American Association on Mental Retardation (AAMR) Ad Hoc Committee on Terminology and Classification published its ninth manual on classification and terminology. This new definition of mental retardation is as follows:

Mental retardation refers to substantial limitations in present functioning. It is characterized by significantly subaverage intellectual functioning, existing concurrently with related limitations in two or more of the following applicable adaptive skills areas: communication, self-care, home living, social skills, community use, self-directions, health and safety, functional academics, leisure and work. Mental retardation manifests before age 18.

This new definition proposes some very significant changes from its predecessors. It is much more *functional* than previous definitions because it (1) stresses the interaction among three major dimensions: a person's capabilities, the environments in which the person functions, and the individual's need for support; (2) refines the concept of adaptive behavior by identifying ten specific adaptive skills areas; and (3) institutes a new three-step process for defining, classifying, and determining systems of support. The new definition also recommends that former levels of severity (mild, moderate, severe, and profound) be discontinued. Table 5.1 provides a clear explanation of how the three-step process of diagnosis, classification, and profile of needed supports is accomplished. Table 5.2 defines and provides examples of the intensities of supports that may be required by various individuals.

PREVALENCE

Estimates of what percentage of the population is mentally retarded vary from one source to another. Beirne-Smith et al. (1994) point out that prevalence variations are impacted by numerous factors, including differences in criteria and methodologies of the researchers and gender, age, community, race, and sociopolitical factors of the individuals being considered for identification in this category. If IQ were the only criterion for defining mental retardation, about 2% of the population would be considered mentally retarded. The federal government reported that for the 1990–91 school year, slightly fewer than 600,000 children were classified as mentally retarded. This represents a little more than 1% of the school age population (U. S. Department of Education 1993) and about 13% of students with disabilities. According to Beirne-Smith et al. (1994), most professionals would suggest prevalence figures of less than 1%. The majority of students in this category have *mild* rather than moderate or severe mental retardation.

One of the more interesting trends in special education since the implementation of PL 94–142 has to do with the mental retardation category. Since the U.S. Department of Education began collecting and compiling data on special education services, there has been a dra-

Table 5.1
The Three-Step Process: Diagnosis, Classification, and Systems of Supports

	STEP 1. Diagnosis of mental retardation *Determines eligibility for supports*
Dimension I Intellectual Functioning and Adaptive Skills	Mental retardation is diagnosed if: 1. The individual's intellectual functioning is approximately 70–75 or below. 2. There are significant disabilities in two or more adaptive skill areas. 3. The age of onset is below 18.
	STEP 2. Classification and description *Identifies strengths and weaknesses and the need for supports*
Dimension II Psychological/Emotional Considerations Dimension III Physical/Health/Etiology Considerations Dimension IV Environmental Considerations	1. Describe the individual's strengths and weaknesses in reference to psychological/emotional considerations. 2. Describe the individual's overall physical health and indicate the condition's etiology. 3. Describe the individual's current environmental placement and the optimal environment that would facilitate his/her continued growth and development.
	STEP 3. Profile and intensities of needed supports *Identifies needed supports* Identify the kind and intensities of supports needed for each of the four dimensions. 1. Dimension I: Intellectual Functioning and Adaptive Skills 2. Dimension II: Psychological/Emotional Considerations 3. Dimension III: Physical Health/Etiology Considerations 4. Dimension IV: Environmental Considerations

Source:From *Mental Retardation: Definition, Classification, and Systems of Supports,* 9th ed. (p. 24) by the Association on Mental Retardation (AAMR), Washington, DC: Author. Reprinted by permission.

Table 5.2
Definition and Examples of Intensities of Supports

Intermittent
Support on an as-needed basis. Characterized by episodic nature, person not always needing the support(s); or short-term supports needed during life-span transitions (e.g., job loss or an acute medical crisis); intermittent supports may be high or low intensity when provided

Limited
An intensity of supports characterized by consistency over time; time-limited but not of an intermittent nature, may require fewer staff members and less cost than more intense levels of support (e.g., time-limited employment training or transitional supports during the school to adult provided period)

Extensive
Supports characterized by regular involvement (e.g., daily in at least some environments (such as work or home) and not time-limited (e.g., long-term support and long-term home living support)

Pervasive
Supports characterized by their constancy, high intensity; provided across environments; potential life-sustaining nature. Pervasive supports typically involve more staff members and intrusiveness than do extensive or time-limited sup-

Source:From *Mental Retardation: Definition, Classification, and Systems of Supports,* 9th ed. (p. 26) by the Association on Mental Retardation (AAMR), Washington, DC: Author. Reprinted by permission.

matic *decrease* in the number of students in the mental retardation category. From the 1976–77 school year until the 1990–91 school year, the number of students identified and served as mentally retarded has declined by about 319,000 (or 39%). This decline is likely due to a number of factors. One is sociopolitical, that is, many school districts may be more conservative in identifying students as mentally retarded, especially if those students are from culturally diverse backgrounds and minority ethnic groups. Another possible reason is that many higher functioning students who were formerly labeled as mentally retarded may now be called learning disabled. The learning disability category is thought to be less stigmatizing than mental retardation, and the students may be able to function very well in resource settings. The third reason for the decline in the number of students labeled mentally retarded may be that recent efforts at prevention and early intervention may be having a significant impact. Increasing awareness of risk factors pre- and postnatally as well as early childhood intervention programs may be resulting in less serious problems in learning and development.

ETIOLOGY

Mental retardation is caused by a number of variables, many of which are unknown. It is likely that for many individuals who are mentally retarded, specific causal factors may not be apparent; or several causes that interact can be identified. In general, however, two categorical schemes can be used to describe the many causes of mental retardation: biological/organic causes and sociocultural causes (Hardman, Drew, Egan, & Wolf, 1993).

Biological or organic causes of mental retardation include maternal infections (e.g., rubella or syphilis), maternal intoxication (resulting in Fetal Alcohol Syndrome), and postnatal infections (e.g., encephalitis). Mental retardation can also be due to chromosomal abnormalities (e.g., trisomy 21, which results in Down syndrome). Physical traumas (e.g., anoxia [oxygen deprivation]) and metabolic disorders (e.g., Phenylketonuria [PKU]) also can cause mental retardation. In addition, disorders such as neurofibromatosis or tuberous sclerosis can also contribute to mental retardation. Environmental toxins (e.g., excessive amounts of lead) and conditions like low birth weight are also contributing factors. Furthermore, there are unknown factors that may result in serious conditions like anencephaly (partial or complete absence of brain tissue) (Hardman et al., 1993).

Despite these many serious biological or organic causes of mental retardation, most individuals who are classified as mentally retarded are considered to be *mildly* mentally retarded, and the causes of their learning problems are not apparent. It is commonly assumed that the mental impairment of these individuals is due to sociocultural factors (sometimes referred to as *psychosocial* variables). Many individuals with mild mental retardation come from low socioeconomic and/or culturally or linguistically different backgrounds. In situations where children do not have adequate nutrition, access to health care, exposure to stimulating educational opportunities, or positive influences or role models who value education, it may be very difficult for them to learn well in school.

For many individuals, there are both sociocultural factors and genetic factors that interact. The term used to described students whose retardation is likely due to both categories of problems is *cultural-familial*. The term implies that the causation is a complex interaction of both environmental and hereditary factors. In fact, there has been a long-standing discussion in special education about whether intelligence is innate or acquired. Often referred to as *nature versus nurture,* the controversy has been important because it impacts educators' beliefs about the efficacy of education and treatment, that is, whether students can benefit significantly from intervention and education. Most authorities agree that intelligence is complex and that it is both acquired and inherited. Nevertheless, environmental influences are extremely important, and educators usually realize that they can have a very powerful impact on students' progress. When individuals with mental retardation are properly taught and given carefully planned assistance, their potential for achieving, learning, and living is enhanced. In this section, realistic expectations for people labeled mildly or moderately retarded will be described, along with the types of treatment and care that are essential for furthering their cognitive, affective, social, motor, and vocational development.

Before proceeding, it is important to emphasize that regardless of the severity of retardation, an individual can be helped and can develop new skills. The child with mental retardation is not likely to blossom or intellectually unfold without special help. With proper intervention, undesirable behaviors can be ameliorated and desirable behaviors can be taught. Moreover, the earlier we get involved, the greater our chance of witnessing improvement.

EARLY INTERVENTION, EXPECTATIONS, AND SOCIOCULTURAL INFLUENCES VERSUS HEREDITY

The Wild Boy

One way to understand the complex nature of sociocultural influences on educational programming for students with mental retardation is to look at some of the landmark historical studies investigating the effects of intervention. The creative and partially successful attempts of Jean Marc Gaspard Itard to educate a 12-year-old *"homme sauvage"* deserve mention in any discussion of mental retardation. In 1799, a wild boy was captured in the forest of Aveyron, France. The boy, later named Victor, behaved in many ways like a wild animal. Victor did not speak or respond to the sound of gunfire, yet he quickly startled at the sound of a cracking nut. Victor did not seem to feel differences between hot and cold, or smell differences between foul and pleasant odors. His moods swung from deep depression to hyper excitement. Itard believed that with proper education Victor could be cured. For 5 years, he worked intensively with Victor and then abandoned his goals, concluding that he had failed. Later, the French Academy of Science recognized Itard's significant accomplishments and requested that he publish a report of his work. The result, written in 1962, was a classic for the field of education, *The Wild Boy of Aveyron.*

Although Itard had failed to "cure" Victor, many very dramatic changes in the boy were evidenced. Victor's behavior was greatly changed, and after much training, he was taught to identify various vowel sounds. Ultimately, he learned to read and write a few words; however, he remained mute. Although Itard regarded his work with Victor unsuccessful, the strategies and activities that he developed are the basis for many of the interventions educators use today.

Studies Related to Sociocultural Influences

Several noted researchers have attempted to determine the relative importance of environmental influences in causing mental retardation. When investigating environmental impact on learning, studies have usually looked at the role of unstimulating, poor environments. It is important to remember that the effects of poverty are different from the effects of cultural minority status (Chan & Rueda, 1979; Garber, 1988). Because culturally, linguistically, and ethnically diverse individuals are so often over represented in poverty groups, this may be difficult to do. The effects of a poverty culture seem to be significant and pervasive, stemming in part from factors like inconsistent parenting practices, lack of stability, stressors related to finding and keeping jobs and paying bills, a sense of fatalism, health problems, and a lack of educational opportunity.

Some of the most interesting research related to environmental influences was performed by Harold Skeels. His early research, begun in the 1930s, is the basis for many of the early intervention programs begun in the 1960s. The Skeels and Dye study (1939) investigated the reversibility of the effects of nonstimulating orphanage environments on children. The study contrasted two groups of children: one that was left in an unstimulating environment with minimal health and medical services and one that received one-on-one care from a surrogate mother trained in how to nurture and care for them. When the groups were retested, the experimental group showed a significant gain in IQ (about 28 points). A follow-up study 25 years later (Skeels, 1966) confirmed that the improvements of the experimental group were lasting and were accompanied by educational progress, stable employment and marriages, and functional independent living. The majority of the contrast group, on the other hand, had a low level of education and were either unemployed or institutionalized. Skeels (1966) concluded:

> It seems obvious that under present-day conditions there are still countless infants with sound biological constitutions and potentialities for development well within the normal range who will become mentally retarded and noncontributing members of society unless appropriate intervention occurs. It is suggested by the findings of this study and others published in the past 20 years that sufficient

knowledge is available to design programs of intervention to coun-
teract the devastating effects of poverty, sociocultural, and maternal
deprivations. The unanswered questions of this study could form
the basis for many life-long research projects. If the tragic fate of
the 12 contrast group children provokes even a single crucial study
that will help prevent such a fate for others their lives will not have
been in vain (pp. 54-55).

Another research and intervention program that addressed the
question of the relationship between environment and mental retardation was the Milwaukee Project. The project was a longitudinal study
examining the influence of family and/or home environments on the
intellectual development of young children. The program focused on
attempts to (1) train mothers to better care for their families and (2)
increase the amount of stimulation provided to infants. Early results
of the project were very encouraging. The experimental children made
significant gains in IQ and were performing better on language, motor,
and cognitive tasks (Garber & Heber, 1973). Unfortunately, follow-up
studies were not as hopeful. Both experimental children and control
children tended to do poorly later in school, and the majority of both
groups were below-average achievers in reading and mathematics by
fourth grade (Garber, 1988). There has also been considerable criticism of the experiment because of possible bias and poor experimental
procedures. Despite the overwhelming skepticism regarding the
integrity of the Milwaukee Project, for many years it had considerable
influence on the development of early intervention programs.

Studies Related to Heredity

There have also been significant studies addressing the role of heredity
in mental retardation. Perhaps the most famous of these was the work
of Jensen (1969), who examined the possible correlation between
intelligence and the genetic base of social classes. The idea that inherited gene pools determine the genetic makeup of future generations
has remained a controversial issue. Questions about genetic determin-
ism based on membership in a class or group and the consequent
implications for genetic engineering are inherently distasteful to many
individuals. Historical movements like the *eugenics* movement, which
advocated mass sterilization of individuals with mental retardation,
have reinforced many people's opinion that viewing intelligence as a
genetically determined quality leads to unwarranted and dangerous
social policies.

Most professionals seem to believe in a middle ground that credits the interaction of both genetic and environmental factors. With such

a highly complex construct as intelligence, it is likely that this moderate point of view is the most accepted.

CHARACTERISTICS OF INDIVIDUALS WITH MENTAL RETARDATION

In presenting some of the characteristics and behaviors exhibited by people labeled mentally retarded, we will discuss some objectives that we believe to be representative of realistic expectations for many of them. Realizing that individuals with mental retardation differ from one another as much as nondisabled people differ among themselves, it is essential to recognize that the discussion will not apply to *all* individuals classified as retarded. The behaviors described are typically displayed at some age level by all people; those with mental retardation often develop at a slower rate or later than do most people.

MILD MENTAL RETARDATION

Generally speaking, people with mild retardation are usually quite capable of caring for their own personal needs. They should be able to carry out everyday activities without the assistance of family, friends, or benefactors. A terminal goal for individuals classified as mildly mentally retarded is often employment and successful adjustment to community living upon the completion of formal schooling.

In terms of cognitive functioning, individuals with mild mental retardation will often have problems in several distinct areas, including memory, generalization ability, and use of learning strategies. Developing learning strategies involves *metacognitive* processes, that is, *learning to learn.* Without these metacognitive skills, which are critical for acquiring new information, school can be a source of difficulty. The demands of school may turn a student with mild mental retardation into what the President's Committee on Mental Retardation (PCMR) called "the six-hour retarded child" (1970). Being classified as mentally retarded may only be appropriate for these students when they are attending school. In *real life* situations requiring social and vocational competencies rather than academic skills, individuals with mild retardation are often very successful.

Other domains may also be problematic for people who are mildly mentally retarded, including:

1. Personal and motivational competencies: self-concept, dependency, failure syndrome

2. Social and behavioral skills: self-direction, responsibility, social relationships

3. General learning problems: attentional variables, mediational strategies

4. Speech and language skills: articulation, receptive and expressive language ability

5. Physical and health dimensions: body measurements, motor skills

Almost all children with mild mental retardation can be effectively educated. In the elementary grades, many students with mild mental retardation can be fully or partially *mainstreamed* (i.e., *integrated, included*) into regular classrooms when these settings are determined appropriate. In a partially self-contained arrangement, students spend some of their instructional day in the regular education setting and the remainder of their time in a special setting with a trained special education teacher. The special education time is usually devoted to helping the student with language, reading, math, or social skill development. During the latter elementary grades, and certainly by the junior high level, special provisions must be made for teaching the essential and practical academic subjects. Students should remain with their normal peers as much as possible, but they may require special programs in language arts, reading, and math.

As children with mental retardation grow to adulthood, the ability to handle leisure time and to enjoy recreational activities can also have a significant impact on their lives. Although they may be able to dance or bowl in organized group situations, adults with mental retardation often end up spending their days watching television. In order to have a balanced, enjoyable life, it is important to develop hobbies and interests and to participate in recreational activities. With appropriate education and training, adults with mild mental retardation can master the life skills necessary for well-rounded, satisfying lives.

Cronin and Patton (1993), in their book on life skills instruction, have provided a thorough guide for professionals who work with adults. Figure 5.1 provides a look at some of the topics pertinent in a life skills course, including personal finance, health and hygiene, and community awareness.

Career education is essential and should begin in the elementary grades and continue throughout the students' schooling and life. Attention to prevocational and vocational skill development should be programmed into the students' academic plan. Instruction in the areas of

Figure 5.1
Life Skills Courses and Select Sample Topics

Life Skills Course	Select Topics
Personal Finance 	maintaining a budget filing tax submitting an application for a loan using credit cards
Practical Math 	performing home repairs/maintenance estimating travel time cooking measuring dosage of prescribed medicine
Health & Hygiene 	dealing with illness administering first aid maintaining one's personal appearance handling stress
Everyday Science 	gardening identifying how things work controlling pests using science in the kitchen
Practical Communication 	using resource materials requesting information writing personal cards and notes taking phone messages
Community Awareness and Involvement 	registering to vote using community resources (e.g., library) attending neighborhood association meetings knowing one's legal rights
Occupational Development 	identifying personal interests and aptitudes preparing a career planning packet practicing interview skills identifying available jobs in the community
Interpersonal Relations 	getting along with others accepting criticism complimenting others engaging in social conversation

Source: From *Life Skills Instruction for All Students With Special Needs: A Practical Guide for Integrating Real Life Content Into the Curriculum* (p. 31) by M. E. Cronin and J. R. Patton, 1993, Austin, TX: Pro-Ed. Reprinted by permission.

general job skills and specific vocational training is essential. By high school, students with mild retardation may remain with their peers in some subjects and focus on vocational training. They should be given an opportunity to learn various types of job skills and be allowed to realistically demonstrate their competence by working on various jobs in the community (i.e., community-based training). Job training can be accomplished through programs that allow students to attend school for part of the day and participate in job training and evaluation and actual employment.

Postsecondary programs and continuing educational opportunities are also important. These programs should teach the person with mild mental retardation to cope with personal problems and provide opportunities for socialization and recreation. Programs should be comprehensive (cover social, motor, cognitive, and academic skills) and continuous (begin early and continue well into adulthood).

MODERATE MENTAL RETARDATION

It is not always helpful or accurate to express people's abilities in either age or grade equivalents because we overlook individual strengths and deficits. However, sometimes people can understand individuals' characteristics when they are viewed developmentally. People with *moderate* mental retardation can sometimes be considered developmentally as approximately 3 or more years behind those who are diagnosed as *mildly* retarded.

Identification of children with more moderate retardation may occur very early. By about age 3, children with moderate mental retardation are so significantly delayed in their development that most are already diagnosed as retarded. At this age, educational programs should include training in self-care skills such as independent bathroom and eating skills, so that children can move toward independence. Preschool children who have moderate mental retardation can usually stand and walk alone but may need help in climbing steps. They generally have a vocabulary of from four to six words, recognize others, play for short periods of time with peers, and communicate many needs with gestures. By age 6, children with moderate mental retardation can usually feed themselves with a spoon (although this may still be messy) and can drink unassisted. They can climb up and down stairs, but still not with alternating feet. They can speak two- or three-word sentences and name simple common objects. Individuals with moderate mental retardation will remain developmentally delayed into their adult lives.

Individuals with moderate mental retardation have traditionally not been placed in regular school classrooms for academic instruction but are often integrated for nonacademic courses. Including children with moderate or severe disabilities into regular classrooms for *all* instruction is part of the political and social movement in education toward *full inclusion.* As this book goes to press, research on the effects of inclusion are not conclusive, but many states have made significant efforts at integrating all students into regular education classes in their home schools. The socialization benefits of increased integration is perhaps the important result when students with disabilities and students without disabilities interact.

Educationally, the program emphasis should be "functionality," that is, improving skills necessary to take care of oneself, to get along with others, and to display other requisite community living and vocational skills. It is very important that transitional planning occur for this group of students. Moreover, the program should strive to get the students or clients to feel good about themselves and ultimately to enjoy their lives.

We typically think of adults with moderate mental retardation as individuals who are capable of varying degrees of employment, including sheltered, supported, or competitive situations. Nevertheless, even into adulthood, these individuals may need supervision in carrying out routine daily activities. Many adults with moderate mental retardation are able to recognize written words and read simple sentences but, for all practical purposes, do not evidence great academic achievement. They can carry on simple conversations and can perform such household chores as dusting, mopping, and cleaning. They can feed, bathe, and dress themselves. By adulthood their gross and fine motor coordination will be developed to the point where they will have good body control. However, social life will be a constant problem. Although individuals with moderate mental retardation are limited in some respects, they may be interesting, challenging, and enjoyable company; however, if left alone they may end up socially isolated.

As one can see, people with mild mental retardation are much closer to nondisabled people in what they can accomplish than are individuals with moderate mental retardation. Also, an individual with mild mental retardation usually *looks* normal. That is, you probably would not be able to tell that someone you have merely seen on the street is labeled mildly retarded. This may not be the case for people with moderate mental retardation. These individuals often look like something is different about them and may have one or many observable, distinctive features (e.g., language problems, poor motor coordination, physical differences, or inappropriate stereotypical behaviors).

The distinctive physical characteristics become more prevalent the more severe the retardation.

CONCLUSIONS

The characteristics and behaviors that we have reported for people with mild and moderate mental retardation do not represent each and every possibility on the continuum of characteristics. For instance, it is not unusual to find a person with mild mental retardation who is incapable of holding a job and who may even experience a great deal of difficulty remaining employed in more sheltered settings. The important thing to remember is that individuals with mental retardation can acquire new skills, learn, and grow intellectually and personally. This developmental process is greatly enhanced when adequate services are provided as early as possible and continue into adulthood.

It is obvious that being retarded is not something one chooses. Having a child with mental retardation is something parents neither hope for nor, in most cases, prepare for. The difficulties that parents encounter are sometimes compounded by the absence of appropriate services or the difficulty in obtaining information and services that are available. The adjustment of parents to the birth of a child with a disability can be made worse by insensitivity and misinformation. Physicians, who are often the first to notice a problem, may not always know what to expect and so cannot tell the parents. By anyone's standards, the birth of a child with mental retardation is a significant event, often leading to both joy and fulfillment as well as difficulties. Individuals with mental retardation are people who are more like than unlike the rest of us. Although they often get caught in life's absurdities and amusing circumstances, they can lead successful and rewarding lives. Because individuals with mental retardation themselves do not enjoy strong political clout, it is important that we act as advocates for them, and teach them to act as advocates for themselves. We must ensure that the public in general and legislators, policy makers, and judges in particular realize that people with mental retardation are entitled to the same rights that every citizen enjoys and the same human dignity that you and I continually demand.

SUGGESTIONS FOR WORKING WITH PERSONS WITH MENTAL RETARDATION

1. Set goals that are realistic for the individual and the community in which the individual lives.

2. Assign tasks that are personally relevant, are carefully sequenced from easy to difficult, and allow the learner to be highly and frequently successful.

3. Recognize the individual's strengths and weaknesses, provide incentives for performance, and establish necessary rules for behavior. Maintain high expectations and don't teach the student to be helpless.

4. Explain required tasks in terms of concrete concepts.

5. When giving instructions be specific: "John, go to the principal's office, give Mrs. Smith the absentee sheet, and come back here."

6. When giving instructions briefly summarize: "Remember John: First, go to the principal's office. Second, give the sheet to Mrs. Smith. Third, come back."

7. When giving instructions, ask what is to be done: "John, tell me what you are to do."

8. When praising, be specific, not general: "John, you did a good job taking the absentee sheet to Mrs. Smith. You went directly to the office, and you came straight back." Don't just make a generic statement about doing a good job.

9. When praising, emphasize "you" rather than "I": "John, you got nine out of ten math problems correct. That took a lot of effort. Keep up the good work."

10. Give constant praise and feedback, especially when the individual is learning a new task.

✦ *PONDER THESE*

1. What are the arguments for and against the following actions:

- *Sterilizing adults with mental retardation*
- *Encouraging matrimony among individuals with mental retardation*
- *Advocating for a community home for adults with mental retardation in your neighborhood*
- *Allowing the initiation of a child with mental retardation into your son's or daughter's Cub Scout or Brownie troop*

- *Invoking the death penalty with an adult who is mentally retarded*

2. *Think about how you could convince a business person to hire an adult with mental retardation. For example, how would you do the following:*
   - *Request cooperation (by phone or personal contact—Would you take your client with you?)*
   - *Describe your client (i.e., Would you use the term retarded?)*
   - *Ask questions about the job description*
   - *Describe the competencies of your client*
   - *Guarantee success*

3. *You are a first grade teacher in a public school. Included in your class is a student (Bill) who is classified as mentally retarded. Bill has some behavioral problems. For example, when he wants something, he takes it, whether another student is using it or not. He is difficult to understand because his speech is not clear. The other students are beginning to make fun of him and are angry at him because he doesn't share. How will you deal with this situation?*

4. *What are some everyday living skills necessary for successful functioning in your community?*

References

American Association on Mental Retardation. (1992). *Mental retardation: Definition, classification, and systems of supports* (9th ed.). Washington, DC: Author.

Beirne-Smith, M., Patton, J. R., & Ittenbach, R. (1994). *Mental retardation* (4th ed.). Englewood Cliffs, NJ: Merrill/Prentice Hall.

Chan, K. S., & Rueda, R. (1979). Poverty and culture in education: Separate but equal. *Exceptional Children, 45,* 422–428.

Cronin, M. E., & Patton, J. R. (1993). *Life skills instruction for all students with special needs: A practical guide for integrating real life content into the curriculum.* Austin, TX: Pro-Ed.

Garber, J. L. (1988). *The Milwaukee project: Preventing mental retardation in children at risk.* Washington, DC: American Association on Mental Retardation.

Garber, J. L., & Heber, R. F. (1973). *The Milwaukee project: Early intervention as a technique to prevent mental retardation.* Storrs: University of Connecticut.

Grossman, H. J. (Ed.). (1983). *Classification in mental retardation.* Washington, DC: American Association on Mental Deficiency.

Hardman, M. L., Drew, C. J., Egan, M. W., & Wolf, B. (1993). *Human exceptionality: Society, school, and family* (4th ed.). Boston: Allyn & Bacon.

Itard, J. M. G. (1962). *The wild boy of Aveyron.* New York: Appleton-Century-Crofts.

Jensen, A. R. (1969). How much can we boost IQ and scholastic achievement? *Harvard Educational Review, 39,* 1–123.

President's Committee on Mental Retardation. (1970). *The six-hour retarded child.* Washington, DC: U.S. Government Printing Office.

Skeels, H. M. (1966). Adult status of children with contrasting early life experiences: A follow-up study. *Monographs of the Society for Research in Child Development, 31*(3, Whole No. 105).

Skeels, H. M., & Dye, H. B. (1939). A study of the effects of differential stimulation on mentally retarded children. *Convention Proceedings of the American Association on Mental Deficiency, 44,* 114–136.

United States Department of Education (1993). *To assure the free appropriate public education of all children with disabilities. Fifteenth annual report to Congress on the implementation of the Individuals with Disabilities Education Act.* Washington, DC: Author.

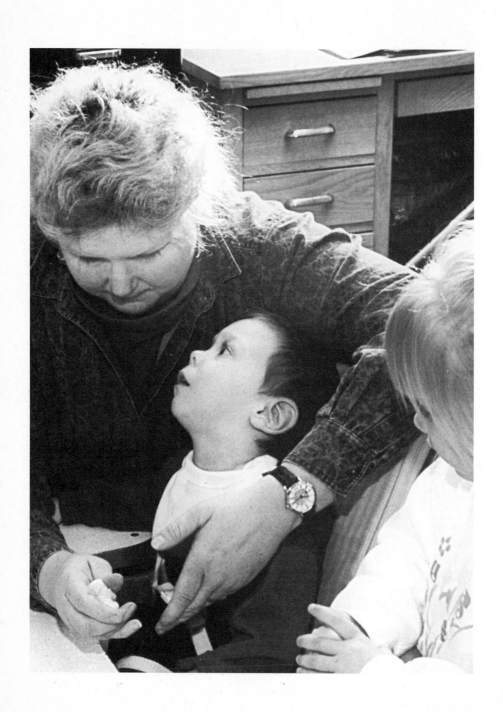

6

AUTISM, PERVASIVE DEVELOPMENTAL DISORDERS, AND OTHER SEVERE DISABILITIES

Frank is a 47-year-old man. When he was 6 years old, his mother took him to one of the state hospitals and dropped him off. She said that she couldn't handle him. She came back to visit him only one time in all the years that he lived at the hospital. Last year, when the state ordered the release of most of the patients in the state hospitals, Frank returned to the community for the first time in 40 years. He was placed in a group home and began to come to our day program for adults. We noticed that he was continually showing up with bruises, so the state began an investigation of his group home and put him on a waiting list for another one. Because of a lack of state funding, the waiting list is 4 years long. Luckily for Frank, he's been placed in a foster home with a very caring and responsible family. Frank doesn't talk at all, and he never remembers to close the door when he goes to the bathroom; but he loves to go bowling and out to lunch, and he always has a smile for the staff. Sometimes I wonder what Frank would be like if he had grown up in a real home and gone to school instead of spending his life in the state hospital.

My husband and I were thrilled when our autistic son, Andy, learned to count. Having gained this skill, Andy would repeat it time and again in any way he could. It became a little boring after the

109

400th time, but we were still pleased with his new ability. Then we received our monthly phone bill with $38 charge for calls to South Bend, Indiana. We didn't know anyone in South Bend, but the number was somehow strangely familiar. Then we realized that to dial South Bend from our Northwest Indiana home, you would need to dial a "one" first. That made the phone number 1-234-5678. Andy had spent $38 practicing his new skill every time my back was turned. I tried to call the number to apologize, but it had been disconnected. I wonder why?[1]

I worked with Albert every day for 3 years in Allen's Restaurant. He was the 57-year-old dishwasher, and he loved to listen to baseball games on the radio while washing dishes. It didn't make any difference what teams were playing; he just enjoyed listening to the play-by-play action while he worked. Before coming to Allen's, he had lived his entire life in the state institution. He couldn't read or write, couldn't make change, and didn't talk very much, although he did know about baseball. He knew most of the famous ballplayers' batting averages, and he knew where each team was on a particular day. He was diagnosed as severely mentally retarded, but I didn't think much about it until I left for a 3-week vacation. When I returned, Albert didn't recognize me. I don't mean he didn't remember my name; I mean he didn't remember me at all. At first my feelings were hurt; later I just figured he had a short memory.

Mary had spent her life in a residential state institution for persons with mental retardation. Because she was in her late 30s, the staff had little hope that she would ever leave the institution. She would sit and rock all day while twisting string between her thumbs and forefingers. One day a local firm received a NASA contract to produce equipment for the space shuttle. While touring the plant, the institution's vocational adjustment coordinator noticed that certain platinum filaments for the equipment had to be twisted by hand. He immediately thought of Mary. The vocational coordinator convinced the plant managers to allow him to train Mary for the job. The managers agreed, and Mary was hired. The amount of training neces-

---

[1]This story was contributed by Jane Kranc, Indiana. Reprinted from *Laughing and Loving With Autism* by R. Wayne Gilpin. Reprinted by permission.

sary to prepare Mary for her new job was minimal. She still spent her days rocking and twisting material. However, she was now paid over $25 an hour for these behaviors.

One of the most difficult patterns of behavior to try to change is physical aggression, especially when it includes self-injurious behavior. Many times, professionals feel very sure that the injury to oneself is done for attention or control, but the behaviors are so dangerous that it is impossible for schools or agencies to ignore them. Four-year-old Rachel had had several labels, including autism, cerebral palsy, mental retardation, and communication impaired. She spent each school day in an early childhood special education program. After school she went to a program for children with autism. Rachel had a self-injurious tantrum pattern that included biting herself, hitting herself in the head, and banging her head on the floor. She would bite her arms so often and so hard that they were black and blue with bruises and bleeding. She would also, on a regular basis, hit and kick her teachers and the other adults in her life.

Her caregivers and parents, after spending a great deal of time in observations, team meetings, and brainstorming sessions, developed a comprehensive plan that involved ignoring her after any aggression toward others, redirecting her during the beginning phases of a tantrum, using a time-out and mild restraint for the self-abuse, and giving her lots of powerful positive reinforcers whenever she did not abuse herself or others. The redirection, time-outs, and positive reinforcement worked quickly, but Rachel really hated it when adults ignored her after she hit or kicked them. Pretty soon, she "upped the ante": if ignored, she would urinate on herself or all over the floor. When that didn't work, she started taking off all of her clothes and scooting around the room. Just about the time that everyone was about to give up, her behavior started to improve. Within 3 months, her aggression had decreased markedly, the tantrums had gone from about 45 minutes to 5 minutes, and her self-abuse had practically disappeared. Rachel made rapid progress in verbal language, and when I checked a month ago, no one could remember the last time she had hurt herself or anyone else.

This chapter is about individuals who have autism, pervasive developmental disorders (PDDs), and other multiple and/or severe disabilities. Because severe disorders are usually very pervasive, we have included information pertinent to a number of interrelated disabilities, including serious emotional disturbance, mental retardation, physical disabilities, visual or hearing impairments, communication problems, cerebral palsy, and behavioral and attention difficulties.

It is difficult to describe and delineate the group of individuals whom we consider as *severely* disabled. To some parents and professionals, the term *severe* implies multiple disabilities; to others it implies extreme cognitive limitations, usually, but not always, in association with other disabilities. More than any other group considered in this book, the individuals discussed in this chapter are a heterogeneous population. However, they usually share at least one important characteristic: they are *functionally impaired,* or limited in the abilities necessary for independent living. Basic self-help and socialization skills necessary for normal everyday life either have not been mastered or cannot be performed.

In the past, individuals with severe disabilities either did not survive infancy, or they survived but were excluded from public education and denied social acceptance. Today, advances in medical technology have made it possible to sustain babies born with very serious medical conditions and very low birth weights. A recent study by doctors at Case Western Reserve University focused on the outcomes of premature infants in particular. Among their findings were the following:

- Half of the smallest premature babies had IQs under 85. In the general population, 15% of people have IQs this low.
- Of the smallest premature babies, 21% were retarded, compared with 1% of the full-term babies.
- Of the smallest premature babies, 25% had extremely poor eyesight, including four babies who were blind. Of the full-term babies, 2% had extremely poor eyesight.
- The smallest premature babies showed signs of behavioral and attention problems, as well as poorer social skills.
- As a result of their problems, 45% of these youngsters required special education (Haney, 1994, p. A6).

Despite the severity of their problems, greater numbers of infants are surviving to adulthood. Our society is learning to cope with the demands they place on our traditional systems and to appreciate what they add to our lives. Pressure for equal civil rights for individuals with disabilities has made it more likely than ever before that individuals with serious physical and cognitive disabilities will live, work, and play alongside everyone else. The development of highly sophisticated communication, mobility, and adaptive devices has increased individuals' chances of obtaining education and employment. In school and in the workplace, improvements in teaching methodology and personnel training, along with some shifts in attitudes, have meant that expectations and opportunities for individuals with severe disabilities have fewer and fewer limits.

HISTORICAL PERSPECTIVE

Individuals who have disabilities that are less severe or less noticeable have historically been more readily accepted and integrated into the mainstream than have people with severe disorders. Because severe disabilities can limit functioning so dramatically, the struggle for acceptance and equality has sometimes been difficult and frustrating. In earlier times, persons with severe disabilities were usually cared for in monasteries or institutions. Some were thought to be witches or possessed by demons and were tortured or killed (Scheerenberger, 1982). During the second quarter of the nineteenth century, attempts were made to educate, train, and reintegrate persons with severe disabilities. Unfortunately, the public attitude toward the efforts of zealous educators became sharply critical. As a result, individuals with severe disabilities became institutional prisoners. This regressive social attitude of separation and confinement persisted for many years.

For a long time, professionals did not have an adequate understanding of the educational potential of persons with severe disabilities, nor did they have the methodology to effect change. As behavioral research and behavioral techniques became more widely accepted and disseminated, professionals began to successfully teach critical basic skills like toileting, self-feeding, dressing, communication movement, and socialization. Teachers, parents, and researchers demonstrated that individuals with severe disabilities *could* learn many useful skills when a systematic and intensive teaching program was employed.

Of course, the gains made with behavioral research alone were not enough to assure appropriate educational services. The movement to establish services was also encouraged by a number of important legal decisions and by powerful legislation. In 1972, a parent organization in Pennsylvania won a victory in the case of *Pennsylvania Association for Retarded Children (PARC) v. Commonwealth of Pennsylvania State Board of Education*. The decision granted all children, including those with mental retardation, the right to an education. The *PARC* case also included the requirement that school districts make efforts to locate children with mental retardation in their communities, ensure their due process rights, and perform regular reevaluations.

Also in 1972, the *Mills v. Board of Education of the District of Columbia* decision extended the right of a free, public education, regardless of the degree of disability, to all exceptionalities. In 1971, the *Wyatt v. Stickney* decision guaranteed the right to appropriate treatment while in a residential facility.

PL 94–142 (1975) (now the IDEA), contained numerous specific provisions for the education of individuals with disabilities. The mandate in the law for a free, public education includes those individuals with the most severe limitations. Determining exactly what constitutes an appropriate education for this group is an ongoing process, reflected in the numerous decisions brought to the courts. The U.S. Court of Appeals rendered a significant decision favorable to the education of the individuals with severe disabilities in the case of *Armstrong v. Kline*. In their decision, the judges struck down the 180-day school year rule of the Pennsylvania Department of Education. Their opinion was that some individuals, as a result of their disabilities, learn very slowly and are negatively affected when their educational programs are interrupted (Stotland & Mancuso, 1981). This decision opened the doors for many parents seeking to obtain extended school-year services for their children with severe disabilities.

Court cases such as *Irving (TX) Independent School district v. Tatro* (1984) and *Timothy W. v. Rochester (NH) Public Schools* (1989) have further defined the responsibility of public education to persons with severe disabilities. In the former case, the U.S. Supreme Court ruled that, in this specific instance, catheterization of a student with spina bifida was a related educational service because it allowed the student to enter a less restrictive environment. The Court found that related services can include anything required by the child to reach, enter, exist, or remain in school. In the latter case, the Court ruled that all children (regardless of the severity of their disability) are entitled to a free, appropriate education at public expense. The Court further held that schools cannot unilaterally exclude certain students on the grounds that they cannot benefit from an education. More recently, the cases of *Daniel R. R. v. El Paso* (1989) and *Sacramento v. Holland* (1992) reaffirmed school districts' responsibility to provide an education for students in the least restrictive environment possible and to put the burden of proof on the districts for demonstrating their good faith efforts at including students in regular education environments.

Parent and professional organizations have also been responsible for achieving services for persons with severe handicaps. The efforts of various state associations for retarded citizens can be seen in the litigation already mentioned. The Association for Retarded Citizens, now called The Arc, has also been effective in its lobbying and informational functions. In 1974, the American Association for the Education of the Severely/Profoundly Handicapped (now called the Association for Persons with Severe Handicaps, or TASH) was established, reflecting the increasing professional interest in the education of these exceptional individuals.

DEFINITION AND PREVALENCE

As yet, a single statement that accurately and succinctly defines severe handicaps does not exist. Earlier in this chapter, the term *functionally impaired* was used to describe individuals who do not have the ability to function independently in a normal living environment. The emergence of the concept of "developmental disabilities" and its emphasis on "substantial functional limitations" further illustrates this point. The meaning of the term *developmental disabilities* overlaps with that of *mental retardation*. As defined in the Developmental Disabilities Assistance and Bill of Rights Act of 1984 (PL 98—527), the term refers to a severe, chronic disability with the following characteristics:

1. It is attributable to a mental or physical impairment or combination of mental and physical impairments.
2. It manifested before the person attained the age of 22.
3. It is likely to continue indefinitely.
4. It results in substantial functional limitations in three or more of the following areas of major life activity:
   - self-care
   - receptive and expressive language
   - learning
   - mobility
   - self-direction
   - capacity for independent living
   - economic self-sufficiency
5. It reflects the person's need for a combination and sequence of special interdisciplinary or generic care, treatment, or other services that are lifelong or of extended duration and are individually planned and coordinated.

Although this definition is very similar to the AAMR definition of mental retardation, it is different in its implication of chronicity and its focus on adults rather than on children.

Pervasive Developmental Disorders

One of the disability domains that is considered severe by almost everyone is the group of associated disorders called pervasive developmental disorders (PDDs). Again, there is overlap among definitions, as there is overlap among the disabling conditions themselves. According to the *Diagnostic and Statistical Manual of Mental Disorders* (4th ed.) (DSM-IV) (American Psychiatric Association, 1994), PDDs are characterized by "severe and pervasive impairment in several areas of development: reciprocal social interaction skills, communication skills, or the presence of stereotyped behavior, interest, and activities" (p. 65). These pervasive developmental disorders include Autistic Disorder, Rett's Disorder, Childhood Disintegrative Disorder, Asperger's Disorder, and any other unspecified PDDs. Because they are so severe, these disorders are usually evident in the first years of life and are often associated with some degree of mental retardation and other general medical conditions such as chromosomal abnormalities, congenital infections, and structural abnormalities of the central nervous system. The most well known of these disorders is Autistic Disorder, or autism.

Autism is characterized by markedly abnormal social interaction and communication skills and a limited repertoire of interests and activities. Among the social behaviors that are problematic are impaired use of nonverbal behaviors such as eye-to-eye contact and use of gestures. In addition, children with autism often have no interest in interactions or friendships with peers. Awareness of others may be impaired, and individuals with autism are often oblivious to others. Communication problems include a delay or absence of spoken language or the use of idiosyncratic language. Echolalic speech, which is inappropriate in the context in which it is used, or stereotypical, repetitive speech is common. The patterns of behavior demonstrated by individuals with Autistic Disorder are also highly unusual. Individuals with autism may perseverate on particular activities and often have unusual mannerisms. Stereotyped body movements like finger flicking or body rocking and fascination with moving objects like spinning wheels are also common among people with autism.

Although the IDEA has established autism as a separate disability category eligible for special education services and autism is a unique and distinct disability, individuals with autism still have many characteristics common to other disability categories. For example, according to Olley (1992), autism usually coexists with mental retardation, and individuals with autism exhibit significant social and language deficits. Occasionally, an individual with autism may display an unusually high ability in a particular area or demonstrate a remarkable memory for specific information. Usually, however, it is rare to find individuals with the "savant" type skills like those portrayed in the movie *Rainman.*

The other pervasive developmental disorders, while similar to Autistic Disorder, are differentiated in the DSM-IV. Rett's Disorder, which has been diagnosed only in females, is very similar to Autistic Disorder. Childhood Disintegrative Disorder follows a different pattern of development; children exhibit normal developmental patterns for about 2 years, then regress. Individuals with Asperger's Disorder are differentiated from individuals with autism on the basis of their lack of delay in language development.

Other Severe Disorders

Cerebral palsy is another disorder that can sometimes, though certainly not always, result in severe impairments in functioning. Generally speaking, individuals with cerebral palsy will have problems with movement and posture. Cerebral palsy is a nonprogressive disorder caused by a lesion or defect to the brain occurring prior to birth, during the birth process, or during the first 4 years of life (Inge, 1987). About two thirds of individuals with cerebral palsy have other associated problems. (This disorder is also addressed in the chapter on physical and health impairments.)

Sometimes, individuals with an emotional/behavioral disorder are described as having a severe disorder, especially with certain forms of psychotic behavior. Those with profound levels of mental retardation are also considered severely disabled, although this only rarely occurs without other accompanying disabilities. Sometimes people with a multiple disability, for example, individuals who are both deaf and blind, are considered to have severely impaired functioning. Again, it is often not the *type* or nature of a disability that results in the *severe* label but rather how limiting the disability is in terms of day-to-day living. Because of the vague and arbitrary nature of this category, determining prevalence figures is a challenge; however, it is a little easier if specific disabilities are considered.

Prevalence

Four or five cases of autism occur per 10,000 births. This makes it a very rare disorder. According to the U.S. Department of Education (1993), during the 1991–92 school year, a total of 5,208 students, ages 6 to 21, were served in the category of autism. This was .1% of the total number of students served under the IDEA. Multiple disabilities and deaf-blindness accounted for less than 1% and about 2.2% of all students with disabilities, respectively. According to the Fifteenth Annual Report to Congress on the Implementation of the IDEA, the multiple disabilities category increased about 80% from 1979 to 1980. In the last 4 years alone, the increase in students served in this category was 28% and was a relatively consistent increase across the nation. In part, this increase might be due to the corresponding decrease in the categories of mental retardation and other health impairments. Determining an accurate prevalence figure for a general type of category like severe disabilities is probably impossible. Based on the U.S. government figures as well as those of various informational and advocacy organizations, it is most likely that about .2% to .5% of the school-aged population would be considered to have severe disabilities.

ETIOLOGY

The specific disorders evidenced by many individuals with severe disabilities can be defined etiologically. This emphasis on a medical description causes some professionals concern because it focuses on causes and conditions instead of functional characteristics and individualized descriptions. Nevertheless, specifying etiology does give the reader some basic knowledge about the nature of severe disabilities, which almost always have an organic basis. Haring (1978) used an organizational structure, still pertinent today, which includes the following conditions as some of the most common causes of severe disabilities:

1. Chromosomal abnormality
2. Genetic disorders
3. Metabolic disorders
4. Infection and intoxicants
5. Neural tube closure (i.e., maldevelopment of the brain and/or spinal cord)
6. Gestational factors (e.g., prematurity, postmaturity, Rh incompatibility)
7. Perinatal difficulties (e.g., lack of oxygen or physical injury during birth)
8. Postnatal difficulties (e.g., infection, disease, physical trauma to the head)
9. Other environmental factors (e.g., extreme sensory deprivation, radiation)

All of these factors can lead to conditions characterized as severe. In addition, other causes of deafness, blindness, severe orthopedic problems, and multiple disorders can also be associated with a severe disability. Many causal factors produce more than one effect. For example, oxygen deprivation or head injury may result in blindness *and* mental retardation *and* motor impairments.

CHARACTERISTICS

Regardless of the label, cause, or disability group, individuals with severe disabilities can be defined by their functional limitations, which were articulated in the definitions above. The developmental disability definition is especially useful because it delineates the areas in which individuals may need assistance and it moves away from causal definitions, which do not guide professionals in their program development. These limitations almost always include serious deficits in self-care, language, learning, mobility, self-direction, capacity for independent living, and economic self-sufficiency. In addition, many individuals with severe disabilities often have ongoing psychosocial needs.

Teachers who work with students who have severe disabilities may see children, adolescents, or young adults who cannot walk, talk, toilet themselves, or feed themselves. They may also see individuals who are medically fragile and require frequent medical interventions in the classroom. They may work with students whose emotional state leaves them violent or out of touch with reality and who require psychotropic drugs. Teachers may enter classrooms with students who cannot see or hear and whose movements are labored and awkward. The range of characteristics is wide, the continuum of severity for each characteristic is infinite, and the combination of disabling conditions is limitless. It is probably most useful to concentrate on the needs of these students and the techniques and programs that can increase their chances for independence and self-sufficiency.

THE NEEDS OF INDIVIDUALS WITH SEVERE DISABILITIES

Education

The "educability" of students with severe disabilities has taken on a whole new meaning in recent years. Pressure brought to bear by legislation, litigation, and advocacy groups has resulted in a political and educational movement toward increased inclusion of individuals with severe disabilities. This inclusion has meant a change from segregated campuses and classes to more integrated settings like regular education classes, content mastery centers, and resource classes. The curriculum, too, is focused on greater integration, with the demands of both the school environment and the community in mind.

Education of students with severe disabilities now includes increasing skills in self-help, vocational training, and community living as well as more traditional functional academics. It is more and more common to see students with severe disabilities in the community for a significant portion of their day. According to Wolfe (1992):

> A community-based outing such as a trip to a fast-food restaurant can provide the students with opportunities to increase his or her competency in skills such as money and word recognition and social situations. Similarly, a student who is blind may spend an equal amount of time in the community acquiring mobility skills and increasing opportunities for independence. The definition of developmental disabilities itself and current best practices together stress the need for functional, age-appropriate skills that will generalize to environments beyond the school doors (p. 127).

Independent Living

The move away from residential placements is also continuing. More and more individuals with severe disabilities are living in the community, often in foster family care, semi-independent and supported living arrangements, group homes, and nursing homes. There is increasing evidence that even individuals with the most severe disabilities can live in the community when given adequate support (Amado, Lakin, & Menke, 1990).

Economic Independence

Another area of importance is the ability to work. Unemployment has traditionally been a problem for individuals with disabilities. Estimates of the unemployment rate for individuals with disabilities has ranged from about 55% to as high as 88% (Wehman, Kregel, & Seyfarth, 1985) and is highest for those with the most severe disabilities. Recently, the movement toward supported employment has increased the employment rate for this group, and teachers have recognized the need for curricula that address prevocational and social skills critical to employability.

Psychosocial Needs

Students who have severe disabilities have many issues related to their quality of life. With the IDEA's recent requirements for increased technological assistance and related services, there is increasing recognition that a traditional educational program is not adequate or appropriate for individuals with severe disabilities. School districts have a greater responsibility than ever before to provide supports, allow for self-determination, and work collaboratively with other agencies and service delivery systems. Individuals with disabilities and their families are working with professionals to design programs that foster independence and self-determination.

Placement Considerations

Traditionally, students with severe disabilities were clustered in a specific site in a district or in specific self-contained classes throughout the district. For administrative purposes, the separate campuses were often easier to manage and specialized facilities, materials, and programs could be centralized. This was especially important for instruction in self-care and vocational skills. However, recent trends have resulted in a shift away from specialized campuses and toward education on home campuses and, often, in regular education classes. Placement decisions must be guided by the "least restrictive environment" clause, and districts must show evidence of attempts in less restrictive environments with support and modifications.

Because all school-aged children (as well as preschoolers) with disabilities must be educated at no cost to the parent, school districts have experienced an influx of individuals with severe disabilities into their schools from special day schools and institutions. For these individuals with severe disabilities, a philosophy of education must be established. This philosophy may be very different from the traditional focus on academic programs that is common for students who are less severely disabled. Education often involves teaching basic self-help behaviors or daily living skills (toileting, self-feeding, etc.) necessary for coping with the demands of the immediate environment. Efforts should be aimed at progress to a less dependent (and consequently more independent) level of functioning. Focusing on the requisite skills for maximum inclusion into school and the community often requires a very systematic, task-analyzed program. Programming should also be age-appropriate and should occur in natural settings, so that generalization and maintenance over time are likely.

The mobility of students may be a consideration in planning for school. Often, special arrangements for transportation must be provided. Since the passage of the ADA, the general public is more familiar with modifications in transportation, communication, and public accommodations, and school districts have often led the way in providing these services. In addition, specially trained assistants may be needed to assist with the children's transportation and also with medical considerations once students are in the classroom. Students may require catheterization, toileting, or changes in position (e.g., from standers to walkers, etc.). Effective use of paraprofessionals is also warranted with children who display extremes of behavior and/or require one-to-one attention. Educating individuals with severe disabilities usually requires a ratio of professionals to children that is optimally around one to three. To help meet this requirement and fulfill a greatly expanded role, paraprofessionals and special assistants must have adequate training and be included as professionals on the team.

Related Services

Technology also plays an increasingly important part in students' progress. With adaptive devices now much more common, students can use switches, touch screens, voice synthesizers, and many other modifications to enhance their communication. Mobility has also been improved by technological advances that have made wheelchairs lighter, more efficient, and easier to control. Continued options for presenting content, like the use of curricula that are computer based instead of traditional book, pencil, and paper are also making a big difference in the spectrum of learning available.

To maximize the progress of persons with severe disabilities, related services personnel are also very important. Service providers may include occupational and physical therapists, speech/language clinicians, audiologists, vision and hearing specialists, orientation and mobility trainers, medical specialists (doctors, nurses, and nutritionists), psychologists, social workers, administrators, and other paraprofessionals. As the inclusion of individuals with severe disabilities into less restrictive environments continues, the services of consultants who visit with students and teachers and coordinate service delivery are also helpful. When behavioral interventions are required and parent cooperation is essential, the consultant can play a key role in fostering a team approach and mediating when differences of opinion arise.

Collaboration and Cooperation Among Service Providers

More than for any other category, individuals with severe disabilities require efforts that are interdisciplinary. As Peterson (1980) pointed out, when the severity of a disability increases, so does the number of disciplines involved in providing services. A transdisciplinary or interdisciplinary model that coordinates the efforts of all of the service delivery professionals is most likely to provide optimum services. As with any group interaction, facilitating cooperation and collaboration with large numbers of professionals who may wish to retain final authority over their particular discipline is a challenging situation. Figure 6.1 presents a list of challenges for service providers that points out some of the many concerns in working with this diverse and sometimes large group of professionals (Wolfe, p. 130).

TEACHER COMPETENCIES AND PREPARATION

The one individual ultimately responsible for the education of students with severe disabilities is the teacher. Good teaching consists of a series of interrelated steps (Hasazi & York, 1978; Strain, McConnell, & Cordisco, 1983) that require considerable organization and planning to be carried out successfully. For children with severe disabilities to learn new behaviors, they must be instructed in a sequential, systematic manner, with appropriate behavioral strategies in operation. Like all effective teaching, working with students who have severe disabilities requires some specific competencies. Although many of the skills required to be competent may already exist in a person's repertoire before embarking in a training program, there are many specialized skills that must be developed. Teacher training programs of any type, but especially those focusing on severe disabilities, have a three-fold obligation: (1) to further develop the existing skills and knowledge base of the teacher-to-be; (2) to establish those skills that do not

Figure 6.1
Challenges for Service Providers

Source: From "Challenges for Service Providers" by P. S. Wolfe, 1992. In P. J. McLaughlin & P. Wehman (Eds.), *Developmental Disabilities: A Handbook for Best Practice* (p. 134), Boston: Andover Medical Publishers. Reprinted by permission.

- Know your community and its needs and values.
- Understand other disciplines such as marketing, business, and personnel management and how these areas can impact on your profession.
- Understand the impact of actions and training occurring in the community. How individuals with developmental disabilities are treated will influence attitudes toward, and expectations for, such individuals.
- Advocate and educate others to the benefits of increased integration.

presently exist but are necessary for successful teaching; and (3) to be accountable in documenting that the certified teachers do in fact have the skills or competencies articulated in the teacher training program.

Competencies

This discussion of what constitutes a professionally competent teacher emphasizes the word *professional*. The distinction demands certain personal qualities, including (1) sound ethical standards, (2) an awareness of and sensitivity to various influences on the child, (3) conscientiousness, (4) organizational skills, (5) an ability to work as part of a team, and (6) an enthusiasm for working with exceptional people. If teachers are to be accepted as true "professionals," then these personal factors should be considered as significant competencies. While difficult to evaluate, these personal characteristics are critical determinants of the quality of education students receive. In addition, of course, there are important minimum teaching competencies that should be required for anyone who works with this population. Figure 6.2 presents a list of competency areas for professionals who work with individuals with developmental disabilities that addresses most of the important skill areas for teachers (Kregel & Sale, 1988).

One of the problems today is that many of the roles played by teachers are well defined and formally addressed by training programs and later by school district administrators. Other roles, however, are less well defined and require high level skills that may not be articulated. For example, dealing effectively with parents may require excellent skills in communication and cooperation, yet may not be addressed in any teacher training classes.

Another problem is that training provided for professionals is often compartmentalized, that is, it does not carry over from one level of disability or one discipline to another. Teaching academic skills to students with mild learning disabilities is not the same as teaching communication skills to a student with autism; yet the training program for each teacher may be exactly the same. Teachers may not understand how vocational rehabilitation counselors work and therapists may not know why teachers do the things that they do, yet all have to work together.

In addition, the *variety* of skills taught in a classroom for students with severe disabilities is an issue. Teachers must be knowledgeable about and competent in using the following:

1. Evaluation procedures for a difficult-to-assess population
2. Task analysis skills for effective goal setting

Figure 6.2
Competency Areas for Professionals Working With Individuals With Developmental Disabilities

1. *Philosophical, legal, and policy issues.* Critical issues surrounding services for individuals with developmental disabilities, such as legislation and litigation, eligibility requirements, definitions, and related services provided by state and local agencies.

2. *Program Development.* Options and programs for individuals with developmental disabilities, assessment of client needs, and coordination of efforts among professional disciplines.

3. *Program Implementation.* Implementation of a service program.

4. *Program Management.* Understanding of legal issues, regulations, processes, and the allocation of personnel, equipment, and resources.

5. *Program Evaluation.* Evaluation of client progress and overall program effectiveness.

6. *Systematic Instruction.* Understanding of use of instructional techniques and use of prompts and reinforcers.

7. *Transition Planning.* Identification and analysis of skills needed in current and future environments of clients.

Source: Adapted from "Preservice Preparation of Supported Employment Professionals" by J. Kregel and P. Sale, 1988. In P. Wehman and M. S. Moon (Eds.), *Vocational Rehabilitation and Supported Employment* (pp. 129–143), Baltimore: Paul H. Brookes. Reprinted by permission.

3. Appropriate curricula in many areas, including self-help, affective, recreational, social, and mobility

4. Effective instructional techniques

5. Behavior management strategies

6. Assistive devices and prosthetic aids

7. Interpersonal skills required in a multidisciplinary context

In general, the trend today is toward more and more education in the community. Greater opportunities for integration as well as the positive effects of learning in the *real* environment make it more important than ever for students with severe disabilities to get out of the classroom and into their neighborhoods. Curricula that focus on (1) self-care skills, (2) recreation and leisure activities, (3) vocational and prevocational competencies (especially the necessary social skills), and (4) skills for community functioning are the norm for these students.

In addition, teachers must also recognize the important role that families play in education. Teachers are sometimes called upon to act as parent-trainers because the educational needs of persons with severe disabilities extend into the home. Parents may need help learning and implementing behavior management skills. Parents also reinforce and provide practice for learning that occurs in the school. The skillful teacher must be able to communicate easily with parents and be sensitive to the many emotional reactions that parents have during their lives with a family member who is severely disabled. Not only does the law require a plan involving family participation, the best interests of the student are served when everyone is working together and when communication is open and frequent.

Teachers must also be able to encourage risk taking with students who have severe disabilities. Often, a pattern of parental overprotection limits the activities of these individuals. While being mindful of the student's limitations, the competent teacher must allow the child to experience everyday situations that involve a certain degree of risk. As Perske (1972) poignantly stated, "Overprotection endangers the . . . person's human dignity and tends to keep him from experiencing the normal taking of risks in life which is necessary for normal human growth and development" (p. 24).

Preparation

It is the responsibility of institutions that train teachers to provide relevant course work and experiences. Most of these professional competencies can be introduced in an academic setting, but maximum mastery can be achieved only if a variety of field experiences are an integral part of the program. Institutions of higher learning also have the opportunity to provide important in-service programs to the school systems and community. The value of such programs for professionals in the field, and for students with severe disabilities, cannot be overemphasized. Competent professionals must continue to be well informed about advances in their field.

Another role that departments of special education can take is that of advocates for high certification standards and for rigorous training problems. Finally, teacher training institutions can assist in developing community services for those who need continuing support after their school years. Issues such as the integration of persons with severe disabilities into the community and the need for models of ongoing training should be concerns of teacher educators.

FUTURE CONSIDERATIONS

Because it seems that our knowledge in behavioral science and technology will keep increasing, it is not difficult to imagine that our knowledge about the learning potential of persons with severe disabilities will also grow. As individuals with severe disabilities demonstrate mastery of various behaviors, new goals that indicate higher levels of functioning or coping can be set.

Appropriate transitional and lifelong planning for these individuals and their families is needed. It is not out of the question to hope for the development of a comprehensive lifelong curriculum for the vocational and personal development of people with severe disabilities.

Continued research must be encouraged, supported, and adequately funded in order to accelerate the pace of development now being experienced. Behavioral technology, which works particularly well with students with severe disabilities, needs to be refined. Efforts to enhance the maintenance and generalization of learned behaviors and to identify alternative reinforcement strategies must continue. Medical research into the etiology, assessment, and prevention of various pathological conditions must also continue.

Major issues related to the lives of persons with severe disabilities remain controversial to this day. Serious questions concerning prenatal screening/intervention, medical technology, and the withholding of treatment postnatally are only a few of the volatile issues yet to be resolved. A major movement toward inclusion of individuals with severe disabilities into mainstream situations is also a reflection of our current social, political, and economic (as well as educational) climate.

SUGGESTIONS FOR WORKING WITH PERSONS WITH SEVERE DISABILITIES

1. Make sure you have a student's attention before beginning any teaching activity.
2. Use age-appropriate materials regardless of the severity of the disability.
3. Set clear goals. Have a plan and stick with it.
4. Use teaching methods that minimize errors. When errors occur, provide corrective feedback.
5. Be consistent. It also helps to follow a planned schedule throughout the day at home as well as at school.
6. Use activities and tasks that are relevant to the child.

7. Teach and assess in natural settings and at natural times whenever possible.

8. Communicate and cooperate with others. The inclusion of parents, other caregivers, and community resources can enhance any student's program.

9. Learn as much as you can about technology. Keeping up with the latest in technological advances in education is a challenge, but for individuals for with serious disabilities, quality of life can be changed by adaptive equipment and devices.

10. In order to promote skill generalization, teach a given skill across a variety of settings, trainers, and materials. After a skill is mastered, plan opportunities for its use on a regular basis.

✦ PONDER THESE

1. *You are a parent and you have a 1-week-old infant who has been diagnosed as having a severe disability. What are your reactions when you receive a sympathy card from friends saying that their thoughts are with you in your time of grief?*

2. *Suppose that you know a parent who has a 4-year-old child with a severe disability. As of now, this child is not receiving any educational services. What would you do?*

3. *Some people believe that premature infants with disabilities so severe that they cannot survive without life-sustaining equipment should not be allowed to live, or stated another way, should be allowed to die. How do you feel about this approach?*

4. *Would you consider an intellectually bright adult with a severe form of cerebral palsy (i.e., substantial motor and communication impairments) to have a severe disability?*

5. *Many people favor full inclusion of all individuals with disabilities, regardless of the severity of the disability or the services required. If you were the parent of a child with a severe disability, how would you feel about this approach?*

References

Amado, A. N., Lakin, K. C., & Menke, J. M. (1990). *Chartbook on services for people with developmental disabilities.* Minneapolis: University of Minnesota, Center for Residential and Community Services.

American Psychiatric Association. (1994). *Diagnostic and statistical manual of mental disorders* (4th ed.). Washington, DC: Author.

Gilpin, R. W. (1993). *Laughing and loving with Autism.* Arlington, TX: Future Education, Inc.

Haney, D. Q. Associated Press. (1994, September 22). Study: Tiniest babies are often disabled. *Austin American Statesman,* p. A6.

Haring, N. G. (1978). The severely handicapped. In N. G. Haring (Ed.), *Behavior of exceptional children* (2nd ed., pp. 195–229). Englewood Cliffs, NJ: Merrill/Prentice Hall.

Hasazi, S., & York, R. (1978). Eleven steps to good teaching. *Teaching Exceptional Children, 10*(3), 63–66.

Inge, K. J. (1987). Atypical motor development and cerebral palsy. In F. Orelove & D. Sobsey (Eds.), *Educating children with multiple disabilities: A transdisciplinary approach* (pp. 43–65). Baltimore: Paul H. Brookes.

Kregel, J., & Sale, P. (1988). Preservice preparation of supported employment professionals. In P. Wehman & M. S. Moon (Eds.), *Vocational rehabilitation and supported employment* (pp. 129–143). Baltimore: Paul H. Brookes.

Olley, J. G. (1992). Autism: Historical overview, definition, and characteristics. In D. E. Berkell (Ed.), *Autism: Identification, education, and treatment* (pp. 3–20). Hillsdale, New Jersey: Lawrence Erlbaum Associates.

Perske, R. (1972). The dignity of risk and the mentally retarded. *Mental Retardation, 10*(1), 24–27.

Peterson, C. P. (1980). Support services. In B. L. Wilcox & R. York (Eds.), *Quality education for severely handicapped: The federal investment* (pp. 136–163). Washington, DC: Bureau of Education for the Handicapped.

Scheerenberger, R. C. (1982). Treatment from ancient times to the present. In P. T. Cegelka & H. J. Prehn (Eds.), *Mental retardation: From categories to people* (pp. 44–75). Englewood Cliffs, NJ: Merrill/Prentice Hall.

Stotland, J. F., & Mancuso, E. (1981). U.S. Court of Appeals decision regarding Armstrong v. Kline: The 180 day rule. *Exceptional Children, 47,* 266–270.

Strain, P., McConnell, S., & Cordisco, L. (1983). Special educators as single-subject researchers. *Exceptional Education Quarterly, 4*(3), 40–51.

U.S. Department of Education (1993). *To assure the free appropriate public education of all children with disabilities. Fifteenth annual report to*

Congress on the implementation of the Individuals with Disabilities Education Act. Washington, DC: Author.

Wehman, P., Kregel, J., & Seyfarth, J. (1985). Transition from school to work for youth with severe handicaps: A follow-up study. *Journal of the Association for Persons with Severe Handicaps, 10,* 132–136.

Wolfe, P. S. (1992). Challenges for service providers. In P. J. McLaughlin & P. Wehman (Eds.), *Developmental disabilities: A handbook for best practices* (pp. 124–141). Boston: Andover Medical Publishers.

TWO

PHYSICAL, SENSORY, AND COMMUNICATIVE IMPAIRMENTS

7

PHYSICAL AND HEALTH
IMPAIRMENTS

A young man, age 15, was being admitted to a short-term residential diagnostic center. The school was concerned because he was experiencing an increase in seizures and questioned the family's compliance with his drug regimen. As the interview with the parents proceeded, the mother expressed her belief about his "fits." "Yes," she said, "he done had more of 'em this last year, but they won't last much longer." When asked what she meant by that, she stated, "Well, he's getting older, you know. And once he's been with a woman, he won't have them fits no more!"
(Who knows, maybe sex is better than Dilantin!)[1]

    People with disabilities are not to be abused, talked down to, or pitied. They are people just like you and me. The film Leo Beuerman[2] *is about a man whose physical disabilities were so extensive that he was described sometimes as "grotesque," or "too horrible to look at." He was small, he weighed less than 90 pounds,*

---

[1]This story was contributed by Carol Grimm, Lockhart, Texas.

[2]*Leo Beuerman*, Centron Educational Films, 1621 West 9th St., Lawrence, Kansas 66044 (13 minutes/color).

and his legs were so bent out of shape that he couldn't walk. He also had poor eyesight and was hard of hearing. Leo lived on a farm in Kansas. Somehow, he learned to drive a tractor, and later he invented a hoist that allowed him to raise himself onto the tractor. He also invented and built a pushcart that enabled him to get around from place to place. Using a hoist to get his cart on the tractor, he would then get on the tractor and drive to town. In town Leo would park his tractor, lower himself and his cart down to the street, get in the cart, and propel himself down the sidewalk to the store-front where he repaired watches and sold pencils. The reason the movie about Leo had such an impact on me is that I can remember buying pencils from him as a kid in school. At that time, I didn't realize how remarkable Leo really was. He just wanted to talk to people, work, and do his own thing. He wanted to be self-sufficient and independent. Here was a man, deformed to the point that, to most people, he was a repulsive sight. However, he was more individual, more free, and more alive than most people.

It was Jimmy's first day in class. Jimmy could not walk due to spina bifida, but he didn't let that get in his way. He was a very proficient crawler. One day, after circle time, the kids were heading for the housekeeping center, and Jimmy was scooting right along with them—in fact, faster than many. One little girl, exasperated that he got to her favorite spot first, indignantly pointed her finger at Jimmy and informed him, "Little boy, we don't run in here."

Ms. Jones had just begun her first elementary teaching job when she went to her doctor complaining of numbness in her legs. After a series of treatments with no improvement, initial test results by the physician indicated multiple sclerosis. The diagnosis proved to be correct. Ms. Jones refused to let the disease end her career. As time went on, the progressive disease affected her arms and legs until she had to use a wheelchair. Ms. Jones continued to teach. The ramps, special toilet equipment, and self-opening doors, originally designed to provide access for students with disabilities in her school, now allowed her to reach her classroom. Not only did Ms. Jones continue her teaching career, but her disability made her more sensitive to the needs of all children. She began to organize her third grade classroom to foster interactions between nondisabled children and their peers with disabilities. As a result of her *innovative techniques and success with all her students, she was selected as her state's outstanding teacher.*

I have a friend, Bobby, who has epilepsy. The medication he takes regularly seems to control the seizures to a great extent; however, he still experiences grand mal tonic-clonic episodes once in a while (approximately once a year). Bobby is athletic and enjoys sports. Interestingly, his favorite leisure time activity is surfing. Now, around here that is not unusual; but for someone who has seizures, it is a bit risky, especially when surfing alone. However, Bobby is not about to let his epilepsy control his life, so his frequent surfboard riding through the breaking waves does not surprise me a bit. Nevertheless, one day when Bobby was talking to my introductory class in special education, I asked him about the danger in going surfing alone and possibly having a grand mal seizure. After a brief hesitation, Bobby replied that he had thought about it and that if he did have a seizure he would probably drown unless someone else could pull him to safety. The class was confused by his matter-of-fact attitude, but they understood his strong feelings about doing what he wanted to do. Then Bobby made everyone sit back and reflect when he concluded his response to my question with this quip: "But at least I'd die happy!"

Since the Vietnam War, various skiing schools have been developed to teach individuals with disabilities how to ski. In the film A Matter of Inconvenience,[3] *a skier with an amputated leg explains how difficult it was for him to make the adjustment from skiing with two legs to skiing with one leg. As he talks about the problems of this transition, you can tell from his face and eyes that he is in deep thought. Slowly he looks up and with a grin says, "One thing though, you don't have to worry about crossing tips."*

American society, perhaps more than any other culture, puts a premium on strong, healthy looking bodies. All forms of media, especially those used for advertising and entertainment, sell products and services by using images of health and attractiveness. We spend millions of dollars each year on beauty aids, cosmetics, tanning lotions,

---

[3]*A Matter of Inconvenience*, Stanfield House, 900 Euclid Avenue, P.O. Box 3208, Santa Monica, CA 90403 (10 minutes/color).

s, running shoes, health equipment, and memberships
,as, all intended to enhance our appearance. As a result,
,uals with physical and health impairments often face a chal-
,enge when they attempt to find full acceptance in their communities.
Integration into school, work, and a full social life can be difficult for
everyone, but the physical and social barriers of our modern society
can make the process complicated and overwhelming for persons with
physical and health disorders. They must deal not only with their disability but also with our social attitudes toward appearances.

DEFINITIONS

This chapter is about physical and health impairments. The various
terms and descriptors used to discuss these disabilities are often complicated, redundant, and confusing. In an attempt to be as clear as
possible, we try to be consistent in using these two general terms. It is
also important to distinguish two other words commonly used in the
media and in ordinary conversation: *disability* and *handicap*. These
two terms have traditionally been differentiated by special education
professionals. A disability was the acknowledged term used to
describe an inherent physical and/or cognitive limitation; a handicap
implied that there were limitations on a person with a disability
because of environmental conditions. Someone with a physical or
health related disability may or may not have a handicap, depending
on the demands of the environment. For example, if an individual who
is mobility impaired and uses a wheelchair works successfully as a
computer data analyst and is not limited by his or her disability, he or
she would not be considered handicapped.

More recently, current attempts at political correctness have had
an important impact on the way individuals with disabilities are
described. When PL 101–476 (the IDEA) was passed in 1990, reautho-
rizing PL 94–142, all references to "handicapped children" were
replaced with "children with disabilities." The IDEA also added the
categories of autism (see Chapter 6) and traumatic brain injury. The
IDEA includes two other relevant categories: orthopedic impairments
and other health impairments. Because of the many specific disorders
included in the physical and health impairment categories, prevalence
figures will be presented as each disorder is described.

Although not generic, the terms *physical impairment* and *health
impairment* refer to a very heterogeneous population that displays a
wide range of conditions. Consequently, our discussion of specific disabilities or conditions will mean that generalizations to all physical or
health impairments may not be valid. Physical or health impairments

can result from many different causes and can be classified in many different ways. For example, impairments may be *congenital* (the child has it from birth) or *acquired* (the child is normal at birth but something happens later). Causes may include genetic factors, physical trauma, oxygen deprivation, chemical agents (poisoning), disease, or some combination of these or other factors. Impairments may also be classified according to the particular organ or organ system involved, for example, neurological impairments (involving the brain or spinal cord or peripheral nerves), cardiovascular conditions (involving the heart and blood vessels), hematological problems (involving the blood), orthopedic conditions (involving the bones and joints), and so on. Some types of disorders can be congenital or acquired, result from a variety of causes, and involve more than one organ system. Thus, you can see that classification of physical and health impairments, while possible, is a topic that cannot be dealt with in much detail in a short space.

Examples of physical impairments include cerebral palsy, muscular dystrophy, multiple sclerosis, spina bifida, traumatic brain injury, spinal cord injuries, and other physical conditions such as amputations, congenital limb deficiencies, and juvenile rheumatoid arthritis. Health impairments include allergies and asthma, cancer, cystic fibrosis, juvenile diabetes, epilepsy, chronic heart conditions, hemophilia, sickle cell anemia, and HIV/AIDS. Some of these disorders could be considered both physical and health disorders and include disorders of neurological, musculoskeletal, and other organic bases.

PHYSICAL IMPAIRMENTS

Hardman, Drew, Egan, and Wolf (1993) provided a simple, straightforward definition of a physical impairment. They describe physical impairments as disorders that " . . . may interfere with an individual's mobility and coordination. They may also affect his or her capacity to communicate, learn, and adjust" (p. 340). It is impossible in this short chapter to adequately discuss the many physical disorders present in children and youth. Therefore, the discussion is limited to traumatic brain injury and cerebral palsy, with a brief mention of spina bifida.

Traumatic Brain Injury

During the 1991–92 school year, approximately 330 students with traumatic brain injury (TBI) were served in special education. Because this was the first year for this category, the figure is very low, and it is impossible to determine patterns of increase or decrease (U.S. Department of Education, 1993). Many students with severe traumatic brain injuries are still being served in programs for students with mental retardation and severe disabilities; those with milder long-term problems may still be in programs for students with learning disabilities or serious emotional disturbance. However, students in the TBI category require an Individualized Educational Program (IEP) that includes all necessary related services.

According to the National Head Injury Foundation, a traumatic brain injury is "an insult to the brain caused by an external force that may produce diminished or altered states of consciousness, which results in impaired cognitive abilities or physical functioning" (1989, p. 2). Traumatic brain injuries include both *closed-head* injuries (like those often caused by automobile accidents) or *open-head* injuries (like gunshot wounds), depending on whether there is penetration of the skull. Brain damage can be either *primary,* which is a direct result of the impact; or *secondary,* which occurs after the initial injury but is still related to it. Knowledge about traumatic brain injuries is valuable for teachers, because students often have long lasting, significant *residual* impairments.

Unfortunately, traumatic brain injury is not a rare occurrence among children. Each year, about one million children sustain traumatic brain injuries. According to Mira, Tucker, and Tyler (1992), this means that 1 in 500 children is hospitalized with a head injury. About 3% of school age children still have residual impairments from brain injuries. Young people between the ages of 15 and 24 face the greatest risk of traumatic brain injury. Among older students, motor vehicle accidents are the leading cause of TBI, but sports related injuries are also common. The other high risk age group for brain injuries is very young children (preschoolers). Causes of brain injury for this group include child abuse and falls. The number of boys who sustain brain injuries is about twice that of girls.

The majority of brain injuries are *mild,* meaning concussions, dizziness, or loss of consciousness without skull fracture. Although not as serious as other brain injuries, mild brain injuries can still result in residual memory and attention problems. *Moderate* brain injuries involve a loss of consciousness from 1 to 24 hours or a skull fracture. Children with moderate head injuries often develop secondary neurological problems like swelling within the brain and usually have long-term residual effects. In *severe* brain injuries, there is a loss of consciousness for more than 24 hours, bruising of the brain tissue, or bleeding within the brain. Children with severe brain injuries are often hospitalized in critical condition and will have motor, language, and cognitive problems after regaining consciousness. They will likely experience lifelong deficits that impact their learning (Mira et al., 1992).

As with any disability, conditions and factors in students' lives will play a role in the outcome of traumatic brain injuries. According to Mira et al. (1992), children who sustain brain injuries reportedly have a higher incidence of prior behavior problems. Overactive and impulsive children often take risks that predispose them to brain injuries. Other risk factors in a child's environment include high levels of family stress, including marital instability and economic problems.

Interventions for TBI vary, depending on the stage of injury. Immediately after injury, the focus is often on sustaining life and minimizing complications, especially if the injury results in coma (unconsciousness lasting more than a short period of time). There seems to be a direct relationship between the length of the coma and the level of cognitive impairment. If the child remains in a coma, therapists may use special stimulation to arouse him or her. After the coma, children often experience posttraumatic amnesia and are seriously disoriented. Efforts must be made to reorient them to their surroundings. Children who sustain traumatic brain injuries may also have other serious medical problems that require intensive intervention.

In the first few months after a traumatic brain injury, children often make rapid recovery. Many of the initial effects of the injury diminish. However, 6 months to 1 year after the injury, many children still evidence a wide range of medical, motor, cognitive, behavioral, and language problems. These problems may persist for many years. Some of the common residual physical problems are seizures, loss of stamina, headaches, hearing or vision impairments, growth problems, and a variety of other effects. Long-term cognitive effects often include problems with memory, attention, language processing, problem solving, and general intellectual functioning. Of these, memory problems are often the most troublesome. Because success in school requires significant long- and short-term memory skills, lingering memory problems can have a serious impact on students' academic achievement. Language problems are also critical for students. Many school tasks involve written or oral language, often in conjunction with other skills. In many ways, students with residual effects of traumatic brain injury resemble their peers with learning disabilities. Expressive and receptive language problems, word retrieval (remembering commonly used words), sequencing skills, and general disorganization are common. Behaviorally, students with brain injuries may display problems similar to those of students with emotional/behavioral disorders. Students often display impulsivity, hyperactivity, poor social interaction skills, and inconsistency of responses.

For school personnel, attending to the needs of students with traumatic brain injuries involves several responsibilities. Hardman et al. (1993) have suggested some relevant interventions, including providing counseling and therapy to help the child cope with the injury and its effects, assisting the child and family in maintaining the gains achieved, and referring the child and family to community agencies for additional services that may be needed. A well-informed staff, a structured, controlled environment, and adaptive equipment and devices are also important in schools. Educators must also be sensitive to the emotional reactions of families. Parents of a child with a brain injury will face a grieving process and an adaptation to loss and may need assistance and understanding from teachers and administrators. Some general suggestions for school personnel who work with students who have had brain injuries are included in Table 7.1.

Cerebral Palsy

The term *cerebral palsy* is used to describe a condition with a wide range of characteristics and a varying level of severity. *Cerebral palsy* literally implies brain paralysis. According to Inge (1992), cerebral palsy is "a nonprogressive disorder caused by a lesion or defect to the brain occurring prior to birth, during the birth process, or during the first four years of life" (p. 30). Numerous causes, occurring before, during, or after birth, may be responsible for this condition. Some of the etiologies include anoxia, infection, intoxication, hemorrhaging, trauma, fever, and prematurity. The resulting physical impairment can range from barely inhibiting to profoundly debilitating. Approximately 2 children in 1000 (.2%) are affected by some form of cerebral palsy (Inge, 1992). Prevalence figures, however, vary widely and may depend on family level of awareness and ability to seek medical attention.

Various forms of cerebral palsy are categorized both by *type* (description of the movement disorder) and by *physical characteristics* (see Table 7.2). Perhaps the biggest problem facing individuals with cerebral palsy is abnormal muscle tone. The muscle tone of a person with cerebral palsy can be either excessive (spastic/hypertonic) or insufficient (hypotonic). Either way, muscle tone is critical for posture and movement. The other important consideration is the individuality of persons who have cerebral palsy. Two people can be categorized with exactly the same type or distribution of the disorder, yet have very different levels of functioning and abilities.

According to Prensky and Palkes (1982), about two thirds of individuals with cerebral palsy also have associated problems. These can include mental retardation, seizures, visual impairments, hearing loss,

Table 7.1
Classroom Suggestions for Teaching Students With Traumatic Brain Injury

- Receptive language

  Limit the amount of information presented at one time.
  Provide simple instructions for only one activity at a time.
  Have the student repeat instructions.

- Expressive language

  Teach the student to rehearse silently before verbally replying.
  Teach the student to look for cues from listeners to ascertain that the student is being understood.
  Teach the student to ask directly if he or she is being understood.

- Maintaining attention

  Provide a study carrel or preferential seating.
  After giving instructions, check for proper attention and understanding by having the student repeat them.
  Teach the student to use self-regulating techniques to maintain attention (e.g., asking "Am I paying attention?" "What is the required task?")

- Impulsiveness

  Teach the student to mentally rehearse steps before beginning an activity.
  Reduce potential distractions.
  Frequently restate and reinforce rules.

- Memory

  Teach the student to use external aids such as notes, memos, daily schedule sheets, and assignment sheets.
  Use visual imagery, when possible, to supplement oral content.
  Teach visual imaging techniques for information presented.
  Provide repetition and frequent review of instruction materials.
  Provide immediate and frequent feedback to enable the student to interpret success or failure.

- Following directions

  Provide the student with both visual and auditory directions.
  Model tasks, whenever possible.
  Break multistep directions into small parts and list them so that the student can refer back when needed.

- Motor skills

  Allow the student to complete a project rather than turn in a written assignment.
  Have the student use a typewriter or a word processor to complete assignments.
  Allow extra time for completing tasks requiring fine-motor skills.
  Assign someone to take notes for the student during lectures.

Source: Adapted from Mira, M.P., Tucker, B.F., & Tuler, J.S. (1992). *Traumatic brain injury teachers and other school personnel*. Austin, TX: Pro-Ed.

Table 7.2
Classifications of Cerebral Palsy (by Type and Distribution)

Descriptive Terminology	Characteristics
Monoplegia	One limb involved
Hemiplegia	One side of body involved
Triplegia	Three limbs involved
Paraplegia	Lower extremities (legs) involved
Diplegia	All limbs involved, but legs more than arms
Quadriplegia	Entire body involved, including all four limbs and trunk
Spastic	Increased muscle tone (hypertonic); slow movement
Athetoid	Involuntary, uncontrolled movements; difficulty maintaining stable posture
Dystonic	Distorted movement; muscle tone that varies between hypotonic and hypertonic
Rigid	Invariable muscle tone; stiff movement
Hypotonic	Low muscle tone; floppy movement
Mixed	More than one type; usually with one predominant

speech and language disorders, and cognitive limitations. Because of the many facets of related disorders, many individuals with cerebral palsy are considered to have multiple disabilities. Although some children with cerebral palsy have normal or above-average intelligence, many are below average in academic functioning. Perhaps more than with any other physical disability, students with cerebral palsy require multidisciplinary interventions. Medical treatment by physicians and nurses, interventions for enhanced mobility provided by occupational and physical therapists, and speech-language therapy available from speech-language professionals are just some of the many interventions necessary for these students.

Advances in computer technology and augmentative communication devices have had an important beneficial impact on the lives of individuals with cerebral palsy. Voice synthesizers, touch screens for computers, light beam control devices, and lighter weight wheelchairs are just some of the inventions that have improved their communication and mobility. As technological advances continue, it is likely that increased integration into school, community and the workplace will be more common.

For teachers and teaching assistants, competencies required for effective education of students with cerebral palsy can include (1) skills required in moving and positioning; (2) abilities related to teaching self-care, including dressing, feeding, and toileting; and (3) knowledge required for appropriate monitoring (for problems like gagging or jaw clenching). Looking ahead, we must focus educational considerations on transition to community living. Employment, housing, and transportation are just a few of the areas of concern if the future is to include independent or semi-independent living.

Other Physical Impairments

Some of the other physical impairments found among school children and youth include spina bifida, spinal cord injuries, and muscular dystrophy. Spina bifida is the most common physical disability of childhood. Spina bifida is a birth defect caused by a prenatal malformation of the spine, resulting in an opening in the vertebral column. The central nervous system is often involved and symptoms can include (1) loss of sensation from the spina bifida protrusion to all areas of the body below it; (2) little or no bladder or bowel control; (3) hydrocephalus, which can be corrected through the implantation of shunts; (4) brittle bones in areas where there is poor circulation due to lack of sensation and physical movement; and/or (5) loss of muscle control below the spine lesion (Paasche, Gorrill, & Strom, 1990). The incidence of spina bifida is approximately 0.5 to 1.0 per thousand live births (Rowley-Kelly & Reigel, 1993). There appear to be multiple causes of spina bifida, including factors related to race, malnutrition, and poverty as well as a family tendency or predisposition. Recent research has focused on deficiencies in the diet of mothers during their pregnancies.

Most students with spina bifida have normal levels of intelligence and are placed in unrestrictive educational settings. Those students with the more serious forms of spina bifida require modifications and adaptive equipment like braces or wheelchairs. Smith, Polloway, Patton, and Dowdy (1994) offer the following suggestions for educators of students with spina bifida:

- Maintain an environment that is *friendly* to individuals with motor impairments (e.g., remove loose floor coverings; make sure floors are not wet).
- Learn how to position students to develop strength and avoid sores.
- Understand the process of clean intermittent bladder catheterization (CIC) and be ready to deal with occasional incontinence.
- Learn how to deal with seizures.
- Ensure full participation of the students in classroom activities.
- Help the student with spina bifida develop a healthy, positive self-concept.
- Communicate with the parents.

HEALTH IMPAIRMENTS

According to Smith and Luckasson (1992), a *health impairment* is a condition in which the body's physical well being is affected, requiring some form of ongoing medical attention. The IDEA notes that health disorders result in "limited strength, vitality or alertness, due to chronic or acute health problems such as a heart condition, tuberculosis, rheumatic fever, nephritis, asthma, sickle cell anemia, hemophilia, epilepsy, lead poisoning, leukemia, or diabetes which adversely affect education performance" (23 Code of Federal Regulations, Section 300.5 [7]).

The following sections are about two specific health impairments: acquired immunodeficiency syndrome (AIDS) and seizure disorders (epilepsy). In addition, two other health impairments will be discussed briefly: asthma and juvenile diabetes.

AIDS (Acquired Immunodeficiency Syndrome)

The human immunodeficiency virus (HIV) causes the disease AIDS. Individuals can be HIV positive and show no signs of the disease; however, children with HIV are likely to develop symptoms of AIDS. According to LeRoy, Powell, and Kelker (1994):

AIDS has escalated from a handful of isolated cases in 1981 to more than 315,000 by June, 1993 (Centers for Disease Control and Prevention, 1993). Estimates are that more than 1 million people are infected with HIV, the agent that causes AIDS. As of June, 1993, AIDS had claimed more than 194,000 victims in the United States, 2,500 of whom were children under the age of 13 (p.37–38).

AIDS is growing fastest among women, adolescents, and young adults. It is difficult to obtain accurate information about the number of AIDS infected children and youth and even more difficult to accurately describe the specific relationships of the disease to disability issues.

HIV is transmitted only through an exchange of body fluids, such as semen, blood, and breast milk. In adults and adolescents, the most common causes of infection are the use of contaminated needles or through sexual contact. Batshaw and Perret (1992) estimated that about 80% of children diagnosed with HIV acquired the infection from their mothers, either prenatally or during the birth process. The other 20% of cases in children are either the result of receiving contaminated blood (usually before 1985) or from sexual partners. There is less likelihood of acquiring the disease from blood products now that they are screened regularly. Infants with HIV will likely develop AIDS before the age of 2, and most will be dead 1 year later. It is expected that as treatments advance, there will be more survivors from this population. Adolescents who acquire HIV sexually or through intravenous drug use are less likely to develop symptoms while still in school; but they still carry the virus (LeRoy et al., 1994).

According to LeRoy et al. (1994, p. 40), some of the typical symptoms of childhood AIDS include:

- Attention difficulties
- Cardiac disease
- Central nervous system damage
- Cognitive deficits
- Cold sores
- Coughing
- Diarrhea (acute and chronic)
- Emotional problems
- Fine and gross motor difficulties
- Hearing problems
- Infections, including frequent bacterial and viral infections; middle ear, eye, and joint infections

- Seizures
- Shortness of breath
- Speech and language delays
- Visual problems
- Weakness
- Weight loss

Some of the unique complications for children with health impairments include social isolation, the effects of long-term hospitalization, parental illness and death (of parents who also have AIDS), family problems, a lack of understanding from the community, and associated learning problems. Children with HIV can be developmentally delayed at birth or may develop normally for a number of years and then begin to evidence delays at a later age. Cognitive impairments such as decreased intellectual levels, specific learning disabilities, mental retardation, visual or spatial deficits, and decreased alertness can cause academic problems in school. Social or behavioral problems can also develop, and may range from lethargy to hyperactivity (Seidel, 1992).

Teachers and administrators should keep abreast of information about the disease and follow the guidelines suggested by the Centers for Disease Control regarding precautions for prevention of HIV. These precautions include (1) careful handling (with nonpermeable gloves) of blood, feces, nasal secretions, sputum, sweat, saliva, tears, urine, and vomitus; (2) use of receptacles with tightly fitting lids and cleanup with a bleach-water combination; and (3) hand washing when skin is exposed to contaminated fluids and drug treatment if an open lesion is exposed to contamination (Centers for Disease Control, 1993). In addition, teachers should maintain ongoing communication with parents and physicians, maintain confidentiality of records, reevaluate frequently, and obtain updated training on a regular basis. Table 7.3 presents a teacher checklist for accommodating students with AIDS (Kelker, Hecimovic, & LeRoy, 1994).

Seizure Disorders (Epilepsy)

A seizure disorder is the result of "an abnormal discharge of electrical energy in the brain" (Hallahan & Kauffman, 1988, p. 340). *Epilepsy* is a disorder that involves recurrent episodes of seizure activity. The prevalence of epilepsy can range from 0.15% to 1% of the population, depending on the definition used.

Epilepsy can be caused by any event that results in brain damage, such as brain lesions, anoxia, trauma, poisoning, or tumors. If etiology

Table 7.3
Teacher Checklist for Accommodating Students With AIDS

- Observe guidelines for confidentiality of information.
- Assess the student for eligibility under IDEA or Section 504.
- Obtain copies of state and local policies for inclusion of students with HIV.
- Get the facts about HIV and how it affects learning.
- Assemble a team to develop an individualized education program (IEP) that addresses educational needs and health-related supports.
- Plan modifications of instructional methods and curriculum to meet the student's individual needs.
- Design ways to include the student who has HIV in typical classroom activities.
- Build flexibility into the student's IEP to allow for hospitalizations and frequent absences.
- Arrange for training in infection control procedures (e.g., universal precautions).
- Educate parents about communicable disease policies and the use of universal precautions.
- Answer students' questions about terminal illness.

Source:From "Designing A Classroom and School Environment for Students With AIDS" by K. Kelker, A. Hecimovic, and C. H. LeRoy, 1994, *Teaching Exceptional Children, 24*(4), p. 52. Reprinted by permission.

can be determined, the term *symptomatic epilepsy* is used; however, if causation cannot be determined, which is true the majority of the time, the appropriate term used is *idiopathic epilepsy*. Even if the original cause of the problem can be determined, the reason for the abnormal discharge of electrical energy under certain conditions (i.e., what triggers a seizure) may remain unknown.

One system for classifying the various forms of epilepsy is based on the localization of the seizure activity in the brain. This system can be briefly described as follows:

1. Generalized seizures: discharge is bilateral and symmetrical or is nonlocalized
2. Partial seizure: discharge is localized
3. Miscellaneous: related to high fever (febrile seizure) or other cause

Included in the generalized seizure category are *grand mal, petit mal, myoclonic,* and *akinetic* seizures. The generalized seizure is characterized by a spontaneous loss of consciousness of varying length and expression.

The grand mal seizure (generalized tonic-clonic) is the type most people think of when they think of epilepsy. The person having a grand mal attack, which is convulsive in nature, usually lets out a cry, loses consciousness, falls, and goes through a short period of muscle contractions of the extremities, trunk, and head. This type of seizure may be preceded by an *aura* (an unusual sensory perception) that can serve as a warning of the onset of a seizure. The grand mal seizure also may include facial contortions, heavy breathing, perspiration, foaming at the mouth, loss of bladder and bowel control, and physical injury if the person strikes against objects while falling or convulsing. This behavior may last up to 5 minutes, after which the individual falls into a deep sleep that is followed by natural sleep. Upon regaining consciousness, the individual may display the following characteristics: disorientation, depression, amnesia of the seizure, nausea, soreness, and exhaustion.

The petit mal (absence) seizure is less dramatic but can have a devastating effect on a student's educational progress. Berg (1982) describes the typical petit mal seizure as "the momentary suspension of all activity, a staring spell, or as some have called them, lapses or absence attacks" (p. 104). Often, this form of epilepsy is misperceived in a classroom setting as daydreaming, inattention, or misbehavior. The lapse of consciousness may last only a few seconds or may continue for up to 30 seconds. Unlike the grand mal seizure, the onset of a petit mal seizure will not be accompanied by the aura phenomenon. Frequently, children will grow out of this type of seizure.

Partial (focal) seizures involve a focal discharge in a localized part of the brain, and as a result produce a specific motor or sensory effect. A *Jacksonian seizure* is an example of a partial seizure and involves a pattern of rhythmic movements that start in one part of the body and progressively spread to other parts. Although not fully understood, psychomotor seizure (complex partial) is considered to be a type of focal seizure and is characterized by inappropriate behaviors such as being verbally incoherent, verbally abusive, or violent. Even though this type of seizure is brief, the behaviors nevertheless are socially unacceptable, and there is a good chance that they will be misinterpreted.

There have been many misconceptions about epilepsy throughout history. Unfortunately, some of these misconceptions still exist. Seeing someone have a convulsion is upsetting and frightening to many people, especially to those uninformed or misinformed about the nature of seizures. Individuals with epilepsy are no more disposed to mental illness than other individuals, and they function quite normally between seizures. Mental retardation occurs in only 10% of this population; most people with epilepsy (approximately 70%) have average or above-average intelligence. Most seizures (80%) can be totally or partially controlled with proper medication. Teachers can assist children who have seizures by ensuring their safety during seizures, by attempting to correct the misperceptions of others, and by being prepared to deal with learning problems that may arise.

Other Health Impairments

This section cannot adequately describe every health impairment in detail. However, asthma, which is a common condition among school age children, and juvenile diabetes, which is less common, are discussed briefly.

Asthma has been described as the leading cause of absenteeism among school children. Estimates are that approximately three million children and youth under the age of 15 have asthma (American Academy of Allergy & Immunology). Characteristic problems include shortness of breath, coughing, and wheezing, due to irritation of the bronchial mucus from allergens or other infections. For some children, asthma attacks are a nuisance; for others, the attacks are life threatening.

Teachers who have students with asthma in their classes should be aware of the side effects of the medications used by students, including headaches, hand tremors, stomachaches, lethargy, and reduced stamina. Allowances should be made for absences, which may be excessive for individual students. In addition, the classroom may harbor many allergens such as chalk dust or animal hair, and should be monitored carefully.

Juvenile diabetes is less familiar to educators. It is a metabolic disorder. Because of insufficient insulin production, individuals with diabetes do not process sugar in a normal way. For many students, management of diabetes includes careful attention to diet and exercise. Urine or blood tests to monitor insulin levels and injections of insulin may be a typical routine for students with more serious diabetes.

Students with diabetes may have problems concentrating and remaining alert in class. According to Paasche et al. (1990), students with juvenile diabetes may also be thin and pale and have abnormal increases in thirst and appetite. Teachers must closely monitor these symptoms and be sure that dietary schedules and restrictions are followed carefully. A student with diabetes should wear a *Medic Alert* bracelet. If a child has received too much insulin or if insulin has been ingested too quickly or without adequate caloric intake, an insulin reaction may occur. Symptoms include tremors, sweating, weakness, dizziness, odd behavior, and (later) unconsciousness or convulsions. Teachers and others should know the procedures for responding to an insulin reaction and should take the child to the hospital quickly if he or she does not improve within a few minutes.

CHARACTERISTICS AND CONCERNS OF STUDENTS WITH PHYSICAL AND HEALTH IMPAIRMENTS

The effects that physical impairments or health problems have on children and their families vary widely, depending on several factors including the following (Hallahan & Kauffman, 1988):

- Severity of the disability
- Support available in the community, family, and school system; attitudes toward the specific disability
- Student's age when the condition was acquired
- Circumstances related to acquiring the disorder
- Progressive or nonprogressive nature of the impairment

As a result, it is often difficult to make generalizations about this disability category. However, there may be some concerns common to most children and youth with physical and health disorders.

Academic Concerns

Having a physical or health impairment does not automatically imply a limitation in cognitive functioning. Although it is true that some children with physical or health impairments also have mental retardation and/or sensory disabilities, many do not. The intellectual ability of most individuals with physical or health impairments is no different from their normal peers. In the past, a physical or health disorder usually resulted in a separate, restrictive placement for students; however, schools today are providing instruction in less restrictive environments in ever increasing numbers. The movement toward inclusion of students with severe disabilities is occurring in many situations, often with increased support of technology and personnel. However, some students still miss school frequently because of medical problems. In these cases, their academic achievement may suffer and remedial efforts may be indicated.

Psychological Concerns

The successful adjustment of a child with a physical or health impairment depends in large part on the actions and attitudes of significant people like parents, siblings, teachers, peers, and the public whom the student encounters in everyday life. Children and youth with physical or health impairments may experience feelings of insecurity, hopelessness, embarrassment, rejection, guilt, low self-esteem, and fear. These feelings may result in efforts to withdraw from interaction (avoidance), hide the stigmatizing impairment, or become overly dependent on others. These reactions can be minimized by sincere and thoughtful intervention, including school situations in which the child is accepted, integrated, and included in the mainstream. In addition, it is also essential that realistic goals be set for the child. Often, the child with a physical or health impairment will fantasize about being "normal" and participating in activities in which "normal" children usually engage.

We are often guilty of reacting to individuals with physical or health impairments with fear, rejection, pity, discrimination, low expectations, or awkwardness. We are probably just uncomfortable! We need to realize that these individuals, while limited in some ways, can nonetheless be valuable contributors to society. Providing opportunities for typical interactions and relationships can minimize the effects of the disability and enhance our own personal growth.

Administrative and Educational Concerns

To provide appropriate services to children with physical or health impairments, changes may need to be made in the educational system. The reorganization of schools and redesign of school buildings has been mandated by the Americans with Disabilities Act (ADA). Barrier free environments, improved communication, and provisions for transportation are all important in schools, just as in the workplace. The successful coordination of many different ancillary services, necessitated by the pervasive nature of some impairments, must also be addressed. Depending on the severity of the impairment, the delivery of educational services may include a hospital program, homebound education, a special school setting, or a regular school setting. Considerations of mobility, transportation, medical services, and adaptive equipment are also important for school administrators. However, integrating the child with a physical or health impairment into regular school settings requires more than making the building accessible. Successful integration requires preparing the school as a whole for this integration, and efforts must focus on education, training, and support.

To maximize learning, alternative teaching methodologies might be needed. Task analysis and behavior modification techniques have proven to be quite successful with many students, including those with health and physical disabilities. *Individualization of instruction* is critical for these students. Adaptive measures that facilitate communication (e.g., use of computers and modified typewriters) and movement (e.g., use of myoelectric arms and wheelchairs controlled by sipping and puffing techniques) are available and can provide children with physical or health disorders with access to information, which is the key to learning. Educational programming for persons with physical impairments are often designed to improve skills in the following areas:

- Occupational and vocational training
- Basic and enriched academics
- Self-help and daily living
- Mobility training
- Communication

All our efforts should be guided by the long-term goal of independent functioning. Although this goal usually implies the need for high level skills, not every individual with a physical impairment will be able to function independently in everyday life. Thus, a program that stresses sequential programming of skills from the most basic to the more advanced is essential.

TRENDS AND ISSUES

Technological Advances

Significant advances have been made in recent years in the areas of medicine, prosthetics/orthotics, adaptive technology, and cosmetology. These advances have had positive effects for many individuals with health and physical impairments. The field of medicine has had a significant impact on this disability group by preventing and treating physical impairments (with surgery, drug therapy, etc.) and health problems (through the use of fetal monitoring, immunizations, and other techniques). In the area of prosthetics, the artificial replacement of missing body parts has enabled many individuals to regain some of the functioning necessary for daily living. The use of prosthetic limbs and other adaptive technological advances, including devices that allow persons with physical impairments to perform many everyday self-help tasks, are constantly being developed and improved. Other examples of engineering advancements are wheelchairs that are operated by miniature computers that can be told what to do; mouth-operated electronic devices that allow quadriplegic persons to perform certain actions from bed by varying their breathing patterns; puffing and sipping devices that can operate a telephone, radio, TV, lamp, typewriter, or door. Cosmetological intervention is also helping some individuals with physical impairments through plastic and reconstructive surgical procedures and through techniques that attempt to minimize the visibility of an impairment.

Costs

Costs for supporting research and providing services for this population are significant. However, these economic matters should be considered from a long-term perspective. For instance, a computerized wheelchair, although expensive, may enable a person to work and function in society. In the long run, this is a cost effective approach. Of even more importance are benefits gained by the individual. It is hard to put a price on someone's independence and long-term adjustment.

CONCLUSIONS

The myriad problems that persons with physical or health impairments face can seem overwhelming. To maximize the benefits of education and training, they must be followed by opportunities to work and live in the community. We must foster a society receptive to individuals with physical and health impairments and find ways for them to become more visible and more accepted. In introducing the reader to physical and health impairments, we are unable to provide you with a *real* understanding of what it is like to be physically or health impaired. So, we would like to conclude with the following thought:

> Physical disability is a minority problem among the young and middle-aged, but among those who reach the life expectancy age of 70, it is a problem of the majority. A very small percentage of us will experience loss of mobility because of diseases like multiple sclerosis or muscular dystrophy; a somewhat larger, but still small percentage, will experience this loss because of accidents; most of us, however, will become old (Cohen, 1977, p. 136).

SUGGESTIONS FOR WORKING WITH PERSONS WHO HAVE PHYSICAL AND/OR HEALTH IMPAIRMENTS

This section is divided into categories based on the specific suggestions relevant to each area.

General Suggestions

1. Treat persons with physical or health impairments as normally as possible.

2. Do not underestimate their abilities because of their physical and/or health limitations.

3. Be aware of the individual's specific situation and the special needs and precautions that are warranted.

4. Be concerned about the psychosocial ramifications associated with the acquisition of a physical or health impairment.

For Wheelchair-Bound Persons

1. Ask wheelchair users if they would like assistance before you help.

2. If conversation lasts more than a few minutes, consider sitting down or kneeling to get yourself on the same level as the wheelchair user.

3. Do not demean or patronize the wheelchair users by patting them on the head.

4. Give clear directions, including distance, weather conditions, and physical obstacles that may hinder travel.

5. When wheelchair users "transfer" out of the wheelchair to a chair, toilet, car, or bed, do not move the wheelchair out of reaching distance.

6. Do not assume that using a wheelchair is in itself a tragedy. It is a means of freedom that allows the user to move about independently.

For Individuals With Traumatic Brain Injury

1. Expect inconsistency, including memory and organizational problems.

2. Help the student by providing structure and support in his/her environment.

3. Try to attend to the student's needs for stress management and social skills training.

4. Modify assignments whenever the student's individual needs require it.

For Individuals With Severe Forms of Cerebral Palsy

1. If the person has difficulties communicating clearly, do not be afraid to ask the person to repeat what was said.

2. Do ask persons with cerebral palsy if they need assistance if they are experiencing difficulty in performing certain activities.

3. Be aware of the person's special needs (e.g., special chair for sitting).

4. Allow for additional time that will probably be needed for accomplishing various tasks (e.g., walking, writing).

5. Individualize the format for assignments, especially requirements for written work.

For Individuals Who Have Convulsive Types of Seizures

1. Remain calm if a person has a seizure.

2. Try to prevent the person from injury by safeguarding the immediate environment.

3. Do not interfere with the person's seizure-related behaviors. Do not force anything into the person's mouth (i.e., between the teeth).

4. If possible, place something soft beneath the person's head, and if possible, turn the person's face to one side to drain saliva.

5. Let the person rest after regaining consciousness.

6. Seek medical assistance if the person seems to pass from one seizure to another without regaining consciousness.

For Individuals With HIV/AIDS

1. Respect the student's and family's right to confidentiality.

2. Train everyone in preventive procedures for handling bodily fluids.

3. Stay in close touch with medical personnel, including the school nurse and the student's physician.

4. Be sensitive to other students' attitudes and behavior toward the student with AIDS. Educate *all* students to avoid prejudicial actions.

5. Make sure that illness related absences are taken into consideration.

✦ *PONDER THESE*

1. *Imagine that you must use a wheelchair for one day; then list all the barriers or obstacles that you would encounter in the course of your typical daily schedule.*

2. *If you catastrophically lost the use of your arms or legs, what functions would you first want to be able to reacquire or relearn?*

3. *Suppose you invited a wheelchair-bound friend over to your home for dinner. What adaptations would you have to make to accommodate your guest?*

4. *Consider how individuals with physical disabilities have been portrayed in various forms of the media (films, television, cartoons, comics, advertisements, etc.). In general, have these portrayals been positive or negative?*

5. *If you were a classroom teacher and you learned that a student in your class had AIDS, but you were not told who it was, how would you feel? How would you handle the situation?*

6. *Assume you have a student in your class who was in a car accident and, as a result, has a traumatic brain injury. He has regular, frequent outbursts of anger, often with no apparent provocation. What would you do? From whom would you seek advice and assistance?*

References

American Academy of Allergy and Immunology (n.d.). *Asthma and the school child* (Tip #19). Milwaukee, WI: Public Education Committee, American Academy of Allergy and Immunology.

Batshaw, M. L., & Perret, Y. M. (1992). *Children with disabilities: A medical primer*. Baltimore: Paul H. Brookes.

Berg, B. O. (1982). Convulsive disorders. In E. E. Bleck & D. A. Nagel (Eds.), *Physically handicapped children: A medical atlas for teachers* (2nd ed., pp. 101–108). New York: Grune & Stratton.

Centers for Disease Control and Prevention (1993). *HIV/AIDS Surveillance Report*, 5(2). Atlanta, GA: U. S. Department of Health and Human Services, Public Health Service.

Cohen, S. (1977). *Special people*. Englewood Cliffs, NJ: Prentice-Hall.

Hallahan, D. P., & Kauffman, J. M. (1988). *Exceptional children: Introduction to special education* (4th ed.). Englewood Cliffs, NJ: Merrill/Prentice-Hall.

Hardman, M. L., Drew, C. J., Egan, M. W., & Wolf, B. (1993). *Human exceptionality* (4th ed.). Boston: Allyn & Bacon.

Individuals with Disabilities Education Act of 1990, PL 101–476, §602[a][19].

Inge, K. J. (1992). Cerebral palsy. In P. J. McLaughlin & P. Wehman (Eds.), *Developmental disabilities: A handbook for best practices* (pp. 30–53). Boston: Andover Medical Publishers.

Kelker, K., Hecimovic, A., & LeRoy, C. H. (1994). Designing a classroom and school environment for students with AIDS: A checklist for teachers. *TEACHING Exceptional Children, 26*(4), 52–55.

LeRoy, C. H., Powell, T. H., & Kelker, P. H. (1994). Meeting our responsibilities in special education. *TEACHING Exceptional Children, 26*(4), 37–44.

Mira, M. P., Tucker, B. F., & Tyler, J. S. (1992). *Traumatic brain injury in children and adolescents: A sourcebook for teachers and other school personnel.* Austin, TX: Pro-Ed.

National Head Injury Foundation Task Force on Special Education. (1989). *An educator's manual: What educators need to know about students with traumatic brain injury.* Southborough, MA: NHIF.

Paasche, C.L., Gorrill, L., & Strom, B. (1990). *Children with special needs in early childhood settings.* Menlo Park, CA: Addison-Wesley.

Prensky, A. L., & Palkes, H. S. (1982). *Care of the neurologically handicapped child: A book for parents and professionals.* New York: Oxford University Press.

Rowley-Kelly, F. L., & Reigel, D. H. (1993). *Teaching the student with Spina Bifida.* Baltimore: Paul H. Brookes.

Seidel, J. F. (1992). Children with HIV-related developmental difficulties. *Phi Delta Kappan, 72,* 38–56.

Smith, D. D., & Luckasson, R. (1992). *Introduction to special education: Teaching in an age of challenge.* Boston: Allyn & Bacon.

Smith, T.E.C., Polloway, E. D., Patton, J. R., & Dowdy, C. A. (1994). *Teaching students with special needs in inclusive settings.* Boston: Allyn & Bacon.

U.S. Department of Education. (1993). *To assure the free appropriate public education of all children with disabilities. Fifteenth annual report to Congress on the implementation of The Individuals with Disabilities Education Act.* Washington, DC: Author.

8

Visual Impairments

Blindness. What sort of image does the word *blindness* evoke? Dark glasses, a guide dog, a tin cup, the groping tap of a red-tipped white cane? The word *blindness* is commonly associated with thoughts of helplessness, pity, and a life of eternal blackness. But is this really blindness? What does blindness mean? To us it means, in part, working with people who are blind and forgetting that they cannot see.

A young couple with visual impairments, with whom my wife and I were friends and professional associates, invited us during the Christmas holidays to an evening at their home. After a time of visiting, we went to the dining area where we enjoyed some refreshments. The colored holiday lights in the windows created a perfect effect for the late evening treats. The next morning, my wife received a very apologetic phone call from an embarrassed hostess. It was not until our host and hostess were retiring for the night that they discovered their light switch was in the off position. It was then that they realized they had fed us in a very dark room.

What I remember most from my philosophy class in my junior year of college is Joe, a student with a visual impairment who sat behind me. He was a likable guy—good sense of humor and very bright. I think he was unable to see at all. He walked with a cane and took all his class notes in Braille—I can still hear the peck, peck, peck of his stylus. One class session about midway through the semester, the professor was flamboyantly explaining a complex theory. He scribbled on the chalkboard to assist him in his instruction. As the professor paused for a moment, Joe raised his hand.

"Yes, Joe."

"I don't quite understand."

"What don't you understand, Joe?"

"The whole thing. It doesn't make any sense."

At this, the professor spun on his heel and frantically drew diagram after diagram, at the same time eloquently explaining the theory. After about 15 minutes, the professor turned around and gasped, "Now do you see?"

Joe stopped pecking with his stylus and calmly replied, "No, I still can't see, but I understand."

The professor cried, "Good!" and then wheeled around and started drawing again.

The Helms were concerned about Susan, their 4-year-old daughter, who was lagging in several developmental areas. Although she seemed to be normal in terms of physical and language development, some of her cognitive skills were far below normal. For example, she couldn't identify letters, shapes, or numbers and could identify only a few common household items (e.g., spoons, knife, chair, bed). An in-depth assessment resulted in a measured IQ of 68 for Susan and a label of mild mental retardation.

Susan was placed in an early childhood program for children with mild handicaps. She remained in special education for several years. At the age of 8, Susan was moved from her early childhood special education program to a primary special education classroom at a local elementary school.

Susan's new teacher, Mr. Williams, soon became convinced that she was not mentally retarded. He enlisted the help of other professors in his school to conduct further evaluations of his student. These assessments revealed that Susan had a serious visual problem. A ophthalmologist eventually discovered that Susan suffered from congenital cataracts.

Surgery soon corrected Susan's primary disability. Susan was reassigned to a program for children with visual problems. Special services and intervention eventually allowed Susan to enter the regular classroom where today she functions well.

Sue, a young college student, desired a means of independent travel that would permit her greater range than by foot. Being legally blind, she obviously could not obtain a driver's license. However, she did have enough remaining vision to ride a bicycle. She purchased a bike and began making frequent trips about the college town and into the surrounding country, often riding several miles. On one occasion she made a visit to our home and decided to return to her dormitory by a new route that took her through the downtown area. As she rode the streets through the main business district, she began noticing numerous friendly people waving and smiling from the sidewalks. They seemed to be waving at her. As she continued, the number of people increased. Then there were crowds, looking, waving, and clapping—for her? Finally, she realized the reason for all the attention. She was riding in the middle of a major holiday parade!

Two adolescent friends attending a school for the blind went for a brief walk on the familiar sidewalks of the immediate neighborhood and left their travel canes behind. During their walk, they encountered an unfamiliar patch of what felt to them like mud. They giggled and walked through it to "dry ground." Imagine the frustration on the face of the homeowner as he looked up from his troweling in time to see two young girls slogging through his freshly poured concrete driveway!

Little Teressa, a first grader, was examining the various objects in a touch-and-tell box. She extracted some shapes from the box—a square, a triangle, and a circle—and described or named them. Finally she came to a cube that was different in shape and texture from those objects she had already handled. She paused, felt it intensely on all sides, and said, "A block. What's this? An H and R Block?"

As a graduate student in special education, I had never met Debbie in person, but I had heard about how independent she was and wanted to be. Debbie, who was totally blind, was preparing to become a teacher of students with visual impairments. At this point in time, I still had much to learn about people with handicaps in general and individuals with visual impairments in particular.

It was an early winter morning and a fresh covering of snow blanketed the ground. I happened to be on my way to the campus center when I came upon Debbie. Debbie was on her way to break-

fast; however, she seemed to be very disoriented and confused. Knowing that Debbie was a very independent person and fearing her wrath, I approached her somewhat timidly, not really sure whether I should ask her if she needed some assistance. Nevertheless, I introduced myself, highlighting our common bond or burden of being fellow graduate students. I then proceeded to ask her if she needed any help.

Debbie told me that she certainly could use some help because the snow had covered the walkway that she normally used to go to the campus center where breakfast was served, thus negating the usefulness of her cane. I was delighted that she had allowed me to provide some assistance. Having had no prior experience as a sighted guide, I was anxious to learn the proper techniques. Debbie told me how to act and so off we went.

Everything went smoothly at first, and I was proud of how well I was doing. Then we came to a set of steps that descended to a lower level. Here I was trying to be so careful that I lost my footing on the icy steps and literally dropped out of the picture. I picked myself up off the ground, climbed back up the steps I had just rocketed over, and regained my position next to Debbie. I was worried that she would simply tell me not to get within 10 feet of her as I was a menace to her safety. However, Debbie was most understanding, and after she realized the reason for my abrupt departure, she got a good laugh out of it.

After I finally escorted her to her destination, without any further mishaps, I realized that I might have needed Debbie's assistance in dealing with the hazards of mobility in the snow as much as she needed mine.

DEFINITION

Visual impairment is a malfunction of the eye or optic nerve that prevents a person from seeing normally. An individual has a visual impairment whenever anomalous development, disease, or injury reduce the ability of the eyes to function. When an individual cannot see normally in at least one eye, the person is considered visually impaired. People who are visually impaired may find that things look dim, blurred, or out of focus. They may have the sensation of seeing only a part of an object or seeing everything masked in a cloud. They may see occasional dark blotches that float or appear to remain in front of the object they are viewing. It may be that they can see things clearly but only straight ahead, as if looking through a drinking straw. Just as there are varying degrees of vision, the ability to use what vision there is also varies among people.

The terms *blindness, visual impairment, low vision,* or *visual handicap* indicate significant visual problems; yet every definition includes varying degrees of vision. In fact, there are more children classified as blind who can see at least a little than there are those who cannot see at all (Jones, 1961).

Today regulations from PL 94–142 have produced the need for two definitions of visual impairment. One definition, the older legal definition, is based on visual acuity and field of vision. The other definition, the more recent one, is based on functional vision for educational purposes.

The first definition was needed to identify those persons who were eligible for benefits through federal programs, such as additional tax exemption, free mailing privileges, special materials from the Library of Congress, the privilege of operating vending stands in federal buildings, the opportunity of receiving special educational materials, and benefits from rehabilitation programs. This definition is still considered the legal definition for receiving benefits:

> The legally blind are defined as those with a central visual acuity for distance of 20/200 or less in the better eye with correction or, if greater than 20/200, a field of vision no greater than 20 degrees in the widest diameter (Hatfield, 1975, p. 4).

Barraga (1977) brought the second functional type of definition to the field by clearly describing the various terms used by professionals, such as *blind, low vision,* and *visually limited.* This approach to defining visual handicaps has been most useful for educational placement and programming. Taylor (1973) divided individuals with severe visual impairments into two categories, the blind and the partially seeing. Those persons who are partially sighted or suffer from low vision make up about 85% of those individuals labeled "legally blind." These persons have some degree of residual vision, but the limits of their sight restrict their mobility, orientation, academic performance, or vocational functioning. Thus, individuals whose vision does not permit the use of print for reading can be educated by the use of Braille and tactile and auditory devices. Persons with partial vision are educated by the use of materials that complement their residual vision, such as large-print books or special illumination.

Formally defining the nature and extent of a visual disorder is directly dependent on (1) visual acuity and (2) visual periphery.

Central visual acuity of $^{20}/_{200}$ or less in the better eye with corrective
glasses or central visual acuity of more than $^{20}/_{200}$ if there is a visual
field deficit in which the peripheral field is constricted to such an
extent that the widest diameter of the visual field subtends an
angular distance no greater than 20 degrees in the better eye
(Colenbrander, 1977).

Acuity generally denotes sharpness or keenness with which one
can recognize given objects at a stated distance. *Peripheral vision* generally denotes the angle or surrounding field with which one can recognize familiar objects. A visual disorder is usually thought of when
visual acuity is less than $^{20}/_{70}$ in the best eye after correction; that is, a
person sees at a distance of twenty feet what the normally sighted person sees at approximately 70 feet. A visual acuity of $^{20}/_{200}$ in the best
eye after correction generally is used as the demarcation for legal
blindness, meaning that this individual sees at 20 feet what the normally sighted person sees at approximately 200 feet. To illustrate, if
two individuals were standing on the goal line of a football field and
looking forward to the seven yard line, the legally blind individual
would see about what the normally sighted individual would see for
two thirds the length down the football field (the opposing 33 yard
line). The acuity range from $^{20}/_{70}$ to $^{20}/_{200}$ feet or more in the best eye
after correction is referred to as legally blind.

Another indicator of blindness is the significant reduction of the
peripheral field, which is normally 160 degrees or better. If this field of
vision falls to 20 degrees or less, an individual generally is classified as
blind; this condition in the lay community is commonly referred to as
tunnel vision.

Many educators find functional definitions far more useful than
clinical definitions. Such definitions focus on visual efficiency, that is,
how well a person with a visual disorder uses his or her existing sight.
Blind individuals possess, at best, only light perception without pro-
jection or are totally lacking in sight. Those persons with low vision
may have significantly impaired sight after correction but possess
enough residual vision to function successfully with instructional/occu-
pational modifications, such as large print or tactile aids.

Individuals with *limited vision* are those persons who are limited
in their visual ability under average circumstances (Barraga, 1986).
These persons may need modification in lighting or high contrast print
to function successfully in the classroom.

Because the above definitions may appear overly technical, most
educational practitioners prefer a simpler definition. They state that
when vision is diminished so as to interfere with the reading of print

in a book (near vision) or the reading of print on the chalkboard (distance vision), the student is visually impaired.

Although there may need to be a definition that is associated with the provision of services, it may be advantageous to describe the condition simply as severe visual impairment and devote more effort to describing the educational procedures and materials required to meet the needs of children with visual impairments.

PREVALENCE

The accuracy of estimates of prevalence in specific impairments is always subject to disagreement due to the ambiguity inherent in existing definitions and identification procedures. Visual impairment is a disability that affects only a small number of the school-aged population. Recent statistics issued by the U.S. Department of Education (1989) indicate that 22,864 students were served under the category "visually handicapped"—terminology used by the federal government. This is approximately 0.05% of the total school population. Most of these students having some type of visual impairment could use printed materials for educational purposes.

Visual impairment becomes a much more prevalent condition when we look at the elderly population. As a result, age becomes a significant factor that must be acknowledged when we speak of the prevalence of visual impairment.

ETIOLOGY

The eye is one of the more intriguing and complex organs of the body. Its derivation comes from the Latin word *oculus* and the Greek word *ophthalmos*, hence the English terms *ocular* and *ophthalmologist*. Early civilizations referred to the eye as the window of the soul. As can be seen in Figure 8.1, the eye is a large sphere actually made up of three distinct layers: the *sclera* and *cones*, the *choroid*, and the *retina*. At the front of the eye is the *cornea*, which gives the sphere its oval shape. Then there is the *iris*, which is a flat bar with circular muscle fibers that dilate and contract the pupil or central opening of the eye. The *lens* is next, directing light rays back to the retina where a camera-like phenomenon transfers the image to the *optic nerve* and onto the *visual cortex* of the occipital lobe of the brain.

As reported by Livingston (1986), most visual problems can be attributed to malformations and malfunctions of the eye. Most visual impairments observed in school-age children are a result of events occurring prior to, during, or shortly after birth (Hatfield, 1963). The

Figure 8.1
The Eye

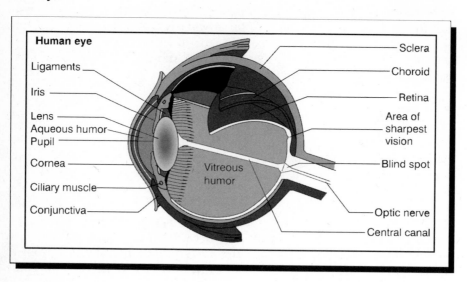

following list categorizes selected types of visual impairments and provides brief explanations of each:

- Refractive problems: Refractive problems occur when light coming through the lens and cornea is not focused precisely on the retina. Such errors are the result of the light being focused in front of or beyond the retina. Refractive errors are related to the shape of the eye itself.

  Myopia—nearsightedness (eyeball too long)

  Hyperopia—farsightedness

  Astigmatism—unevenness in surfaces of cornea or lens

- Lens abnormalities (or accommodation errors): These errors are related to the way in which the lens of the eye changes during the process of focusing light waves.

  Dislocation

  Cataracts—clouding of the lens

  Retinopathy of prematurity (retrolental fibroplasia)—scar tissue behind the lens (overconcentration of oxygen)

- Retinal defects: These defects are related to damage or destruction of the retinal portion of the eye. Visual acuity and reductions in the field of vision are the most common types of manifestations.

Retinitis pigmentosa—progressive degeneration of retina

Diabetic retinopathy—interference of blood supply to retina

Macular degeneration—blood vessels of macula (part of retina) are damaged (loss of central vision)

- Muscle control problems: These problems refer to the use and control of the six muscles that control eye movement. Double vision and many problems with depth perception are related to difficulties with muscular control.

Strabismus—cross-eyed

Nystagmus—involuntary, rapid, rhythmic, side-to-side eye movements

Amblyopia—"lazy eye"

- Miscellaneous

Glaucoma—pressure due to a build-up of eye fluid

Trauma—damage due to accidents, and so on

Color vision—inability to detect certain colors

VISUAL IMPAIRMENT IN PERSPECTIVE

The vignettes at the beginning of this chapter illustrate several points about visual impairment; these and other points will be further developed in this section.

Most individuals with visual impairments can see. Only a small portion of those who are legally or educationally blind are totally blind or without vision.

Most individuals with visual impairments have all their other senses; that is, they are normal. Having a visual impairment, even total blindness, does not impair or improve one's sense of hearing, smell, taste, or touch. An individual with a severe visual impairment is not endowed with a "sixth" sense, as some believe. If such a person does do some things in different ways from most, it may be a very natural way of using the other senses in place of lost vision.

Most people who are totally blind, by making use of hearing, touch, smell, and kinesthetic perception, can learn much about their environments. With good orientation and mobility skills and experience, those with little or no vision can use a cane as an aid for crossing intersections, taking walks, making shopping trips, and getting to just about any place within walking distance. Their hands help them to learn about a lot of things if they are just permitted to touch, handle, and move objects that are about them.

Often, the biggest block to living and learning naturally, for persons with visual impairments, is other people who have normal vision. Family and friends, in their attempts to be helpful, too often forget the needs of a person with a visual impairment. For example, rather than permit a man with a visual impairment to take an elbow, they may push him across the intersection; or they may take the same man's order from his sighted friend across the table; or they may insist upon "look, but don't touch."

As a group, people who are visually impaired comprise a normal range of personalities, interests, and abilities. Some people with visual impairments are gifted, some are retarded, and most are intellectually normal. There are those who are emotionally disturbed and others with learning disabilities. We have athletes and scholars with visual impairments. There are those who are socially adept, delinquent, prolific, dull, fascinating, obnoxious, or any other combination.

People with severe visual impairments have been successful in nearly every activity and vocation. However, society still judges these people not so much by their abilities as by their perceived differences. Because they are judged incapable *before* the fact, adults with severe visual impairments often find locating jobs difficult and obtaining desirable employment nearly impossible.

Severe visual impairment can handicap people in their early experiences and in their ability to get from place to place. Important early experiences can be denied to children with visual impairments if they are not permitted to be active and to use all of their senses to the maximum, thus often affecting concept and language development. Active early childhood and preschool experiences are important factors in assuring normal development for children with visual impairments.

The difficulty in establishing one's position in the environment (orientation) and in moving from place to place (mobility) are two of the most direct handicaps caused by visual impairment. Some individuals with visual impairments are limited only in their ability to operate a motor vehicle, while for others, visual impairment may cause a major mobility impediment.

Visual impairment can occur as one of the impairments in a person with multiple handicaps. In about half the cases, severe visual impairment occurs as one of several difficulties in persons with multiple handicaps.

The child with multiple impairments (e.g., deaf-blind) presents a unique educational problem. In many cases, particularly if the impairments are severe, instruction must be highly individualized. Impairments come in all degrees of severity and in nearly every possible combination. Each additional impairment presents its own unique hurdle to normal growth and development, in addition to the problems that result from the particular combination of impairments.

To date, too little is still understood about children with multiple handicaps. This misunderstanding has led in some cases to the misplacement and inappropriate treatment of these individuals. There are cases of persons who are deaf-blind with normal cognitive abilities being placed in special units of residential institutions designed for individuals who are mentally retarded. It is probably safe to say that, for some people with multiple handicaps, too little has been done to assure their maximum potential for development.

EDUCATIONAL AND PRACTICAL CONCERNS

Education

The curriculum for students with visual impairment should be consistent with the regular education curriculum; however, additional instruction in certain areas of specific need may also be necessary. Hatlin and Curry (1987) state that daily living skills, independent living skills, personal management skills, and social skills development must be of prime importance. Mobility training is included to teach individuals with visual impairments the most efficient means of interacting with their environment (Lowenfeld, 1971; Lyndon & McGraw, 1973). Depending on the extent of impairment, the curriculum may also include the use of Braille (the system of raised dots representing letters and symbols) for reading and writing, as well as the utilization of talking books, compressed speech, magnified print, embossed materials, and other technological advances. Most teaching methods found effective with normal-seeing students are effective with students with visual impairments. The obvious difference occurs with visual presentation that must be adapted or modified to utilize auditory or tactual sensory channels (Napier, 1973).

Among the majority of those persons identified as visually impaired, the utilization of residual sight is a key component in any intervention. Such practices as frequent breaks to reduce eye fatigue, a mixture of multisensory activities (i.e., visual, auditory, tactile, etc.), and the use of materials that offer a high visual contrast are among the practical and viable instructional adaptations available to the teacher.

In addition, optical aids (requiring a prescription) and non-optical aids are available to the instructor. These aids include such things as large print textbooks, bold line paper, closed circuit television, and text magnifiers (special lenses). Further, technology, including Braille keyboards for computers or specialized monitor adaptations for enlarging the screen, is being employed for use with visually impaired students.

The issue of best placement of students who are visually impaired has provoked much debate over the years. With the implementation of PL 94–142, more students with milder problems have been provided services in the regular school settings, often in regular education classrooms. However, this has not always been the case. Furthermore, the question of best placement is more complicated for those students with more severe forms of impairment.

The question of residential versus day school for the visually impaired has engendered a quiet debate. Until the midpoint of this century, the majority of children with severe visual impairments who received a quality education were educated at residential schools for the blind. Since that time, increased numbers of children with severe visual impairments are being educated in local day school programs (Jones & Collins, 1966) or in regular public school settings (Heward & Orlansky, 1988), resulting in fewer numbers of students attending residential schools.

McIntire (1985) outlines the possible future impact of residential schools for those persons with visual impairments. The role of residential programs will, necessarily, change over time due to the effect of expanded technology, the inclusion movement, and the quality process.

The major considerations of the debate are analyzed as follows:

Favoring day schools:

1. It is important that children live at home with their families.
2. Dormitory living is detrimental to healthy development.
3. Segregation from normally seeing peers deprives children with visual impairments of important experiences needed for normal development.
4. Larger local high schools can provide a wider range of curricular offerings than most small residential schools.

Favoring residential schools:

1. Only the residential school is in a direct position to influence what learning takes place between the end of one school day and the beginning of the next.
2. The child can receive more individualized instruction than in the day schools where classes are often much larger.
3. Education will be better when the teachers can devote their entire interest and training to working with persons who are visually impaired.

4. If the number of children or the number of disabling conditions increases, those with visual impairments will become a neglected minority, eventually losing out on educational services and materials as money is spent elsewhere.

To summarize, in order to ensure a nonrestrictive environment for persons with visual impairments, it is necessary (1) to provide placement alternatives that are flexible and varied and (2) to consider the skill level of the person when selecting the most appropriate setting. The needs of children who are visually impaired must not be overlooked in the selection of educational placement.

Facets of Everyday Living

In addition to the educational needs of individuals who are visually impaired, other practical considerations must be addressed. Many everyday activities sighted persons routinely perform may have to be done in different ways by those with limited or no vision. For example, the selection and matching up of clothes will have to be determined in alternative ways. Some individuals use Braille tags; others simply buy clothes of certain colors that go together, then separate their closets accordingly. The acts of eating and drinking will be executed in modified ways. Telling time is accomplished by using specially designed watches with hands and raised dots (not Braille configurations) that can be touched.

Many typical household appliances will also need to be modified. The American Foundation for the Blind publishes a catalog entitled *Aids and Appliances for the Blind and Visually Impaired* that lists many such everyday items.

SUGGESTIONS FOR WORKING WITH PERSONS WHO HAVE VISUAL IMPAIRMENTS

The following suggestions have been divided into sections based on the nature of the recommendation.

General Suggestions

1. If a person with a visual impairment seems to be having problems (e.g., disorientation), ask whether you can be of any assistance. The worst that can happen is that she or he will say "No."

2. When acting as a sighted guide (a) let the person who is visually impaired take your arm rather than grabbing his or her

arm and pushing; and (b) approach steps and other similar environmental realities at right angles.

3. Assist persons in getting into a chair or a car by placing their hand in the appropriate location (i.e., on the back of the chair or on the roof of the car).

4. Be sure to talk directly to the person and not to other companions. This is especially important for those working in restaurants who sometimes avoid talking to persons with visual impairments.

5. When you enter or leave a room in which the only other person present is visually impaired/blind, let the other person know you have come in or are leaving.

Educational Suggestions

1. Seat students with visual impairments in settings that maximize any residual vision and that avoid glare from the sun or lighting.

2. Try to minimize the reliance on visual materials when lecturing, and if they are needed, explain them fully.

3. Be careful not to talk at too quick a pace for students who use a slate and stylus for taking notes in Braille.

4. Avoid using materials that have low contrast features (such as purple ditto sheets) or glossy surfaces.

5. It may be necessary to allow students with visual impairments to take more breaks than usual. Their eyes may fatigue at quicker rates than students without visual impairments.

6. For students with visual impairments who can use printed materials, use large-print materials and broad-tipped markers that contrast with the color of your materials.

7. Encourage students to tape record your presentations and to use readers if available.

8. Utilize the services of Recordings for the Blind as this organization has put much printed material on tape.

◆ *PONDER THESE*

1. If a child without travel vision entered your class, what specific things would you have to teach him in order for him to adapt successfully to the classroom? How might you and the children in your class have to change your habits or behaviors to facilitate the child's adaptation?

2. *Imagine that you are a self-sufficient adult who is blind. How would you feel about receiving a special tax exemption simply because you are categorized as legally blind? Would you work for legislation providing special exemptions for persons categorized as handicapped (e.g., those who are deaf) in other ways?*

3. *If you suddenly lost your vision, what special problems would you encounter in performing such everyday activities as eating, dressing and grooming, toileting, communicating, and getting around? What would you do for recreation?*

4. *Highlight the advantages and disadvantages of the following mobility techniques used by people who are blind or visually limited: sighted guide, guide dog, cane.*

5. *Find out how a person with congenital blindness dreams.*

INFORMATION/RESOURCES

1. American Foundation for the Blind
   15 W. 16th St.
   New York, New York 10011

2. American Printing House for the Blind, Inc.
   P.O. Box 6085
   Louisville, Kentucky 40206

3. Library of Congress National Library Service for the Blind and Physically Handicapped
   1291 Taylor St., NW
   Washington, DC 20542

4. National Association for the Visually Handicapped
   22 W. 21st Street
   New York, New York 10010

5. Recording for the Blind
   20 Rozel Road
   Princeton, New Jersey 08540

References

American Foundation for the Blind. (1986). *Aids and Appliances for the Blind and Visually Impaired*. New York: Author.

Barraga, N. C. (1977). *Visual handicaps and learning: A developmental approach*. Belmont, CA: Wadsworth.

Barraga, N. C. (1986). Sensory perceptual development. In G. T. Scholl (Ed.), *Foundations of education for the blind youth: Theory to practice*. New York: American Federation for the Blind.

Colenbrander, A. (1977). Dimensions of visual performance. *Archives of the American Academy of Ophthalmology, 83*, 332–346.

Hatfield, E. M. (1963). Causes of blindness in school children. *Sight-Saving Review, 33*, 218–33.

Hatfield, E. M. (1975). Why are they blind? *Sight-Saving Review, 45*, 3–22.

Hatlin, P. H., & Curry, S. A. (1987). In support of specialized programs for blind and visually impaired children: The impact of vision loss on learning. *Journal of Visual Impairment and Blindness, 81*, 7–13.

Heward, W. L., & Orlansky, M. D. (1996). *Exceptional children: An introductory survey of special education* (5th ed.). Englewood Cliffs, NJ: Merrill/Prentice Hall.

Jones, J. W. (1961). *Blind children, degree of vision, mode of reading*. Washington, DC: U.S. Government Printing Office.

Jones, J. W., & Collins, A. P. (1966). *Educational programs for visually handicapped children*. Washington, DC: U.S. Government Printing Office.

Livingston, R. (1986). Visual impairments. In N. G. Haring & L. P. McCormick (Eds.), *Exceptional children and youth* (4th ed., pp. 397–429). Englewood Cliffs, NJ: Merrill/Prentice Hall.

Lowenfeld, B. (1971). *Our blind children, growing and learning with them* (3rd ed.). Springfield, IL: Charles C. Thomas.

Lyndon, W. T., & McGraw, M. L. (1973). *Concept development for visually handicapped children*. New York: American Foundation for the Blind.

McIntire, J. C. (1985). The future role of residential schools for visually impaired students. *Journal of Visual Impairment and Blindness, 79*, 161–164.

Napier, G. D. (1973). Special subject adjustment and skills. In B. Lowenfeld (Ed.), *The visually handicapped child in school* (pp. 221–277). New York: John Day.

Taylor, J. L. (1973). Educational programs. In B. Lowenfeld (Ed.), *The visually handicapped child in school* (pp. 155–184). New York: John Day.

U.S. Department of Education. (1989). *Eleventh annual report to Congress on the implementation of the Education of the Handicapped Act*. Washington, DC: U.S. Government Printing Office.

9

HEARING IMPAIRMENT

At the age of 3, David began undergoing speech therapy. Each week his mother took him to the session, sat through as an observer, and then took him home. At the first visit, the therapist, who was aware of the fact that David had a little experience in speechreading (lip reading), chose to test the skills by initiating a simple command, "Close door." David watched the therapist's face intently but made no move to carry out the command. The command was repeated and, again, no response. This continued for a while until it became obvious that both the therapist and David were confused. Not daring to initiate other commands or try other words under the circumstances, the therapist suggested to the mother that perhaps David was disturbed by the new situation. Calmly looking into the therapist's eyes, the mother patiently suggested, "Try 'shut door.'"

We were being trained to be teachers of children with hearing impairments. We had completed our course work and were preparing to do student teaching at a residential school. We had been trained strictly in teaching speech and speechreading (lip reading) without the use of signs or gestures. However, students and staff at the school made considerable use of manual signs and finger spelling, none of which we understood. A few of us were given assignments at the secondary level, which was particularly difficult since the use of signs at that level was considerable.

We were all having difficulty mastering sign language in addition to our student teaching assignments. To improve our ability, we practiced these skills by reading the Ann Landers column to our fellow student teachers in the evening. It was a laborious task and each day's column seemed to take forever.

During our learning period, one of my fellow student teachers returned to our dormitory at the end of an exhaustive day. She was embarrassed, concerned, and wondering aloud, "What do they think of me?" Only after considerable coaxing did the story come out. Her responsibility was to teach arithmetic. Because of her difficulty with manual signs and the inability of many students to speechread, she had devised a plan to use the overhead projector in writing out each problem for the students. Things went well until she indicated the operation of addition by writing the plus sign. This was greeted by a room full of blank faces. Try as she might, she was unable to make the children understand that they were to add. Exasperated, she finally decided to resort to finger spelling the word add. Suddenly the room was astir with children's snickering and laughing. What had she done? There in the middle of a lesson, standing before all those young attentive faces, she suddenly realized that she had just signed the letters "a-s-s"!

I had just completed a university program in teaching children who are deaf, and the summer was mine to relax and prepare specifically for my first teaching experience in the fall. I was well armed with techniques and materials and very anxious to apply them to my class of early elementary children.

The first day of school finally arrived. Was I prepared! The room was ready, and I was at school well before the hour. My course work and student teaching experiences had taught me well that children who were deaf of the age of those I was soon to teach have difficulty in reading and require much work if they are ever to be able to speak. I also knew that a part of teaching children who are deaf involves surrounding them with a world of language. I thought that while my children might be unable to hear me and produce only the gross approximations to words in their speaking, I would greet each child at the door with a "good morning." As they entered the room, I positioned myself so that my face was clearly visible, and I carefully spoke and formed the words "good morning." I anxiously watched each small face for any sign of recognition or attempt at response.

Response I got. To each greeting there was a well-spoken "Good morning, Mr. ——." I had just introduced myself to my class, only to discover that they were not deaf but were an excited, talking, hearing group of children with hearing impairments.

A few years ago, I was hired to interpret for a priest with a hearing impairment. He was to come to a Catholic church up in Mililani, Hawaii. Through a friend, I was able to meet with him earlier than scheduled so I could become familiar with him, his style of signing, and what his needs were going to be.

Being the friendly lady that I am, I began to share with him who I was, what I did, and so on. He did the same. We sat in the church lounge. He began to tell me about his busy schedule, when I told him I was still shy/embarrassed, about interpreting in front of large audiences. The sentence began, "I am shy/embarrassed. . . ." The sign for shy/embarrassed is the back of your hand brushing against your right cheek, starting from your chin and moving upward. You need only do this one time. Being as nervous as I was, I did not start at the chin and move upward; rather I started at the temple of the face and stroked downward.

It was at this point that the priest's eyes got extremely large with shock, he looked confused, and then he laughed. Now I was shocked, confused, and needed an explanation. He told me to repeat what I had just signed. I did. He asked me what I was trying to say. I spelled it out, and it was at this point that he told me what I'd done. What I had signed was not only incorrect but especially inappropriate for a priest. I had signed not that I was shy/embarrassed, but that I was a prostitute. Now I was really embarrassed![1]

I was most impressed with Phyllis's emotional maturity and language facility. Her speechreading was excellent and proved a boon to her close friends. She often related conversations that were taking place well out of earshot, across the dining room or lounge. Besides working at her studies, Phyllis was enjoying an active social life. During the course of college, she began dating one special fellow. After a period of time during which she had been seeing her friend quite regularly, she returned one night a little discouraged. She and John had broken up. As she explained, going places

---

[1]This story was contributed by Karen Ruff.

together was enjoyable, and they liked each other's company, but always having to say "good night" or exchange "sweet nothings" while sitting under a light was just too much for John to handle.[2]

DEFINITION

Whenever children are prevented from hearing environmental sounds because of malfunction of the ear or of the associated nerves, they experience some form of hearing impairment. Hearing impairments can be temporary or permanent, mild or profound. In discussing the problem of defining and classifying hearing impairment, Myklebust (1964) proposed that four variables be considered: (1) degree of impairment, (2) age at onset, (3) cause, and (4) physical origin. The variables of degree of impairment and age at onset have the most direct relevance for education. Both are accounted for in the definition provided by Streng, Fitch, Hedgecock, Phillips, and Carrell (1958).

The child who is born with little or no hearing, or who has suffered the loss early in infancy before speech and language patterns are acquired, is said to be deaf. One who is born with normal hearing and reaches the age where he can produce and comprehend speech but subsequently loses his hearing is described as deafened. The hard of hearing are those with reduced hearing acuity either since birth or acquired at any time during life (p. 9).

More recent definitions continue to stress the development of spoken language as it is related to hearing impairment. *Hearing impairment* is a generic term indicating a hearing disability that may range in severity from mild to profound. It consists of two categories, *deaf* and *hard of hearing*. A person who is *deaf* is one whose hearing disability precludes successful processing of linguistic information through audition, with or without a hearing aid. A person who is *hard of hearing* is one who, generally with the use of a hearing aid, has residual hearing sufficient to enable successful processing of information through audition. This residual hearing is in fact a reduction in an individual's auditory acuity and/or of audible sounds.

---

[2]Special gratitude is extended to Lois Schoeny and Lynn Mann, experienced teachers of children with hearing impairments, who kindly contributed some of the anecdotal material used in this chapter.

PREVALENCE

It is estimated that 5% of the school age population possesses some degree of hearing impairment (Silverman & Lane, 1970). Of this 5%, approximately 1% to 1.5% are in need of special education services. Unfortunately, only 0.13% of the school population was receiving services as reported by the Department of Education to Congress in the 1989 annual report. There are a great number of children who have hearing impairments that *need attention* but who *do not require special education placement* because their impairments are minor or correctable.

ETIOLOGY

In a study of school age children with hearing impairments enrolled in special education programs, more than half had impaired hearing at birth. The etiology was undetermined for approximately 38% (Myklebust, 1964). Reviews of the literature indicate 25% to 50% of all childhood deafness is due to heredity (Hoemann & Briga, 1981). This figure is explained to a certain degree by the high incidence of marriage among people who are hearing impaired.

The ear itself consists of three parts: the outer ear, the middle ear, and the inner ear. Malfunctions in the middle and/or inner ear result in learning impairments. The middle ear consists of four parts: the tympanic membrane (ear drum), the malleus (hammer), the incus (anvil), and the stapes (stirrup). These organs transmit sound waves through vibration to the inner ear. The inner ear consists of the vestibular mechanism made up of the semicircular canals (related to balance) and the cochlea, which is involved in hearing. It is the cochlea that receives the vibrations from the middle ear and transmits a signal to the brain via the auditory nerve.

Impairments of hearing in the outer or middle ear (conductive), even when that portion of the auditory system is totally nonfunctional, leave some potential for using residual hearing (Myklebust, 1964), whereas impaired hearing resulting from loss of inner-ear or nerve functions (sensorineural) can be a more serious, irreversible type of hearing loss.

Hearing impairments can result from a variety of causes. Excess ear wax and placement of small objects in the ear by children are frequent causes of conductive hearing impairments, as is otitis media, an inflammation of the middle ear (Davis, 1970). Pregnant women contracting rubella during the first trimester frequently give birth to children with sensorineural hearing loss (Northern & Downs, 1974).

Figure 9.1
The Ear

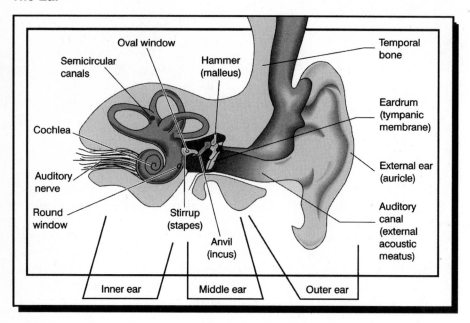

Some childhood diseases that involve viral infections of the upper respiratory tract also can cause hearing loss. Other causes include the use of certain antibiotics (McGee, 1968), excessive exposure to loud noises, viral infections of the pregnant mother prior to the child's birth, and Rh incompatibility (Davis, 1970).

ASSESSMENT

Although parents, teachers, and other key individuals in a child's life may suspect that a hearing problem may exist, it is usually an audiologist who conducts the more accurate and elaborate assessment procedures. As Hallahan and Kauffman (1988) have pointed out, there are three general types of hearing tests: pure-tone audiometry, speech audiometry, and specialized tests designed for use with very young children.

Pure-tone audiometry assesses an individual's hearing sensitivity (loudness) at various frequencies. Intensity of sound is measured in decibel (dB) units and frequency is measured in Hertz (Hz) units. The intensity of sounds that we come into contact with every day range from 0 dB (the zero hearing threshold) to well over 100 dB (very loud sounds like auto horns). The frequencies of most speech sounds that are important to humans fall between 125 to 8000 Hz. Pure-tone tests can be administered either by earphones (air conduction) or by placing a vibrating device on the person's forehead (bone conduction). By administering these two types of tests, an audiologist can determine if the hearing loss is conductive or sensorineural.

Speech audiometry is simply a test of whether a person can understand speech. At the heart of this procedure is an attempt to determine at which dB level the examinee is able to understand speech (known as the speech reception threshold).

Inherent in these assessment techniques is the examinee's ability to respond to the stimulus situation. For very young children, this voluntary response may not be possible. Three techniques that have been developed for utilization with this age group include play audiometry, reflex audiometry, and evoked-response audiometry (Hallahan & Kauffman, 1988).

Other *specialized audiometric tests* are used with individuals who have multiple handicaps or who have severe disabilities. These tests do not require a specific behavioral response from the child and therefore can facilitate assessment.

Tympanometry is an auditory test that yields information related to the resistance of the tympanic membrane or its ability to conduct vibrations into the middle ear mechanism. Stapedial reflex testing employs pure tone signals and measures the reflex response of the stapedial muscle to these signals. Both of these auditory tests use an impedance audiometer as the instrument of evaluation.

An additional auditory assessment technique, which requires the use of an electroencephalograph and a computer, is the evolved response technique. This technique is used to examine changes in brain wave patterns in response to specific sound stimuli.

IMPRESSIONS

Many times people have certain incorrect impressions about children with hearing impairments, such as (1) children who are deaf cannot hear; (2) children who cannot hear cannot talk; and (3) children who are deaf are also retarded. These three notions have direct educational and social implications; therefore, they will receive focal attention in this chapter.

Children who are deaf cannot hear. Children classified as profoundly hearing impaired may still have some ability to hear. They may be able to hear loud noises such as automobile horns or slamming doors. The ability to hear even this much may provide vital information to alert or warn the child of danger. Of all children with hearing impairments, relatively few can properly be labeled profoundly deaf. Many have enough usable hearing to develop language. The typical breakdown of degrees of hearing impairment is as follows:

Classification	Degree of dB Loss
Mild	26–54
Moderate	55–69
Severe	70–89
Profound	90+

There are two ways in which children with hearing impairments can be helped with respect to the information they receive. First, they can be helped to understand and use what sounds they can hear. Then, of course, if the hearing impairment is such that the variety of sounds can be increased through amplification, they can be given access to more information through use of the hearing aid. However, it is worth noting that hearing aids amplify all sounds in the environment. As a result, while these devices provide a useful function to many people who are hearing impaired, they have limitations as well. For these reasons, it is important that children with hearing impairments be identified as soon as possible and that they be exposed to experiences in listening and interpreting sounds (auditory training).

Children who are deaf cannot talk. In language acquisition, receptive language precedes expressive language. Children who are profoundly deaf, because they cannot receive language aurally, are handicapped in their expression of the language. However, children with all degrees of hearing impairment are able to and do learn to communicate.

With amplification and auditory training, children who are hard of hearing can usually use their hearing to develop spoken language. They can and do talk. Some children who are deaf, with the benefit of little or no residual hearing, are able to develop successful speechreading (lip reading) and some speaking skills. Although ability in speechreading is difficult and skill level may vary, the acquisition of clear, intelligible speech by the child born profoundly deaf is usually a laborious task. Both receptive and expressive language are available to persons who are profoundly hearing impaired through the use of sign language. American Sign Language (ASL) is a system that includes thousands of conceptual signs; it is not a word-by-word representation of the English language having syntactic and semantic differences.

Although this system is popular with adults who are hearing impaired, it may not be suitable for children who are beginning to learn the English language. The importance of this task for later learning (e.g., reading) should be obvious. Other sign languages such as morphemic-based Signing Exact English (SEE II) also exist. Another recognizable system is the manual alphabet (also known as finger spelling). This includes individual finger signs for each letter of the alphabet and numbers from 1–10 as in Figure 9.2.[3]

For a long time there has been great controversy over whether educators should rely strictly upon oral language (oralism) or should use manual sign language (manualism) when teaching children who are deaf. Unfortunately, the issue has not, as yet, been resolved. There is some trend toward a combined use of oral and manual methods in a procedure identified as "total communication."

Total communication is a communication approach that combines manual and aural-oral methods. That is, it combines signing with all the components of aural-oral programming. In essence, total communication relies on any form or communication mode that facilitates mutual understanding between persons. Most proponents of total communication support the notion of establishing the program as early in a child's life as possible to establish and reinforce the basic communication pathways quickly.

Children who are deaf are also retarded. The measurement of intelligence has traditionally relied heavily upon language, and language is precisely the area of greatest handicap for the child with a serious hearing impairment. Both professionals and laypersons have wrongly inferred that because persons who are hearing impaired evidence a language deficit there may also be an intellectual or cognitive deficit. More recent, broader conceptualizations of intelligence include considerations of nonverbal or performance aspects (Myklebust, 1964). With language factors accounted for, the intelligence of children with hearing impairments approximates the norm for hearing children (McConnell, 1973; Wiley, 1971).

Observations of behavior of individuals who are profoundly deaf may also give the impression of retardation. A child who fails to respond to another's voice, fails to respond to very loud noises, demonstrates problems in balance, or produces strange vocalizations may mistakenly be judged as mentally retarded. These behaviors alone or in combination actually may indicate serious hearing problems. The alert observer should have the child checked for hearing loss.

---

[3]From the Pennsylvania Society for the Advancement of the Deaf.

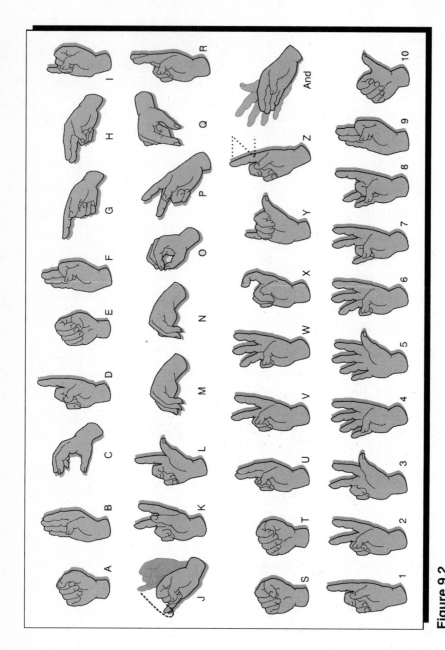

Figure 9.2
Finger signs for the alphabet and numbers 1–10.

COGNITION AND COMMUNICATION

The mistaken impressions of the preceding discussion highlight areas of educational need for children with hearing impairments. Programs benefitting such children should include some or all of the following elements: (1) early identification, (2) parent counseling and participation, (3) concept development, (4) preschool education, (5) auditory training, (6) speech training, and (7) speechreading and/or sign language.

Early identification of the child with a hearing impairment is essential in order to initiate auditory and speech training before lack of exposure to language results in a more serious deprivation. Gentile (1972) found that students of high school age who are deaf averaged fourth-grade level on a test of comprehension and averaged sixth-grade level on a test of computation. Early and intensive intervention in the area of language development is imperative for the child with a hearing impairment to approach normal achievement in academic areas. Assistance in providing concrete hearing and language experiences can serve to enrich the child's total fund of information, enhancing intellectual and social growth. Parents should participate directly in providing these experiences.

The development of basic social skills is not so much a matter of the hearing impairment itself but that of how individuals in the environment respond (Hoemann & Briga, 1981). Matters are further complicated because children who are hearing impaired cannot easily communicate their feelings of isolation, rejection, and frustration (Meadow, 1975). Emphasis upon exposure can help foster healthy social and interpersonal relationships. It can also minimize the limitation hearing impairment places upon the amount of information that the child obtains from the environment.

Children who are hearing impaired need activities that contribute to conceptual development. Skills should include comparisons of sizes, shapes, and colors of objects (Evelsizer, 1972). An understanding of these concepts will increase the opportunities for meaningful experiences in which there is variety, novelty, and occasion for selection. Such experiences can contribute to development of divergent thinking and evaluation. It is in these two areas, divergent thinking and evaluation, that hearing impairment most directly and generally affects intelligence (Myklebust, 1964). In addition, Lowenbraun (1988) states that the pragmatic abilities of hearing impaired students are not as well developed as those of their hearing peers.

Furth (1973) suggests that development of cognition and intelligence should precede emphasis upon language under the theoretical framework that thought precedes language. Placing primary emphasis upon early identification and diagnosis, conceptual development, auditory training, and building a base of general experiences should be consistent with such a conceptualization.

It has been the experience of educators of those who are hearing impaired that early work on language is important to language development in the child (McConnell, 1973). The longer the deprivation, the greater the handicap. Approaches to language may include speechreading and speech training in which the child is exposed in a systematic way to oral language. One advantage of acquiring ability in speech and speechreading rather than just manual communication skills is that it enables the child to communicate with normally hearing persons.

The use of sign language in the form of manual signs or finger spelling permits the child who is deaf to communicate with other individuals who are deaf. Signs and gestures may be used when total lack of hearing, visual impairment, or reduced mental functioning render an individual unable to acquire speech and speechreading skills with reasonable facility. Although some educators tend to feel that use of manual signs may retard or interfere with development of speaking and speechreading skills if introduced early (McConnell, 1973), there is some evidence that use of manualism may not interfere and perhaps may even facilitate overall language development (Alterman, 1970; Meadow, 1968; Struckless & Birch, 1966; Vernon & Koh, 1970).

Finally, technology has begun to play a major role in intervention for persons with hearing impairments. Hearing aids have long been employed to enhance the auditory ability of persons with conductive losses. However, recently, Assistive Listening Devices (ALDs) and closed captioning have expanded educational opportunities and access for hearing impaired individuals. Also, telecommunication devices for the deaf (TDDs) have created new means of communicating for this group. With the aid of these devices, persons with hearing impairments can now enjoy the local or national news on television, listen to lectures in college classes, and "call" their Congressman in Washington, D.C., to express their opinion on pending legislation.

POSTSCRIPT

It would be a mistake to argue that children with hearing impairments are just like all other children. They are not. By virtue of their exceptionalities they are different. Boothroyd (1982) points out that what begins as a sensory problem has consequences that can create:

1. A perceptual problem
2. A speech problem
3. A communication problem
4. A cognitive problem
5. A social problem
6. An emotional problem
7. An educational problem
8. An intellectual problem
9. A vocational problem

These problems are often compounded by:

10. Parental problems
11. Societal problems

The personal and social success of persons who are hearing impaired depends upon the degree to which we as individuals and as a society will accept their differences and upon the quality of methods, techniques, and devices developed to ameliorate their handicapping condition.

SUGGESTIONS FOR WORKING WITH PERSONS WHO HAVE HEARING IMPAIRMENT

General

1. Write messages or key phrases down if necessary.
2. Talk directly to the person with a hearing impairment when there is an interpreter.
3. Use gestures and facial expressions as much as possible.
4. Consider trimming facial hair if you work with hearing impaired people on a regular basis.
5. Get the person's attention by waving your hand or tapping him or her on the shoulder.
6. Familiarize yourself with the basic operation of a person's hearing aid as well as the capabilities of the person using it.
7. Speak naturally and clearly; do not overdramatize or overenunciate.

Educational

1. Seat persons with hearing impairments appropriately. This usually means near the speaker or interpreter.
2. Do not stand in front of a window or light source as this makes speechreading difficult.
3. Avoid talking while writing on a chalkboard (i.e., face the person with a hearing impairment while talking).
4. Discuss new concepts and provide new vocabulary in advance.
5. Use visual aids whenever possible.
6. Occasionally ask students who are hearing impaired to repeat what you have said to determine whether they understood.

✦ PONDER THESE

1. *Think of some methods you could use to determine the possibility of a hearing loss in young children.*
2. *Discuss the pros and cons of teaching communication skills to people who are deaf using the following methods:*

   Oral communication

   Manual communication (e.g., signing and finger spelling)

   Simultaneous oral and manual communication

3. *Investigate the impact of technology on the lives of individuals who are hearing impaired. Consider areas like:*

   Using telephones

   Computer technology

   Medical advances (e.g., cochlear implants)

4. *List the major concerns that arise for a person with a profound hearing impairment in the following situations:*

   Driving

   Staying at a hotel or motel

   Responding to someone knocking at the door

   Crossing the street

   Playing softball

INFORMATION/RESOURCES

1. Captioned Films/Videos for the Deaf
   Modern Talking Picture Service, Inc.
   5000 Park Street North
   St. Petersburg, Florida 33708

2. DEAFTEK, USA
   P.O. Box 2431
   Farmington, Massachusetts 01701

3. National Association for the Deaf
   814 Thayer Avenue
   Silver Spring, Maryland 20910

4. National Captioning Institute
   5203 Leesburg Pike
   Falls Church, Virginia 22041

5. National Information Center on Deafness
   Gallaudet University
   800 Florida Avenue, NE
   Washington, DC 20002

6. Software To Go
   Precollege Program
   Gallaudet University
   800 Florida Avenue, NE
   Washington, DC 20002

References

Alterman, A. I. (1970). Language and the education of children with early profound deafness. *American Annals of the Deaf, 115*, 514–521.

Boothroyd, A. (1982). *Hearing impairments in young children.* Englewood Cliffs, NJ: Merrill/Prentice-Hall.

Davis, H. (1970). Abnormal hearing and deafness. In H. Davis & S. R. Silverman (Eds.), *Hearing and deafness* (3rd ed., pp. 87–146). New York: Holt, Rinehart & Winston.

Evelsizer, R. L. (1972). Hearing impairment in the young child. In A. H. Adams (Ed.), *Threshold learning abilities: Diagnostic and instructional procedures for specific early learning disabilities.* Englewood Cliffs, NJ: Merrill/Prentice Hall.

Furth, H. G. (1973). *Deafness and learning: A psychosocial approach.* Belmont, CA: Wadsworth.

Gentile, A. (1972). Academic achievement test results or a national testing program for hearing impaired students: 1971. *Annual Survey of Hearing Impaired Children and Youth*. Gallaudet College Office Demographic Studies, Ser. D, No. 9.

Hallahan, D. P., & Kauffman, J. M. (1988). *Exceptional children: Introduction to special education* (4th ed.). Englewood Cliffs, NJ: Merrill/Prentice-Hall.

Hoemann, J. W., & Briga, J. S. (1981). Hearing impairments. In J. M. Kauffman & D. P. Hallahan (Eds.), *Handbook of special education* (pp. 222–247). Englewood Cliffs, NJ: Merrill/Prentice-Hall.

Lowenbraun, S. (1988). Hearing impaired. In E. L. Meyen & T. McSkirtic (Eds.), *Exceptional children and youth: An introduction*. Denver: Love.

McConnell, F. (1973). Children with hearing disabilities. In L. M. Dunn (Ed.), *Exceptional children in the schools: Special education in transition* (2nd ed., pp. 351–410). New York: Holt, Rinehart & Winston.

McGee, T. M. (1968). Ototoxic antibiotics. *Volta Review, 70*, 667–671.

Meadow, K. P. (1968). Early manual communication in relation to the deaf child's intellectual, social, and communicative functioning. *American Annals of the Deaf, 113*, 29–41.

Meadow. K. P. (1975). Development of deaf children. In E. M. Hetherington (Ed.), *Review of child development research* (Vol. 5, pp. 441–508). Chicago: University of Chicago.

Myklebust, H. R. (1964). *The psychology of deafness: Sensory deprivation, learning and adjustment* (2nd ed.). New York: Grune & Stratton.

Northern, J. L., & Downs, M. P. (1974). *Hearing in children*. Baltimore: Williams and Wilkins.

Silverman, S. R., & Lane, H. S. (1970). Deaf children. In H. Davis and S. R. Silverman (Eds.), *Hearing and deafness* (3rd ed., pp. 433–482). New York: Holt, Rinehart & Winston.

Streng, A., Fitch, W. J., Hedgecock, L. D., Phillips, J. W., & Carrell, J. A. (1958). *Hearing therapy for children* (2nd ed.). New York: Grune & Stratton.

Struckless, E. R., & Birch, J. W. (1966). The influence of early manual communication on the linguistic development of deaf children. *American Annals of the Deaf, 111*, 499–504.

U.S. Department of Education. (1989). *Eleventh annual report to Congress on the implementation of P. L. 94–142: The Education for All Handicapped Children Act*. Washington, DC: U.S. Government Printing Office.

Vernon, M., & Koh, S. D. (1970). Early manual communication and deaf children's achievement. *American Annals of the Deaf, 115,* 527–536.

Wiley, J. A. (1971). A psychology of auditory impairment. In W. M. Cruickshank (Ed.), *Psychology of exceptional children and youth* (3rd ed., pp. 414–439). Englewood Cliffs, NJ: Merrill/Prentice-Hall.

10
COMMUNICATION DISORDERS

Our anecdotes to this point have depicted what it is like to work with people who are handicapped. We have not attempted to convey directly what it is like to have a disability. Almost everyone has at some time or other experienced some embarrassment, guilt, frustration, anxiety, or pride stemming from verbal interaction with others. Few of us, however, have felt the overwhelming emotions that accompany severe difficulties in oral communication. Listening and talking are such ubiquitous social experiences that we tend to underestimate the handicap that can result from even minor speech deviations. We find it relatively easy to form an empathic relationship with an individual who has an obvious physical, emotional, or mental disorder, but we tend to feel that the individual with a speech disorder suffers no lasting penalty and could easily overcome the difficulty with a little determination. Consequently, we have chosen the following anecdotes to call your attention to the feelings and problems of children with speech and language disorders and their families.

My son, John, was always a delightful child. From the time he began to toddle around the house, his wonderful personality and intellect were apparent. It wasn't until he was approaching his second birthday that my wife and I became concerned. He rarely spoke. He followed directions and seemed to understand, but rarely tried to communicate, and when he did, it was in gibberish. Our family doctor told us "he's just a little slow in the development of oral language." But there was little improvement over time.

As John grew older and began to articulate clearly, the problem became more worrisome to us. When he spoke, his words were out of order, and his use of nouns and pronouns was, at best, inconsistent. Statements like "He's happy 'cause his am going" and "I'll maybe get go a new toy" were typical of his statements. After consulting with a speech clinician at a local university, the results of a language evaluation revealed that John had a language disorder. John had, in essence, learned a set of language rules that differed significantly from those of English. For John, the syntax and semantic rules of English either did not apply or were being modified in his utterances.

My wife and I were devastated. Something was wrong with our child, and we couldn't do anything about it. We began months of long, grueling language therapy with John, both in the speech clinic and through carryover at home.

Finally, John's language improved to the point that it was within "normal" limits. However, to this day he has reading problems (though his schoolwork in other areas is excellent). I can see his frustration, and I know how some teachers and students regard him. It hurts me so. They only see his problems. They'll never see beyond them to the wonderful person he really is.

I must be pretty tough because I'm not in the bug house. The constant experience of starting to say something and never having it come out when I want it to should have driven me crazy long ago. I can't even say my own name. Once in a while I get a little streak of easy speech and then wham, I'm plugged, tripped up, helpless, making silent mouth openings like a goldfish. It's like trying to play the piano with half the keys sticking. I can't even get used to it because sometimes I can fear a word and out it pops; then again when I am expecting smooth speech and everything's going all right, boom I'm stuck. It sure's exasperating (p. 72).[1]

---

[1]From *Speech Correction: Principles and Methods*, 4th ed. (pp. 41–42, 61–63, 72, 181, 384–385) by Charles Van Riper, 1963, Englewood Cliffs, NJ: Prentice-Hall, Inc. Copyright © 1963. Reprinted by permission.

Even when I was a little girl I remember being ashamed of my speech. And every time I opened my mouth I shamed my mother. I can't tell you how awful it felt. If I talked, I did wrong. It was that simple. I kept thinking I must be awful bad to have to talk like that. I remember praying to God and asking him to forgive me for whatever it was I must have done. I remember trying hard to remember what it was, and not being able to find it (p. 61).[1]

The most wonderful thing about being able to pronounce my sounds now is that people aren't always saying "What? What's that?" I bet I've heard that fifty thousand times. Often they'd shout at me as though I were deaf and that usually made me talk worse. Or they'd answer "Yes" when that just didn't make sense. I still occasionally find myself getting set for these reactions and steeling myself against them and being surprised when other people just listen (p. 72).[1]

After I came to high school from the country, everybody laughed at me whenever I tried to recite. After that I pretended to be dumb and always said "I don't know" when the teacher called on me. That's why I quit school (p. 42).[1]

Therapist: *When you were stuck that time, what were your feelings?*

Subject: *I don't know. All, All mmmmmmmmmmmmixed up, I ggggguess.*

Therapist: *You probably felt helpless . . . sort of as though your mouth had frozen shut . . .*

Subject: *And, and I cccccouldn't open it, Yeah.*

Therapist: *You couldn't open it. It was almost as though you had lost the ability to move a part of yourself when you wanted to . . . Sure must be frustrating . . .*

Subject: *Sssure is. BBBBBurns me up. I, I, I, jjjust hate mmmmm . . . Oh skip it . . . I don't know.*

Therapist: *(Acceptingly) It almost makes you hate yourself when you get stuck like that.*

Subject: *Yeah, dih-dih-sigusted with mmmmmmyself and everything else . . .*

Therapist: *Some stutterers even find themselves hating the person they are talking to.*

Subject: *Yyyyeah, I,I,I,I, I wwwwwas huh-huh-huh-hating yyyyyyyyou just then.*
Therapist: *Uh huh. I know.*
Subject: *(Blurting it out) How, how come you know all these th-things? (pp. 384–385)[1]*

When I was 15, I participated with a group of five other boys in a stuttering therapy program. All of us in the group had a common problem—Mrs. Shinn, the lady who worked in our favorite ice cream parlor. We'd go into the store to order a strawberry cone and say, "I want a st-st-st-st-st- . . . ," and before we could finish the word she'd hand us a strawberry cone. Sometimes she'd even say, "Yeah, I know, strawberry." Well, that's pretty irritating to have someone think she can always predict what you're going to say. It's even worse when someone finishes a sentence for you. Much as we liked the ice cream she dished out, we all started to hate old Mrs. Shinn. So we thought of a way to teach her a lesson. One day we went into the ice cream parlor one after another. Each of us said the same thing. "I want a st-st-st-st-st- . . . " and just as Mrs. Shinn was about to hand us the strawberry cone we finished, " . . . st-st-st-chocolate cone." From that day on, she always let us finish our orders before she started to dip.[2]

Speech and language disorders are particularly complex problems. For this reason speech-language therapists typically receive rigorous training and are required to meet high professional standards. Correction of speech and language disorders is carried out in many different, often multidisciplinary settings. Therefore, in many universities, training programs for speech-language pathologists are located in departments other than special education, such as departments of speech pathology and audiology. Basic knowledge of speech and language disorders and their correction is important for all professionals working with persons who are disabled, because many individuals with other primary handicaps, such as mental retardation and emotional disturbance, also experience difficulties in speech and language.

---

[2]This anecdote was contributed by C. Lee Woods, Ph.D.

DEFINITION

Often the concepts of communication, language, and speech are confused. It is imperative for professionals and lay people to employ the proper use of these terms. Hallahan & Kauffman (1986) aptly differentiate these concepts:

> Speech and language are tools used for purposes of communication. Communication requires . . . sending . . . and receiving . . . meaningful messages . . . Language is the communication of ideas through an arbitrary system of symbols that are used according to semantic and grammatical rules . . . Speech is the behavior of forming and sequencing the sounds of oral language (p. 194).

We can consider speech as a part of oral language, in a subcategory of the more generic use of the term *language*. In this chapter, we will be most concerned with oral language—a system of communication incorporating spoken sounds.

Unfortunately, the identification of a speech or language impairment can be a matter of subjective judgment. Just how much a language or speech pattern must differ from normal before it becomes a disorder often depends upon characteristics of both the listener and the speaker. For instance, a mother having grown accustomed to her 9-year-old's unusual articulation may overlook the fact that the child's speech is unintelligible to his peers. Moreover, whether a speech difference is considered a disorder depends upon the age of the speaker. That is, in a 3-year-old, faulty articulation is normal and certainly would not be thought of as a disorder, as it might be for an older child. Van Riper (1978) notes that abnormal speech is so different from normal speech that it (1) draws the listener's attention to itself rather than to what is being said and (2) interferes with communication, or it (3) produces distress in the speaker or the listener. Defective speech is conspicuous, unintelligible, or uncomfortable.

In spite of difficulties involved in precisely defining speech and language disorders, usable definitions have been developed by speech-language pathologists. McLean (1978) notes that the identification and classification of communication disorders, while not an easy task, is usually based on two comparisons:

> Judgments of which children should be considered to have a communication disorder requiring special education or clinical programming are made from two basic comparisons. The first is a comparison of the child's language with the standard language form of the culture. The second is a comparison of the child's language with the language of other children at the same age level (p. 271).

ETIOLOGY

The cause of speech and language disorders may be either biological or functional. *Biological* etiologies involve known neurological deficits or structural malformations such as cleft palate, cleft lip, enlarged adenoids, hearing impairment, cerebral palsy, damage to various muscles that are used in articulation (dysarthria) or phonation, deformities of the vocal organs, and ear infections, to name a few.

Most disorders of speech and language, however, have no known biological cause and are, therefore, termed *functional* disorders. This implies that there is a definite functional loss of a certain ability, but it cannot be attributed to any organic cause. Functional disorders may include articulation and voice problems, stuttering, and specific language disabilities. Many theories, attempting to explain the etiology of various problems, have been offered, but no single explanation is generally accepted at this time.

LANGUAGE DISORDERS

The American Speech and Hearing Association (1982) classifies communication disorders as either organic (physically based) or functional (environmentally based). However, to fully understand how language is disordered, we must know what constitutes normal language.

The development of language begins with the early cry of an infant and progresses through stages of differentiated crying, babbling, vocal play, single words, holophrastic speech (a single word representing a whole phrase or sentence), syntactical utterances, multiword expressions, and sentences. Recently, there has been some discussion of whether language comprehension precedes language production. The prevailing attitude seems to favor an interactive mechanism. That is, children progress through these stages in a predictable manner; however, this process is very complex and problems can occur. Because language acquisition is greatly complex, there are conflicting theories of language development. Individuals such as Chomsky, Skinner, Bloom, Nelson, and Bruner all have theories to explain the hows and whys of language development (see Schiefelbusch & McCormick, 1981). Research does not yet conclusively support any single orientation; we must therefore await the further investigation of this complex phenomenon.

Language problems occur in all the following areas: oral, written, and even gestural. However, our concern with the various aspects of oral language disabilities relates to Hull and Hull's (1973) description:

> Disability in oral language occurs when an individual is unable to comprehend meaningful ideas which have been spoken or when he is unable to use spoken words to effectively express meaningful ideas (p. 303).

In other words, this individual is not effectively able to use the elemental symbols of oral language.

Naremore (1980) notes that in thinking about different types of language disorders one should keep in mind these three things: (1) the language and nonlanguage behaviors a child imitates, because a lot of language learning involves learning to imitate; (2) the language the child comprehends, because receptive language (understanding what is heard) is so important in early learning; and (3) the language the child uses spontaneously, because effective communication in natural situations is the ultimate goal of language remediation.

In addition to these three points, Naremore suggests four classes of disordered language. First, some children do not develop receptive and/or expressive language by the age of 3 years as most children (Bangs, 1982). The *absence of language* may be due to deafness, brain damage, mental retardation, or childhood psychosis. Regardless of the cause, the important thing is that the child shows no signs of understanding or being able to use language. These children need direct instruction in how to make speech sounds and say words. They also need to be given many opportunities to hear and use language. And these opportunities must be structured to teach the child how language is used for communication—to influence the environment for a desired result (for example, to get something the child wants).

A second class of language disorder is *qualitatively different language*. That is, the child may make speech sounds and even have an extensive vocabulary but not know how to use language to communicate effectively. Speech may be echolalic (parrotlike repetition of what is heard) or just not make sense or not accurately convey meaning. Such difficulties may have any number of causes, and often the causes are not really known in a specific case. Whatever the cause, a child with qualitatively different language needs remedial instruction in the *functions* of language—how it is used in social contexts (i.e., pragmatic language) and how it is related to thinking and behaving.

Delayed language, a third type of disorder, means that the child appears to be acquiring language by the normal processes and in the normal sequence, but at a significantly later age than most children. Finally, *interrupted language development*—the child has acquired language normally but loses it due, for example, to hearing impairment or brain damage—is another class of disorder. Again, the cause of the language disorder may or may not be known. Certainly, language instruction may be different for a hearing child than for one who is deaf. But, in any case, a remedial language training program must take into account what the child knows about, how the child talks about those things, and how the child communicates his wishes, intentions, demands, feelings, and so on (see Schiefelbusch & McCormick, 1981).

SPEECH IMPAIRMENT

"Speech is defective when it is ungrammatical, unintelligible, culturally or personally unsatisfactory, or abusive of the speech mechanism" (Perkins, 1971, p. 4). Remember that *unintelligible* and *unsatisfactory*, terms used in the preceding statement, are subjective descriptors. Just as beauty is in the eye of the beholder, defective speech can be in the ear of the listener. Speech can vary along numerous dimensions. Several that are the basis of classification of speech disorders include phonological disorders, voice disorders, and fluency problems. And these classifications are not mutually exclusive because an individual may exhibit more than one type of speech problem.

Phonological Disorders

Phonology has to do with the way speech sounds are made (articulation). Phonological disorders consist of omissions (e.g., "tha" for "that"), substitutions (e.g., "thnake" for "snake"), and distortions (e.g., "s" produced by lateralized emission of air). Children with phonological difficulties are sometimes described as using "baby talk," being "tongue-tied," or not "talking plain." The causes of phonological difficulties include slow development, missing teeth, cleft palate or lip, neurological impairment, emotional problems, and faulty learning. In the vast majority of cases with which a speech-language pathologist works, the phonological problem is functional; that is, the etiology is unknown. It must be remembered that some children may not master all of the speech sounds until approximately 8 years of age. It is not uncommon or pathological for children between the ages of 5 and 8 to misarticulate some sounds and for children younger than 3 years of age to be unintelligible except to their parents. When evaluating a child's phonology, one must always keep in mind the child's overall developmental level.

Voice Disorders

Phonation or voice is the tonal or musical quality produced by vibration of the vocal folds. Voice disorders can affect pitch, loudness, and tonal quality, and cause the voice to have the sound of nasality and hoarseness (Perkins, 1980). More specifically, deviations along these dimensions may involve abuse of the larynx, interference with communication, or unpleasantness to the ear. The individual's voice may consistently be too high- or low-pitched, too loud or too soft, too monotone, or too breathy, harsh, or hoarse. These disorders of voice may be caused by malformation, injury or disease of the vocal folds, psychological factors, hearing loss, and so forth. Damage to the vocal folds can result from the person's persistent misuse of the voice, for example, through excessive screaming. It is also possible for voice disorders to arise from faulty learning.

Disorders of Speech Flow

The dimensions of speech flow include sequence, duration, rate, rhythm, and fluency (Perkins, 1980). Normal speech is perceived as relatively fluent or smooth-flowing with various natural interruptions. All of us have experienced difficulties in speech fluency, usually when we try to speak too quickly or forget what we were saying in mid-sentence.

The most common problem associated with speech fluency is stuttering. Dysfluencies or disruptions in the flow of speech are one aspect of stuttering. Normal speech contains disruptions of rhythm or dysfluencies, but when these occur so frequently and severely that the listener's attention is drawn to them and they interfere with communication, the speaker may be considered to have a speech problem. The speech disruptions that characterize stuttering include repetitions or prolongations of sound, word, syllable, or speech posture, and/or avoidance and struggle behaviors. Stuttering has been classified into two types: (1) "primary" involving the normal, dysfluent repetitions characteristic of a young child and (2) "secondary" referring to the more severe speech impairments that are compounded by the dysfluent nonspeech behaviors just noted.

Usually caused by a complex interaction of factors, stuttering involves social, emotional, and physiological reactions in both speaker and listener. Among the few facts about stuttering that we do know are:

1. Stuttering is a natural phenomenon of childhood. In learning speech and language, all children become dysfluent to some degree. Many children develop patterns of dysfluency that are transitory but do, nevertheless, cause their parents grave concern. In almost all cases, stuttering begins before adolescence, and, by late adolescence, approximately three fourths of children who stutter stop spontaneously. This phenomenon occurs

independently of the assistance of speech-language pathologists or other professionals.

2. Most individuals who stutter have particular trouble with certain words or specific situations. For instance, speaking to strangers or talking on the phone may pose great difficulties, but reading aloud or singing are not affected.

3. Stuttering is more prevalent among boys than girls. Various studies have reported boy/girl ratios ranging from 3:1 to 8:1.

4. Stuttering runs in families. This may or may not be due to hereditary factors. One should remember that religious beliefs also run in families, but religion is not transmitted genetically.

5. There are numerous theories of stuttering, with none sufficient to explain all cases. Hereditary, psychoanalytical, organic, and learning theories have been proposed. It is also believed by some researchers that children become stutterers primarily because parents show exaggerated concern for the young child's normal dysfluencies ("diagnosogenic" theory).

6. Although a large number of treatment methods have been applied, none has been universally successful. Therapeutic efforts have included systematic desensitization, negative practice, ego building, psychotherapy, operant conditioning, voluntary control, modification of stuttering patterns, chemotherapy, surgery, hypnosis, and rhythmic speech. Although no universal "cure" has been found, it appears that some of the most successful treatments known to date are those based on learning principles.

MULTIPLE DISORDERS

Often speech and language disorders will be found together in an individual. Both problems often occur simultaneously under certain handicapping conditions.

Disorders Associated With Hearing Impairment

If a child has a significant hearing impairment, speech may be characterized by voice disorders and articulation problems. This child is most likely to misarticulate unvoiced high frequency sounds such as "s," "f," "p," "t," and "sh." For this individual, the task of learning the sounds of language is severely impeded by the hearing difficulty. If the impairment is too severe, it may be necessary to use another language system such as signing.

Disorders Associated With Cerebral Palsy

The type of brain damage that results in cerebral palsy may make it difficult or impossible for the child to control the muscles necessary for proper phonation and articulation. The speech of such individuals may be characterized by fluctuating patterns of pitch, timing, intensity, and phonology. In addition, both cognitive and perceptual motor difficulties may inhibit the acquisition of language and speech. However, because of the considerable variance of this population, some individuals will display severe impairment while others with milder forms of cerebral palsy will demonstrate normal speech and language abilities.

Disorders Associated With Cleft Palate or Cleft Lip

Cleft palate is a structural defect in the palate or roof of the mouth that may make it difficult or impossible for the individual to close off the nasal air passage, which is necessary for proper phonology. Speech associated with an unrepaired or inadequately repaired cleft palate is hypernasal; that is, too much air escapes through the nose as the person talks. Cleft lip (often inappropriately referred to as a "harelip") is a structural defect in the upper lip that, if unrepaired, may also result in defective articulation. Both cleft palate and cleft lip result from failure of the bone and/or soft tissue of the palate or lip to fuse during approximately the first trimester of pregnancy. Language facility in the young child may be hindered by the communication problems stemming from these physical disorders.

Disorders Associated With Mental Retardation, Emotional Disturbance, and Learning Disabilities

Children who are mentally retarded may exhibit speech problems and delays in language development. These individuals will more likely develop greater speech problems than normal children of the same developmental age. It is also a fact that as the severity of the retardation increases, so does the probability that the individual will have significant speech and/or language problems. Children with severe emotional disturbance may display peculiar language patterns such as meaningless statements, parrotlike speech (echolalia), or frequent, inappropriate use of personal pronouns. Although the distinction between language disabilities and learning disabilities is not clearly demarcated, there is a strong relationship. Many professionals believe that language disorders may be the focal issue in regard to learning disabilities.

PREVALENCE

It was reported by the U.S. Department of Education (1989) that 2.28% of the 1987–88 school population was determined eligible for speech services. However, most authorities estimate that 5% of school age students have some type of speech handicap. The estimated breakdown (of school age population) of specific speech problems is:

phonological disorders	1–3%
voice disorders	1–2%
stuttering	less than 1%

The prevalence of language disorders is difficult to estimate because there are no satisfactory figures for this impairment at present. The issue of determining a prevalence figure for language disorders becomes compounded by the significant overlap of language problems and learning disabilities.

SPEECH AND LANGUAGE PROBLEMS

Speech therapists perform their services in a wide variety of settings, including elementary and secondary schools, speech and hearing clinics, residential facilities, and rehabilitation hospitals. As one might expect, schools serve the largest number of individuals needing intervention. However, only those students with the most severe communication disorders or multiple disabilities require more than "pull out" services (Michael & Paul, 1991).

School speech and language programs are the most feasible means of providing services to children. Working together, teachers and speech-language specialists can identify and provide assistance to large numbers of children who otherwise might never be taken to a speech center. Unfortunately, because most school systems face chronic shortages of speech-language therapists, only those children with the most severe speech or language handicaps are typically served by them on a regular basis. However, most of these students have only mild associated disabilities or are solely speech/language disordered. Many students who are severely retarded and in need of speech/language therapy do not receive appropriate services. Many times the focus of intervention is on the primary disability (i.e., mental retardation) at the expense of the secondary disability. Some children with speech and language impairments may receive assistance from a learning disabilities specialist or resource teacher if the particular school is able to provide this type of service.

Teachers, then, play a vital role in assisting those children not seen regularly by the speech-language therapist. After a careful assessment of the child's speech, the specialist can recommend activities that the child can work on in the classroom. Only through the cooperative efforts of teacher and specialist can assistance be provided for all children with speech and language handicaps.

Speech/language intervention is a specific type of related service mentioned in the Individuals with Disabilities Education Act (IDEA). Intervention currently focuses on the pragmatics or functionality of speech/language training, speech/language training in naturalistic settings, and instruction that focuses on the context or environment as it relates to speech/language. In combining these principles with behavioral procedures, interventions can emphasize (1) the development of speech/language skills peculiar to the current and future needs of the client, (2) the generalization of acquired speech/language to new environments, and (3) the enhancement of the client's motivation to communicate with others.

POSTSCRIPT

We have outlined only major disorders of speech and language and the major etiological factors contributing to these conditions. There are other less common or more specific disorders and etiological factors that are beyond the scope of this chapter. Moreover, within each of the broad categories we have outlined, there is a wide variation in degree of severity of the handicap. Additionally, an individual's speech may be disordered by more than one of the conditions already discussed. For more detailed treatment of speech and language impairments, see Devany, Rincover, and Lovaas (1981), Hixon, Shriberg, and Saxman (1980), Schiefelbusch and McCormick (1981), Tarver and Ellsworth (1981), or Van Riper (1978).

Speech is one of an individual's most personal attributes. Certainly, as the anecdotes at the beginning of this chapter demonstrate, having a speech problem can be extremely embarrassing and painful. When people continually respond more to the sound than to the content of speech, a person's desire to communicate thoughts and feelings can be inhibited. Although children with speech disorders may choose a world of silence rather than face the disturbing reactions on a listener's face, they can, with help, overcome or learn to cope with their difficulties. At times, they can make light of their situation. Having a speech or language disorder, like having any other disability, does not exclude a child from the world of fun and humor.

SUGGESTIONS FOR WORKING WITH PERSONS WHO HAVE SPEECH/LANGUAGE DISORDERS

General

1. Teachers, parents, and friends should be informed of what skills and/or behaviors the therapist is targeting so they can appropriately respond and reinforce them in educational settings, at home, or in the community.
2. Listen attentively and patiently when the person is talking. Give the person time.
3. If you do not understand what the individual said, explain what you did understand and ask for clarification of the rest.
4. Remember that the person with a speech/language impairment has trouble talking, not hearing; do not shout or yell.
5. Laugh with, but not at, the individual who has a speech/language impairment.

Working With Those Who Stutter

1. Accept them as they are.
2. Look at and not away from them when they talk. Obvious uneasiness can make them uncomfortable.
3. Encourage but do not force them to talk.
4. Do not say things for them. That is, do not complete their words or statements when they get hung up.
5. Build their self-confidence by emphasizing their assets.
6. Encourage them to participate in group activities.
7. Create an environment in which these individuals can feel comfortable. Let them know that you are aware of but accept their problem.

✦ PONDER THESE

1. *We judge one another's speech to a large degree on the basis of what we are accustomed to hearing. Which, if any, of the following individuals would you judge to have defective speech? What specific characteristics of their speech distract you from the content of what they have to say?*

Jimmy Carter	Norm Crosby
Mel Tillis	Jimmy Stewart
Stevie Nicks	Charo
Barbara Walters	Pee Wee Herman

2. *Imagine that a parent comes to you with one of the following descriptions of a child's speech or language.
What specific questions would you ask the parent to
help you determine whether the child may in fact need
the services of a speech-language specialist?*

   *"Now my little boy—he just don't talk plain so you can
   understand him."*

   "Melinda stutters."

   "Fred sounds like he's talking through his nose."

   *"I don't know what's the matter. She just hardly ever
   talks. I mean almost never! She doesn't say more than a
   couple of words in a day, and sometimes you can't even
   understand those."*

3. *To get some idea of what it is like to have a speech
impairment, try one of the following activities. In public
or in the company of strangers or on the telephone,
speak with a severe phonological or voice deviation or
with marked dysfluency (stutter). Describe your listener's reactions and the feelings they engendered in
you.*

INFORMATION/RESOURCES

1. American Speech-Language-Hearing Association
   1080 Rockville Pike
   Rockville, Maryland 20852

2. Trace Research and Development Center
   University of Wisconsin/Madison
   5151 Waisman Center
   1500 Highland Avenue
   Madison, Wisconsin 53705

3. Phonic Ear, Inc.
    3880 Cypress Drive
    Petaluma, California 94954

4. Sentient Speech Systems Technology, Inc.
    2100 Wharton Street
    Suite 630
    Pittsburgh, Pennsylvania 15203

5. Innocomp
    33195 Wagon Wheel Drive
    Solon, Ohio 44139

References

American Speech and Hearing Association. (1982). Definitions: Communicative disorders and variations. *ASHA, 24,* 949–950.

Bangs, T. E. (1982). *Language and learning disorders of the preacademic child with curriculum guide* (2nd ed.). Englewood Cliffs, NJ: Merrill/Prentice-Hall.

Devany, J. M., Rincover, A., & Lovaas, O. I. (1981). Teaching speech to nonverbal children. In J. M. Kauffman & D. P. Hallahan (Eds.), *Handbook of special education* (pp. 512–529). Englewood Cliffs, NJ: Merrill/Prentice-Hall.

Hallahan, D. P., & Kauffman, J. M. (1986). *Exceptional children: Introduction to special education* (3rd ed.). Englewood Cliffs, NJ: Merrill/Prentice-Hall.

Hixon, T. J., Shriberg, L. D., & Saxman, J. H. (Eds.). (1980). *Introduction to communication disorders.* Englewood Cliffs, NJ: Merrill/Prentice-Hall.

Hull, F. M., & Hull, M. E. (1973). Children with oral communication disabilities. In L. M. Dunn (Ed.), *Exceptional children in the schools* (2nd ed., pp. 299–348). New York: Holt, Rinehart, & Winston.

McLean, J. E. (1978). Language structure and communication disorders. In M. G. Haring (Ed.), *Behavior of exceptional children* (2nd ed., pp. 253–288). Englewood Cliffs, NJ: Merrill/Prentice Hall.

Michael, M. G., & Paul, P. V. (1991). Early intervention for infants with deaf-blindness. *Exceptional Children, 57*(3), 200–210.

Naremore, R. C. (1980). Language disorders. In T. J. Hixon, L. D. Shriberg, & J. H. Saxman (Eds.), *Introduction to communication disorders.* Englewood Cliffs, NJ: Merrill/Prentice-Hall.

Perkins, W. H. (1971). *Speech pathology: An applied behavioral science.* St. Louis: Mosby.

Perkins, W. H. (1980). Disorders of speech flow. In T. J. Hixon, L. D. Shriberg, & J. H. Saxman (Eds.), *Introduction to communication disorders.* Englewood Cliffs, NJ: Merrill/Prentice-Hall.

Schiefelbusch, R. L., & McCormick, L. P. (1981). Language and speech disorders. In J. M. Kauffman & D. P. Hallahan (Eds.), *Handbook of special education* (pp. 108–140). Englewood Cliffs, NJ: Merrill/Prentice-Hall.

Tarver, S. G., & Ellsworth, P. S. (1981). Written and oral language for verbal children. In J. M. Kauffman & D. P. Hallahan (Eds.), *Handbook of special education.* (pp. 491–511). Englewood Cliffs, NJ: Merrill/Prentice-Hall.

U.S. Department of Education. (1989). *Eleventh annual report to Congress on the implementation of P.L.94–142: The Education for all Handicapped Children Act.* Washington, DC: U.S. Government Printing Office.

Van Riper, C. (1978). *Speech correction: Principles and methods* (6th ed.). Englewood Cliffs, NJ: Merrill/Prentice-Hall.

THREE

OTHER EXCEPTIONAL AREAS

11

GIFTEDNESS

I was standing at the front of the room explaining how the earth revolves and how, because of its huge size, it is difficult for us to realize that it is actually round. All of a sudden Spencer blurted out, "The earth isn't round."

I curtly replied, "Ha, do you think it's flat?"

He matter-of-factly said, "No, it's a truncated sphere."

I quickly changed the subject. While the children were at recess I had a chance to grab a soft drink in the teacher's lounge. While sipping my drink, I looked up the word "truncated" in the dictionary. I'm still not sure if he was right, but it sounded good; so good that I wasn't going to make an issue of it. Spencer said the darndest things.

At 4 Ellie was reading on a third-grade level. At 5 she could complete long arithmetic problems in her head. At 6 she played sonatinas on the piano. At 7 she said, "At Sunday school they told us that God created all the things in the world. I already knew that, so I didn't learn anything new. What I'm anxious to know is how did he make everything. Do you know what I mean? When are they going to teach me how *he created all these things?"*

Not long ago, I was invited to go on a "reef walk" with a class of gifted third- and fourth-graders. It was a very educational experience.

While we were wading in shallow water, we came upon a familiar marine organism commonly called a feather duster (tube worm). Forgetting that these students had vocabularies well advanced of their nongifted age peers, I was ready to say something like, "Look how that thing hangs on the rock."

Before I could get my highly descriptive statement out, Eddie, who always amazes us with his comments, offered the following: "Notice how securely anchored the organism is to the stationary coral."

All I could reply was: "Yes, I did."

It was explained quite clearly to his father that Albert would never make a success of anything, and when Albert was expelled from the "gymnasium" he was emphatically told, "Your presence in the class is disruptive and affects the other students." According to Clark (1971, p. 12) Albert's last name was Einstein.

Barlow (1952), quoting from the mid-nineteenth-century Chamber's Journal, reported the arithmetical examination given to Truman Stafford, a child prodigy. The examination was given by the Rev. H. W. Adams when Truman was 10 years old.

> I had only to read the sum to him once. . . . Let this fact be remembered in connection with some of the long and blind sums I shall hereafter name, and see if it does not show his amazing power of conception and comprehension. The questions given him became continually harder. What number is that which, being divided by the product of its digits, the quotient is 3; and if 18 be added, the digits will be inverted? He flew out of his chair, whirled around, rolled up his eyes and said in about a minute, 24. Multiply in your head 365,365,365,365,365,365 by 365,365,365,365,365,365. He flew around the room like a top, pulled his pantaloons over the tops of his boots, bit his hands, rolled his eyes in their sockets, sometimes smiling and talking, and then seeming to be in an agony, until, in not more than one minute said he,
> 133,491,850,208,566,925,016,658,299,951,583,225! (p. 43)

Mr. Palcuzzi, principal of the Jefferson Elementary School, once got tired of hearing objections to special provisions for gifted children, so he decided to spice an otherwise mild PTA meeting with his proposal for the gifted. The elements of the Palcuzzi program were as follows:

1. Children should be grouped by ability.
2. Part of the school day should be given over to special instruction.
3. Talented students should be allowed time to share their talents with children of other schools in the area or even of other schools throughout the state. (The school, that is, taxpayers, will pay the transportation costs.)
4. A child should be advanced according to his talents, rather than according to his age.
5. These children should have special teachers, specially trained and highly salaried.

As might be expected, the "Palcuzzi program" was subjected to a barrage of criticism:

"What about the youngster who isn't able to fit into the special group; won't his ego be damaged?"

"How about the special cost; how could you justify transportation costs that would have to be paid by moving a special group of students from one school to another?"

"Mightn't we be endangering the child by having him interact with children who are much more mature than he is?"

"Wouldn't the other teachers complain if we gave more money to the instructors of this group?"

After listening for 10 or 15 minutes, Mr. Palcuzzi dropped his bomb! He said that he wasn't describing a new program for the intellectually gifted, but a program the school system had been enthusiastically supporting for a number of years—the program for gifted basketball players! Gallagher (1975) refers to this as the "Palcuzzi Ploy" (p. 83).

The Palcuzzi Ploy illustrates the very real problem of selling the general public on committing to the development of more appropriate educational programs for the gifted. There has been a tendency to view *equal* education for all as being the *same* educational practices for all, even though a major objective of public school education is to provide programs that will allow all individuals to develop their potential. When students reach a certain intellectual criterion we tend to say, "Enough is enough! You only need to learn so much and we don't need a bunch of intellectual elitists around anyway."

Students who are gifted are generally perceived as being capable of shifting for themselves. In fact, many people feel that they will learn even under the most adverse learning conditions. The fact of the matter is that these students possess a unique array of learning characteristics that are best utilized through nontraditional teaching techniques. In other words, the learning and thinking of gifted pupils are best facilitated through a *special* education.

Students who are gifted continue to be an underidentified and underserved group for whom there are not federal mandates for services. Many students are not identified because of ineffective assessment procedures as well as an unawareness on the part of teachers and parents of what constitutes giftedness. For those students who are identified, their programs may not be comprehensive and sometimes not suited for their particular type of giftedness.

Albert Einstein was bored in school and maintained a below-average to mediocre school record. Thomas Edison, at the age of 7, was at the bottom of his class. His mother got so upset with the school that she pulled him out of class and taught him at home. He was never again admitted to a public school. Stories like these tend to confirm the popular belief that persons who are gifted can and will learn on their own in spite of problematic school experiences.

But what about the gifted students who do not make it? The talented children who lose interest in school because they are bored and unchallenged? What about Dorothy J., a middle-aged Cahuilla Indian woman? In spite of Dorothy's fear of teachers and lack of knowledge of English, she completed high school. As reported by Martinson (1973), "She is co-author, with university professors, of several books in linguistics, ethnobotany, and music and has served as a university lecturer in both the United States and abroad. Meanwhile, because she lacks formal higher education, she earns a living on an assembly line in a factory near her reservation" (p. 205).

DEFINITION

It would seem that there are as many definitions of the gifted as there are authorities in the field. In fact, there is considerable disagreement about which terms should be used to describe giftedness. Furthermore, much discussion has focused on whether high IQ alone should define giftedness or whether other characteristics like high creativity, achievement, motivation, or special talents (for example, in music, dance, athletics, or interpersonal relationships) should be considered. The definition that has been used most widely in the United States was first submitted to Congress in 1972. Its lingering impact warrants its presentation below.

> The term "gifted and talented children" means children and when-
> ever applicable, youth, who are identified at the preschool, elemen-
> tary, or secondary level as possessing demonstrated or potential
> abilities that give evidence of high performance capabilities in areas
> such as intellectual, creative, specific academic, or leadership abil-
> ity, or in the performing and visual arts, and who by reason
> thereof, require services or activities not ordinarily provided by the
> school.

The federal definition may be misleading in some respects. No one has devised a technically adequate measure to determine "potential abilities," particularly in areas such as leadership ability. And while the federal definition gives the impression that there are many *independent* features of giftedness, in reality many of the characteristics listed (e.g., intellectual, creative, and specific academic abilities) are highly correlated. It is also noteworthy to point out that the psychomotor domain is absent from the definition. It was felt that this area is addressed sufficiently through other programs such as athletics.

Specific definitions of giftedness have changed over the years. Early definitions relied almost exclusively on IQ. Contemporary definitions typically refer to creativity, motivation, and/or exceptional performance in some culturally valued activity as well. All definitions state that gifted students are clearly superior in some ability area to most others of the same age. How far superior they should be, who should be the comparison group for judging superiority, and in what specific ways they should be superior have become the debatable issues in defining giftedness.

Renzulli, Reis, and Smith (1981) have suggested that giftedness should be conceptualized in a multifaceted way. They suggested that gifted individuals should demonstrate or show potential in the following areas:

1. High ability (includes intelligence)
2. High creativity (implies the development and application of innovative ideas)

3. High task commitment (related to high degree of motivation and diligence)

Gardner (1983) has proposed the concept of "multiple intelligences." He and his colleagues have identified seven different areas in which one can demonstrate specific degrees of ability. The different intelligences, examples of occupations that might relate to each area, and a short description of the intelligence are presented in Table 11.1. Although these different intelligences have not yet been empirically validated, they do provide a foundation for looking at individuals in a more expansive way by equally distributing the importance of different types of abilities.

A conceptualization of giftedness that combines Renzulli's ideas with those of Gardner's is depicted in Figure 11.1. It acknowledges the different types of intelligence (Gardner) and provides a mechanism for considering giftedness in any of the areas by requiring that a person display certain features or dimensions (Renzulli's "creativity," "motivation," and "task commitment"). This conceptualization clarifies the often ambiguous relationship between giftedness and creativity by suggesting that the development and application of innovative ideas are part of any type of giftedness.

PREVALENCE

The number of students or individuals in the general population who are gifted is unknown. It is logical to conclude that prevalence figures will be influenced by how giftedness is defined, how it is measured, and who is assessed. Government sources do not indicate clearly what percentage of the population is thought to be gifted, although figures of 3% to 5% are often cited to describe the extent of giftedness in the school population (National Center for Educational Statistics, 1989).

IDENTIFICATION

Teachers play an important role in the identification of students who are gifted, as they are often the ones who recognize that a person is gifted and initiate the confirmation process. Certain types of behaviors might suggest that a student is gifted, thus requiring a more in-depth assessment.

Once a student is nominated by a teacher to be considered for gifted programming, other information is typically gathered to determine eligibility. Sources of information can include formal tests; informal assessments; interviews with teachers, parents, and peers; and actual student products including portfolios.

Table 11.1
Multiple Intelligence

Intelligence	End-States	Core Components
Logical-mathematical	Scientist Mathematician	Sensitivity to, and capacity to discern, logical or numerical patterns; ability to handle long chains of reasoning.
Linguistic	Poet Journalist	Sensitivity to the sounds, rhythms, and meanings of words; sensitivity to the different functions of language.
Musical	Composer Violinist	Abilities to produce and appreciate rhythm, pitch, and timbre; appreciation of the forms of musical expressiveness.
Spatial	Navigator Sculptor	Capacities to perceive the visual-spatial world accurately and to perform transformations on one's initial perceptions.
Bodily-kinesthetic	Dancer Athlete	Abilities to control one's body movements and to handle objects skillfully.
Interpersonal	Therapist Salesman	Capacities to discern and respond appropriately to the moods, temperaments, motivations, and desires of other people.
Intrapersonal	Person with detailed, accurate self-knowledge	Access to one's own feelings and the ability to discriminate among them and draw upon them to guide behavior; knowledge of one's own strengths, weaknesses, desires, and intelligences.

Source: From "Multiple Intelligences Go To School: Educational Implications of the Theory of Multiple Intelligences" by H. Gardner and T. Hatch, 1989, *Educational Researcher, 18*(8), p. 6. Copyright 1989 by the American Educational Research Association. Reprinted by permission.

Figure 11.1
Conceptualization of Giftedness

Type of Giftedness	Knowledge	Dimensions Creativity	Motivation	Task commitment
Logical-mathematical				
Linguistic				
Musical				
Spatial				
Bodily-kinesthetic				
Interpersonal				
Intrapersonal				

Although it might be said that identifying gifted students has been often overlooked in education, this definitely is the case with certain groups of children (Wolf & Stephens, 1986). Four different groups of students are typically underrepresented in gifted education, including children who are culturally different, female, disabled, or underachieving. There are gifted learners in all these groups, and efforts must be undertaken to identify them.

ORIGINS OF SELECTED TYPES OF GIFTEDNESS

Galton's (1869) classic contribution to the quantitative psychological study of giftedness touched off the nature-nurture controversy. His examination of adult geniuses lent support to the argument for a hereditary cause. In the years after his study, environmental aspects were accentuated by the majority of authorities in the field of giftedness. However, it was observed that gifted individuals walked, talked, and read much earlier than "normals," and such early acceleration in behavioral development was difficult to attribute primarily to environmental events. Yet it was also observed that the environments in which the majority of the gifted developed were unquestionably wholesome and stimulating.

Because the nature-nurture controversy became so complex and conjured up emotional overtones, a pragmatic resolution evolved, as indicated below.

> . . . in the relationship between genetics and environment, genetics
> sets boundary lines of intellectual performance—an upper limit
> and lower limit—that an individual will be able to achieve. Whether
> the individual is near the top of that boundary line or near the bot-
> tom is dependent on his or her environmental circumstances (Gal-
> lagher & Gallagher, 1994).

Although the logic of this approach seems irrefutable, Jensen (1966, 1969) insisted that genes and prenatal development account for 80% of the variance in intelligence and that environment accounts for only 20% of the variance. Citing research studies, growth figures, and models of intelligence, Jensen presented a convincing case. Torrance (1971) summarizes Jensen's position as follows:

> He especially questioned the idea that IQ differences are almost
> entirely a result of environmental differences and the cultural bias
> of intelligence tests. As in his earlier papers, he argued that envi-
> ronmental factors are less important in determining IQ than
> genetic factors. After examining the recent research concerning
> compensatory educational programs for young children, Jensen
> concluded that extreme environmental deprivation can keep a child
> from performing up to his genetic potential, but an enriched educa-
> tional program cannot push the child above the potential. Jensen
> argues, however, that there are other mental abilities not included
> in intelligence tests that might be capitalized upon in educational
> programs. He believes that current educational attempts to boost
> IQ have been misdirected, and he advocates the development of
> educational methods that are based on other mental abilities
> besides IQ (p. 550).

Early childhood studies have established that environmental fac-tors can have a significant influence on intelligence and school success (Schweinhart & Weikart, 1985). Just how much environmental versus genetic factors play in determining functional intelligence has yet to be established. While researchers and educators debate the question of how much the environment affects intelligence, a growing number of parents currently are doing their best to create "superbabies." Glenn Doman (1984) in *How to Multiply Your Baby's Intelligence* tells par-ents that high and low intelligence are products of the environment and to produce superior intellectual abilities in their children, parents should present stimulating learning activities from birth onward.

David Elkind (1981), in reaction to the drive for early development of abilities, warns parents that too much early pressure to learn can create depression in young children. Certainly both educators and parents continue to await clarification on how much early stimulation and skill training are appropriate in developing children's full capacity for superior functioning and emotional well-being.

CHARACTERISTICS

Individuals who are gifted may display a wide variety of specific interests, aptitudes, knowledge, and skills. When examining lists of possible characteristics, we run the risk of overgeneralizing that all students who are gifted show evidence of these features. Nevertheless, some distinguishable characteristics are noticeable in many students so identified.

Terman's Study

In describing gifted persons, however they are defined, mention must be made of Terman's monumental contribution, *Genetic Studies of Genius* (Burks, Jensen, & Terman, 1930; Cox, 1926; Terman, 1925; Terman & Oden, 1947; Terman & Oden, 1959). Terman actually devoted his life to the study of 1,528 gifted (high IQ) children, following them for 35 years from 1920 to his death in 1956. This five-volume study is expected to continue to the year 2010. The study is noted not only for its large sample size and longitudinal contribution but also for its consistent accuracy. The findings of Terman's investigation have been confirmed and reconfirmed.

Terman's study counteracts the stereotypic concept that gifted individuals are physically weak, are small in stature, wear glasses, read all the time, are not interesting to be around, and are "bookwormish." Terman's findings indicate not only that the gifted are superior in intellect but also that they are physically, socially, emotionally, and morally advanced.

Terman's gifted subjects were reported to be taller, stronger, and heavier than nongifted children. They walked earlier and had a lower incidence of sensory defects, malnutrition, and poor posture. They came from above-average to high-income homes, and their parents were well educated. When compared with the general population, they had a low incidence of delinquency, mental illness, and alcoholism. These individuals seemed to be more happily married, to have fewer divorces, and to have fewer offspring. Of over 1,500 offspring, there is a reported mean IQ of 132, with only 2% falling below 100 and 33⅓%

scoring over 140. After studying Terman's classic work, you cannot help but wonder what causes giftedness.

Contemporary Perspective

We enter a word of caution here—gifted children are not necessarily superchildren. Some do, in fact, fit a negative stereotype that has often been perpetuated by the media. Individuals may vary from the generally superior description one gets from Terman's studies. Some gifted children are physically or emotionally labile. Those with *extremely* high intelligence (IQ over 180) may be particularly prone to difficulties in social adjustment simply because their advanced abilities are so *exceedingly* rare among persons their age (see Hollingworth, 1942).

Clark (1992) has developed a list of characteristics that individuals who are gifted may display. These characteristics are divided into five areas, as shown in Table 11.2. Note how some of these seemingly desirable characteristics could have negative repercussions in a classroom or workplace situation.

Some Thoughts About Creativity

Because there exists a low tolerance for nonconformity in our society, creativity may often be discouraged. Torrance (1965) attempted to accelerate creativeness in children by offering them $2 prizes for stories that were interesting, exciting, and unusual. He found that children would produce such stories when reinforced for doing so. By using reinforcement techniques, other researchers too have found that creativity in story writing, easel painting, block building, and selection of word combinations can be increased (Baer, Rowbury, & Goetz, 1976; Brigham, Graubard, & Stans, 1972; Glover & Gary, 1976; Goetz & Salmonson, 1972).

Torrance and others have demonstrated that creative thinking abilities need to be energized and guided and that the earlier this is done the better. Unfortunately, creativity is not being identified by conventional methods of measurement and evaluation.

DIFFERENTIAL PROGRAMMING

Placement

While students with disabilities can arouse concern in others to address their needs, students who are gifted are usually left to fend for themselves in the general classroom with their chronological peers. In schools today, students who are gifted are most likely to spend the

Table 11.2
Differentiating Characteristics of the Gifted

I.	The cognitive domain	• Extraordinary quantity of information; unusual retentiveness
		• Advanced comprehension
		• Unusually varied interests and curiosity
		• High level of language development
		• High level of verbal ability
		• Unusual capacity for processing information
		• Accelerated pace of thought processes
		• Flexible thought processes
		• Comprehensive synthesis
		• Early ability to delay closure
		• Heightened capacity for seeing unusual and diverse relationships, integration of ideas, and disciplines
		• Ability to generate original ideas and solutions
		• Early differential patterns for thought processing (e.g., thinking in alternatives; abstract terms; sensing consequences; making generalizations; visual thinking; use of metaphors and analogies)
		• Early ability to use and form conceptual frameworks
		• An evaluative approach toward oneself and others
		• Unusual intensity; persistent goal-directed behavior
II.	The affective domain	• Large accumulation of information about emotions that have not been brought to awareness
		• Unusual sensitivity to the expectations and feelings of others
		• Keen sense of humor—may be gentle or hostile
		• Heightened self-awareness, accompanied by feelings of being different
		• Idealism and a sense of justice, which appear at an early age

Source:From *Growing Up Gifted,* Fourth Edition, by Barbara Clark. Copyright 1992 by Merrill/Prentice Hall. Reprinted by permission.

greater part of their instructional day in a general education classroom setting with some differential programming available for part of the day. For this reason it is critical that general educators become more knowledgeable of, skilled at, and comfortable with teaching students who are gifted.

**Table 11.2
continued**

II.	The affective domain continued	• Earlier development of an inner locus of control and satisfaction
		• Unusual emotional depth and intensity
		• High expectations of self and others, often leading to high levels of frustration with self, others, and situations; perfectionism
		• Strong need for consistency between abstract values and personal actions
		• Advanced levels of moral judgment
		• Strongly motivated by self-actualization needs
		• Advanced cognitive and affective capacity for conceptualizing and solving societial problems
		• Leadership
		• Solutions to social and environmental problems
		• Involvement with the metaneeds of society (e.g., injustice, beauty, truth)
III.	The physical/ sensing domain	• Unusual quantity of input from the environment through a heightened sensory awareness
		• Unusual discrepancy between physical and intellectual development
		• Low tolerance for the lag between their standards and their athletic skills
		• Cartesian split—can include neglect of physical well-being and avoidance of physical activity
IV.	The intuitive domain	• Early involvement and concern for intuitive knowing, and metaphysical ideas and phenomena
		• Open to experiences in this area; will experiment with psychic and metaphysical phenomenon
		• Creativity apparent in all areas of endeavor
		• Ability to predict; interest in future

Students who are gifted may be capable of learning at such a high level of cognition that traditional instruction for students of their age is often not meeting their needs and is considered boring, tedious, and redundant. It is no wonder that many case histories of very bright individuals reveal that at some time in their lives they experienced difficulties in school. Kirk (1972) reported that Norbert Wiener, one of the great men in cybernetics, read *Alice in Wonderland* and *The Arabian Nights* by age 4 but was refused admission to school because he was not old enough. At age 7, he was placed in the third grade. At age 18, he received his Ph.D. in mathematics.

Even though the general education setting is an important setting in which to address the needs of students who are gifted, it "should not, cannot, and must not be the *only* setting in which appropriate services are provided" (Maker, 1993, p. 4). These students need programming that is different "in depth, scope, pace, self-directedness of expectations" (Lopez & MacKenzie, 1993, p. 288).

Rationale for Differential Programming

As listed by Ward (1962), the logic of special education services for the gifted is based on the following assumptions and observed facts:

1. Gifted children as a group differ from others in learning ability; they learn faster and remember more, and they tend to think more deeply with and about what they learn.

2. As adults, gifted persons tend to remain similarly advanced beyond the average and tend to assume distinctive social roles as leaders in the reconstruction and advancement of whatever lines of activity they pursue.

3. The regular school curriculum only barely approximates the demands of either the greater learning capacity or the anticipated social roles of gifted persons.

4. An educational program *can* be devised which *does* more adequately meet these basic demands, and which on the whole being uniquely suited to the gifted is both unnecessary for and impossible of accomplishment by students of lesser ability.

5. Differential educational provisions for the gifted promise to discover more gifted persons, to improve their education, and to launch them earlier into their chosen careers so that society, as well as the persons themselves, may enjoy longer the fruits of their productive and creative labors (p. 22).

Ward's points, though written nearly three decades ago, are hard to argue against; nearly all current educational programs for students who are gifted are built around most or all of his assumptions. Getzels and Dillon (1973) list nearly 30 specific programs and practices, but we will discuss only 3: acceleration, enrichment, and special grouping.

Types of Differential Programming

Acceleration. By this means the student is introduced to content, concepts, and educational experiences sooner than is done with other students of the same age. There are many types of accelerative practices, some of which include early entrance to school, grade skipping, self-paced instruction, curriculum compacting (faster movement through a given curriculum), mentorships, advanced placement, credit by examination, and correspondence courses (Southern & Jones, 1991). Research seems clearly to support acceleration, but programs of this type can be met with criticism and disfavor.

> Apparently the cultural values favoring a standard period of dependency and formal education are stronger than the social or individual need for achievement and independence. This is an instance of the more general case one remarks throughout education: when research findings clash with cultural values, the values are more likely to prevail (Getzels & Dillon, 1973, p. 717).

Although administrative arrangements for handling any student—disabled, normal, or gifted—assist or interfere with instruction, the major educational concerns focus on what goes on in the classroom. No administrative manipulation of environmental variables can *assure* learning. This is not to minimize the importance of administrative approaches, but it is commonly recognized that although appropriate facilities, materials, and wholesome environmental conditions are necessary, these important facets are no substitute for a conscientious, sensitive, skillful, and competent teacher.

Enrichment. This approach uses techniques that provide topics, skill development, materials, or experiences that extend the depth of coverage beyond that typically presented in the existing curriculum. This practice is commonly used in general education settings where it may be the easiest type of intervention to implement. Enrichment activities are sometimes categorized as horizontal or vertical. *Horizontal enrichment* refers to providing *more* educational experiences at the same level of difficulty, while *vertical enrichment* refers to providing higher-level activities of increasing complexity. This latter type of enrichment activity might more properly be considered a type of acceleration technique (Southern & Jones, 1991).

Renzulli (1977) observes that much of what passes as enrichment (i.e., the horizontal kind) is actually a waste of gifted students' time. He has proposed a three-stage model for enrichment activities. Two levels of enrichment (general exploratory activities and group exercises to increase creativity, affective awareness, and problem solving skills) are appropriate for *all* children, including the gifted. But a third type, individual and small-group investigations of real-life problems, is particularly suited for students who are gifted. In this kind of enrichment, the child actually carries out an experiment or project as a chemist, politician, writer, meteorologist, or what have you. The child *becomes* a professional or artisan, working like an adult counterpart and producing valuable information or creating a valuable product.

Perhaps children are gifted some of the time (they may not always meet the dimensions described in Figure 11.1) or in some specific areas (not in others). This idea has led Renzulli et al. (1981) to propose a "revolving door" plan for enrichment. This plan means children will be phased in and out of the special third level of enrichment (the real-life investigations or projects) as they demonstrate their ability and interest by producing something valuable. If and when a "gifted" student does not display the motivation, creativity, or knowledge to pursue a particular project at this level, then he or she returns to the general education classroom activities and another child who meets the necessary criteria for the project is included in the special enrichment.

Ability grouping.   In this method, those who are gifted are separated into more homogeneous groupings for at least part of the instructional day (VanTassel-Baska, 1989). One example of this technique is cluster grouping. The practice allows students with similar interests and enthusiasm to explore topics from different perspectives and to stimulate the creative thinking of others in the group.

The benefits of such grouping warrant continued consideration of such an approach. However, Getzels and Dillon (1973), in quoting Gold, warn, "Grouping apparently is a helpful but not automatically effective instructional adjustment; achievement seems to improve only when grouping is accompanied by a differentiation in teacher quality, curriculum, guidance and method" (p. 716).

As the "Palcuzzi Ploy" illustrates (see the vignette at the beginning of this chapter), American schools support ability grouping in athletics but are less supportive of such grouping in academics. Legal action in the 1960s and 1970s tended to eliminate special "tracking" or ability grouping on the grounds that it is a discriminatory practice. The feeling of many Americans seems to be that equality should be the overriding concern in public education. But, as Gallagher and Weiss (1979, p. 2) noted, "society's notion of 'equality' tends to be destructive of giftedness in elementary and secondary school." It seems likely that public schools will maintain an emphasis on inclusion and heterogeneous grouping—for both students who are disabled and those who are gifted. The practice of special grouping will be found most often in private schools where the forced policy of equality is handled differently.

FINAL THOUGHTS

Individuals who are gifted are very bright, yet they too need attention and selected support, and their learning and thinking can most certainly be inhibited or suppressed. If we are to do what we say *should* be done, that is, develop each individual to her optimum or maximum potential, then we must take another look at our educational services for students who are gifted.

Not only is differential instruction important to gifted individuals themselves, it is essential for society. We are living in a world that becomes more complex every day. Conflict, violence, drugs, alcoholism, overpopulation, and pollution are problems that threaten our very survival. How may these problems be resolved now and in the future? It is extremely likely that we will turn to today's gifted students and hope they will come up with some answers. Should we not provide these future leaders, scientists, health providers with the best possible preparation?

In the 1950s, during the era of Sputnik, the nation turned to gifted individuals for solutions to problems in the physical sciences (e.g., space exploration). The public at that time supported differential educational programs for gifted students, especially those in science and engineering. Unfortunately, the programs were short lived, as the United States quickly caught up in the space race. At present, it is the social sciences that need a booster shot. We should now begin to train and entice our gifted individuals into the area of social science exploration.

Maslow's (1971) analogy of how tall our species can grow and how fast we can run brings the value and importance of those who are gifted into meaningful perspective.

> If we want to answer the question how tall can the human species grow, then obviously it is well to pick out the ones who are already tallest and study them. If we want to know how fast a human being can run, then it is no use to average out the speed of a "good sample" of the population, it is far better to collect Olympic gold-medal winners and see how well they can do. If we want to know the possibilities for spiritual growth, value growth, or moral development in human beings, then I maintain that we can learn most by studying our most moral, ethical, or saintly people.

> On the whole I think it is fair to say that human history is a
> record of the ways in which human nature has been sold short.
> The highest possibilities of human nature have practically always
> been underrated. Even when "good specimens," the saints and
> sages and great leaders of history, have been available for study, the
> temptation too often has been to consider them not human but
> supernaturally endowed.[1]

As we begin to think about gifted individuals as a human
resource to solve society's problems, we must be aware that we have
no right to harness their intellectual talents at the cost of their basic
freedoms. Getzels (1957) reminds us that there comes a time when we
must look at the gifted as people and not be compelled to figure out
how we can get the most out of them. Hopefully, if they are properly
treated in our educational settings, gifted persons will find gratification
as well as intriguing challenges in all learning.

SUGGESTIONS FOR WORKING WITH PERSONS WHO ARE GIFTED

1. In helping an underachieving student become motivated, present ideas and tasks in terms of the needs and interests of the child.
2. Help individuals set realistic goals.
3. Give students choices in deciding learning goals and activities. Choices give the student an opportunity to develop self-esteem and a sense of competency.
4. Do not expect perfection. Gifted individuals need to know that mistakes are a natural part of growing and learning.
5. Provide extra activities and experiences for students who are gifted, but be thoughtful about scheduling. Be sure the gifted student does not become overscheduled.
6. Be sure the gifted student and the other children in her class or neighborhood understand that she is more like them than different. Like everyone else, the gifted child sometimes has feelings of fear and inadequacy, a huge need for love and acceptance, and the desire to play and have fun.

---

[1]From *The Farther Reaches of Human Nature* (p. 7) by A. Maslow, 1971, New York: Viking Press. Copyright 1971 by Viking Press. Reprinted by permission.

7. Be sure that educational experiences challenge the student and awaken her interest in learning. Watch for signs of boredom. Gifted children need schools to be exciting, not places where they must sit through long hours of learning activities below their level.

8. Provide opportunities for creative problem solving.

9. Avoid comparisons of the gifted child and youth with others, particularly siblings.

10. Help the gifted person develop a respectful attitude toward the feelings, skills, and abilities of her nongifted peers.

11. Help the gifted student develop leadership skills.

12. Appreciate the gifted student simply for being a fine human being. Communicate that you like the individual, not just because of her superior ability, but because she is just a good person and a delight to spend time with.

✦ *PONDER THESE*

1. *By what criteria could the following individuals be judged to be gifted?*

Thomas Jefferson	*Yo Yo Ma*
Jesse Jackson	*John Grisham*
Tom Hanks	*Cal Ripken*
Spike Lee	*Gloria Estefan*
Bill Gates	*Mother Teresa*

2. *Is it possible to become nationally known—a household word—without being gifted?*

3. *Read some accounts, factual or fictional, of giftedness (e.g., The Child Buyer by Lewis Hersey or Mental Prodigies by Fred Barlow). How would you handle the children described if they were in a regular public school class?*

4. *Plan a hypothetical educational program to make children gifted. Would the opposite of your program make children retarded?*

References

Baer, D. M., Rowbury, T. G., & Goetz, E. M. (1976). Behavioral traps in the preschool: A proposal for research. In A. D. Pick (Ed.), *Minnesota Symposia on Child Psychology* (Vol. 10, pp. 3–27), Minneapolis: University of Minnesota.

Barlow, F. (1952). *Mental prodigies.* New York: Greenwood.

Brigham, T. A., Graubard, P. S., & Stans, A. (1972). Analysis of effects of sequential reinforcement contingencies on aspects of composition. *Journal of Applied Behavior Analysis, 5,* 421–427.

Burks, B., Jensen, D., & Terman, L. M. (1930). The promise of youth. *Genetic studies of genius* (Vol. 3). Palo Alto, CA: Stanford University.

Clark, R. W. (1971). *Einstein: The life and times.* New York: World.

Congressional Record. (1978, October 10), H–12179.

Cox, C. M. (1926). The early mental traits of 300 geniuses. *Genetic studies of genius* (Vol. 2). Palo Alto, CA: Stanford University.

Doman, G. (1984). *How to multiply your baby's intelligence.* New York: Doubleday.

Elkind, D. (1981). *The hurried child.* Reading, MA: Addison-Wesley.

Gallagher, J. J. (1975). *Teaching the gifted child* (2nd ed.). Boston: Allyn & Bacon.

Gallagher, J. J., & Gallagher, S. A. (1994). *Teaching the gifted child.* Boston: Allyn & Bacon.

Gallagher, J. J., & Weiss, P. (1979). *The education of gifted and talented students. A history and prospectus.* Washington, DC: Council for Basic Education.

Galton, F. (1869). *Hereditary genius: An inquiry into its laws and consequences.* London: Macmillan.

Gardner, H. (1983. *Frames of mind: The theory of multiple intelligences.* New York: Basic Books.

Getzels, J. W. (1957). Social values and individual motives: The dilemma of the gifted. *School Review, 65,* 60–63.

Getzels, J. W., & Dillon, J. T. (1973). The nature of giftedness and the education of the gifted. In R. M. W. Travers (Ed.), *Second handbook of research on teaching.* Chicago: Rand McNally.

Getzels, J. W., & Jackson, P. W. (1962). *Creativity and intelligence: Explorations with gifted students.* New York: Wiley.

Glover, J., & Gary, A. L. (1976). Procedures to increase some aspects of creativity. *Journal of Applied Behavior Analysis, 9,* 79–84.

Goetz, E. M., & Salmonson, M. M. (1972). The effect of general and descriptive reinforcement on "creativity" in easel painting. In G. Semb (Ed.), *Behavioral analysis in education—1972.* Lawrence: University of Kansas Department of Human Development.

Hollingworth, L. S. (1942). *Children above 180 IQ, Stanford-Binet: Origin and development.* Yonkers-on-Hudson, NY: World Book.

Jensen, A. R. (1966). Verbal mediation and educational potential. *Psychology in the Schools, 3,* 99–109.

Jensen, A. R. (1969). How much can we boost IQ and scholastic achievement? *Harvard Educational Review, 39,* 1–119.

Kirk, S. A. (1972). *Educating exceptional children* (rev. ed.). Boston: Houghton Mifflin.

Lopez, R., & MacKenzie, J. (1993). A learning center approach to individualized instruction for gifted students. In C. J. Maker (Ed.), *Critical issues in gifted education: Vol. 3. Programs for the gifted in regular classrooms* (pp. 282–295). Austin: Pro-Ed.

Maker, C. J. (Ed.). (1993). *Critical issues in gifted education: Vol. 3. Programs for the gifted in regular classrooms.* Austin: Pro-Ed.

Martinson, R. A. (1973). Children with superior cognitive abilities. In L. M. Dunn (Ed.), *Exceptional children in the schools* (2nd ed., pp. 191–241). New York: Holt, Rinehart & Winston.

Maslow, A. H. (1971). *The farther reaches of human nature.* New York: Viking.

National Center for Education Statistics. (1989). *Digest of educational statistics, 1989.* Washington, DC: U.S. Department of Education, Office of Research and Improvement.

Renzulli, J. S. (1977). *The enrichment triad model: A guide for developing defensible programs for the gifted and talented.* Wethersfield, CT: Creative Learning.

Renzulli, J. S. (1978). What makes giftedness? Re-examining a definition. *Phi Delta Kappan, 60,* 180–184, 261.

Renzulli, J. S., Reis, S. M., & Smith, L. H. (1981). *The revolving door identification model.* Mansfield Center, CT: Creative Learning.

Schweinhart, L. J., & Weikart, D. P. (1985). Evidence that good early childhood programs work. *Phi Delta Kappan, 66,* 545–551.

Southern, W. T., & Jones, E. D. (1991). *Academic acceleration of gifted children.* New York: Teachers College Press.

Terman, L. M. (1925). Mental and physical traits of a thousand gifted children. *Genetic studies of genius* (Vol. 1). Palo Alto, CA: Stanford University.

Terman, L. M., & Oden, M. H. (1947). The gifted child grows up. *Genetic studies of genius* (Vol. 4). Palo Alto, CA: Stanford University.

Terman, L. M., & Oden, M. H. (1959). The gifted group at mid-life. *Genetic studies of genius* (Vol. 5). Palo Alto, CA: Stanford University.

Torrance, E. P. (1965). *Rewarding creative behavior: Experiments in classroom creativity.* Englewood Cliffs, NJ: Merrill/Prentice-Hall.

Torrance, E. P. (1971). Psychology of gifted children and youth. In W. M. Cruickshank (Ed.), *Psychology of exceptional children and youth* (3rd ed., pp. 528–564). Englewood Cliffs, NJ: Merrill/Prentice-Hall.

VanTassel-Baska, J. (1989). Appropriate curriculum for gifted learners. *Educational Leadership,* 13–15.

Ward, V. S. (Ed.). (1962). *The gifted student: A manual for program improvement.* Charlottesville, VA: Southern Regional Educational Board.

Wolf, J. S., & Stephens, T. M. (1986). Gifted and talented. In N. G. Haring & L. P. McCormick (Eds.), *Exceptional children and youth* (4th ed., pp. 431–473). Englewood Cliffs, NJ: Merrill/Prentice Hall.

12

CULTURAL DIVERSITY

As many educators know, there is such a phenomenon as a culture of poverty—that is, customs, behaviors, and beliefs that result not from ethnic or racial differences but from socioeconomic differences. The lesson was taught to me by Ben. Every Friday afternoon, I took my class somewhere fun or interesting. This particular day, we went to a casual restaurant across the lake. Even though the lake was only about 5 miles from downtown, none of my students had ever been there. The people at the restaurant were great. We got the best table on the deck, with a spectacular view for miles. While we were munching on chips and salsa, I checked out the kids for good table manners. Only one of them, Ben, hadn't used his napkin and already had crumbs and salsa all over his face. I quietly reminded him that he needed to use his napkin. He looked right at me, then went on eating as though I hadn't said a word. I told him again to unroll his napkin and silverware and wipe his face. He looked at me with great confusion but still made no movement. I finally moved over near him, handed him his napkin, and told him (a little more strongly) to please use it. He finally smiled at me and wiped his face. When I asked what had taken him so long, he explained that he hadn't known that the piece of white cloth was a napkin. The

LaVonne I. Neal, University of Texas at Austin, contributed to this chapter.

only kind of napkins he had ever seen were the folded paper kind that come in plastic packages. He couldn't believe that he was really supposed to wipe his face on a piece of starched cloth.

My first year teaching middle school was an interesting experience. As one of the two African Americans on the staff, my perceptions of appropriate behavior and those of my peers sometimes differed. One day, I watched as two eighth grade African American boys greeted each other with body bumps, handshakes, slaps on the back, and loud voices. While I smiled at the boys' enthusiastic camaraderie, my Anglo colleague grew agitated and nervous. She turned to me and remarked that she thought that the boys' behavior was offensive and potentially disruptive. What was perfectly normal and appropriate to me was both too loud and too physical to her.

My first job as an educational consultant involved a trip out west, to a small town in the middle of nowhere. A colleague and I had been hired to visit a school in order to help them deal with a student who had serious behavioral problems. The school district supervisor picked us up at the airport and spent the next hour driving and describing the subject of our consultation. The young man in question had done various nefarious things and had managed to work his way out of both a regular class and a self-contained special education class. He was spending his days in a 12' x 12' room with his own teacher and aide because of his highly disruptive actions. We were anxious to get a look at this young man and were expecting to meet a large, menacing, aggressive bully with no social skills and an explosive temper. Imagine our surprise when we met Luis, a small 6-year-old Hispanic boy. We settled in, spent some time observing, then started asking questions. Before long, we stopped and looked at each other, having come to the same conclusion. Luis's behaviors had certainly escalated, but they undoubtedly had something to do with the fact that he spoke no English. In fact, no one in his family spoke English. And none of his teachers spoke Spanish. Luis couldn't understand anything that anyone at school said to him, nor could they understand anything he said to them. He never did anything he was told because he didn't know what he was being told to do. My friend and I were both amazed that in the late 1980s something like this could still happen. We have used this example time and time again when we do teacher training. The lesson to me is that we always need to look at the big picture and not make assumptions about why kids do what they do.

In many Latin American families, children are taught to speak respectfully to their elders, especially teachers. For example, whenever responding to a female teacher, most Hispanic students would never just say, "Sí," or "No." They would say "Sí, Señorita" or "No, Señorita." When they begin to use English, the natural translation is "Yes, Miss" or "No, Miss." Despite the students' best efforts to be polite, many Anglo teachers still take offense. One of the teachers on my team reprimanded a student for addressing her only as "Miss" without using her surname. Very frustrated with what she perceived as a lack of respect, she told the student that she had a last name and would not respond until addressed with her surname after the "Miss." The student, who had made a conscious effort to be as polite as possible, was left not knowing what he had done wrong.

One of the students I know who attends an after school program for students with autism has made some important changes during the last year. Until then, Denise, who is Chinese American, refused to do much of anything that anyone asked her to do. She would sit when asked to stand and stand when asked to sit. She had the staff going crazy because she would sit in a corner and refuse to do anything they asked. Denise also refused do anything at home. Although she was 11 years old and capable of learning to help herself, she was still carried around, dressed, and spoon fed by her grandmother, an elderly woman who speaks only Chinese. Denise's family had problems communicating with teachers and other professionals and was very reluctant to ask questions or to participate in her programming. In addition, they viewed Denise's autism as a very private matter and never asked for help in dealing with her. Everyone was thrilled when we hired a Chinese American staff member. Not only can she communicate well with Denise's family, but she also spends 2 hours a day in their home. She has shown the parents and the grandmother that it is important to teach Denise to take care of herself and not to do everything for her. Last week, we saw videotapes of Denise's home training and were all amazed. This girl who 1 year ago was pinching, running, spitting, and refusing to do anything independently is now setting the table, helping to cook dinner, cleaning up, brushing her teeth, and dressing herself. Her parents are very excited. We all believe that without the help of a Chinese American staff member, Denise might never have learned even a little of what she now knows.

For a significant number of exceptional children, school is the agent that differentiates them from the "normal" students. Many students who are identified as mentally retarded, learning disabled, or emotionally disturbed are not so identified until they enter school. For these students, school seems to become the *cause of* and not the *solution to* their learning problems. The academic and behavioral demands they encounter are major impediments to success.

For still another segment of the school age population school is a major obstacle. However, these students may not lack the requisite academic and behavioral skills for appropriate achievement. Rather, they happen to have been raised in families whose cultural heritage differs from that of the majority of their peers. This fact can have a dramatic impact on a student's schooling.

Interestingly, some students can be included in both of the groups mentioned above. They can have academic or behavioral difficulties as well as cultural differences. In effect, these students have dual disabilities: their recognized disability and their cultural divergence from their peers (Chinn & Kamp, 1982; Fair & Sullivan, 1980). Moreover, because the families from which many of these students come are poor, it has also been suggested that these students actually might be in triple jeopardy due to their handicap, their ethnicity, and their low socioeconomic status (Baca & Chinn, 1982).

The increasing recognition of diversity within American society poses a significant challenge: how to create a cohesive and democratic society while at the same time allowing citizens to maintain their ethnic, cultural, socioeconomic, and primordial identities. Multicultural education has emerged as a vehicle for including diverse groups and transforming the nation's educational institutions. Multicultural education tries to create equal educational opportunities for all students by ensuring that the total school environment reflects the diversity of groups in classroom, schools, and the society as a whole (Banks, 1994).

INTRODUCTION

This chapter examines three general areas: cultural diversity, multicultural education, and the complexities of exceptionality in relation to cultural differences. Although this area of public and professional interest has been receiving much attention within the last few years, there is an appreciable lack of programming and research. For this reason, the "state of the art" on providing appropriate services for culturally different students with handicaps is only beginning to be formulated. Unquestionably, many issues must be addressed before substantial progress can be made.

There are three guiding principles from which efforts to educate culturally different students with disabilities have emerged. These principles are desegregation, equal educational opportunity, and appropriate education. The first of these, desegregation, initially surfaced in the 1954 Supreme Court decision in *Brown v. Topeka Board of Education*. Segregated education for certain students was declared unconstitutional. The second principle, equal educational opportunity (related in many ways to desegregation), was firmly established in three landmark cases, *Diana v. State Board of Education* (1970), *Larry P. v. Riles* (1972), and *Lau v. Nichols* (1974). These cases prohibited the use of discriminatory tests to diagnose and place Hispanic, African American, and Asian American children into classes for the mentally retarded. The third factor, an appropriate education, is mandated in the Individuals with Disabilities Education Act (IDEA, originally PL 94–142). This federal legislation guaranteed that all students with disabilities are entitled to an education tailored to their particular needs and abilities. Furthermore, this law safeguards the rights of both students and parents.

These forces notwithstanding, the nature of cultural diversity in relation to exceptionality is not nearly as clear or straightforward as we would like. As a matter of fact, there are a number of problems. Consequently, it is well worth looking more closely at problems surrounding this issue. If we can understand the problems, perhaps we can do something about them.

THE NATURE OF CULTURAL DIVERSITY: DEFINITION AND PREVALENCE

The United States is a nation that prides itself on the fact that the many people who first came to this country were from a variety of ethnic backgrounds, were able to live in relative harmony, and collectively were able to build a strong, democratic society. Over the years, the ethnicity of these people was largely subsumed; everyone was an American. Nevertheless, while we do not today think of people of Italian heritage as an ethnic minority, we do think of other groups, such as American Indians, Asian Americans, African Americans, and Hispanics, in this way. Very recently, we have also witnessed the immigration of other people such as Southeast Asians, Haitians, and Cubans.

What makes these people different? Basically it stems from culture. Hilliard (1980) provided a succinct yet acceptable conceptualization of culture. "*Culture* means the distinctive creativity of a particular group of people. *Creativity* includes world view, values, style, and above all language" (p. 585). Therefore, it follows that the variables of culture cited by Hilliard will differ, at times significantly, across ethnic groups. Unfortunately, customs and social values can set individuals apart from the majority in negatively perceived ways.

At one level, cultural diversity is a desirable feature of life. Exposure to diversity exposes us to different people and customs. However, when cultural differences are great and/or when they are set in the context of formal schooling, significant problems often arise. Aragon (1974) referred to this situation as "cultural conflict." In our country, the major discrepancy is between the culture of various minority groups and the Anglo American culture upon which the public school system is based and implemented throughout the country. Although discussing IQ testing, Gonzalez (1974) used a term that is quite apropos for referring to the fact that our schools are oriented in a single direction—in other words, *Anglocentric*.

An example of how cultural values can differ across various groups follows. Selected items related to how "an individual" is viewed from five cultural perspectives are presented in Table 12.1.

The fundamental cause of cultural conflict comes from trying to achieve a "cultural fit." As the vignettes demonstrate, we often attempt to fit culturally diverse students into a system that is frequently at odds with the way they are, the way they think, and the way they behave. If we truly adhere to the ideal that each student's individuality must be taken into consideration when programming for their educational needs, then it is hypocritical to ignore their cultural heritage.

It is important to remember that just being culturally different does not automatically make one eligible for special education. As mentioned before, it is certainly possible for minority students to have disabilities as well. The perplexing dilemma is distinguishing culturally diverse students with linguistic differences (i.e., non-English proficient [NEP] or limited-English proficient [LEP]) from students who have true language or learning disabilities.

One of the most important factors related to a student's likelihood of ending up in special education relates to socioeconomic status. Children who live in poverty face a number of interactive variables, including (1) a greater likelihood of poor prenatal care and a corresponding likelihood of complications during and after birth; (2) continuing problems related to health and cognitive development, including malnutrition, toxic agents like lead, and poor parental care; and (3) a lack of stimulation and exposure to educational experiences. Because of the direct link between poverty and cultural/ethnic background, students from ethnic and cultural minorities face compounded risks. In 1989, 31.6% of the African American population and 26.8% of the Hispanic population in the United States lived below

Table 12.1
Comparison of Hispanic, Asian, African American, Native American, and Mainstream U.S. Values

Mainstream U.S.	Hispanic	Asian	Black	Native American
Nuclear-family-oriented	Extended-family-oriented	Extended-family-oriented	Nuclear- and extended-family-oriented	Extended family and large network units: clan, tribe
Individualistic	Family comes before the individual	Family central focus	Expressive individuality tied to family and community	Belief in rights of individual as well as others
Children socialized to be independent and competitive	Children taught to be obedient, cooperative, and dependent	Children taught to be obedient, cooperative, and dependent	Children taught dependence on family and community	Children are encouraged to be independent, to make decisions
Competition is valued	Cooperation is valued	Cooperation is valued	Loyalty to family and network	Cooperation is valued
Time is valuable; events are tightly scheduled	Time is flexible; events are not tightly scheduled	Time is "elastic," can be stretched or contracted	Most have mainstream time concept, some have flexible time concept	Spatial temporal concept of time; present-oriented
Direct eye contact	Children lower their eyes when reprimanded	Lack of eye contact in deference to authority	Physical touching and verbal expression of emotions	Limited eye contact and physical touching
Direct ways of dealing with issues	Indirect ways of dealing with issues	Indirect, subtle response	Direct and spontaneous expression of feelings	Indirect, no interruptions, use of silence
Likelihood parents to value education	For low-income families, daily survival is more important than education	Parents value education	Parents respond well if school demonstrates interest	Parents are influenced by staff sensitive to their values and needs
Tendency to use and trust outside agencies	Use family and religious personnel, then outside agencies	Agencies are last resort—usually when problem is extremely serious	Takes time to develop trust, but if staff is sensitive, they will listen	Extended family first, then outside agencies as last resort

Source: Adapted from *Developing Cross-Cultural Competence* by E. W. Lynch and M. J. Hanson, 1992, Baltimore: Paul H. Brookes. P.O. Box 10624, Baltimore, MD 21285-0624. Adapted by permission.

the poverty level, compared to 10.1% of the white population (U.S. Bureau of the Census, 1990).

Rapid population growth is occurring among several culturally or ethnically diverse backgrounds, including Hispanic/Latinos, African Americans, and Asians (U.S. Bureau of the Census, 1990). Because the population growth rates of some of these groups are dramatically higher than those for the white population, the public school systems in many states and cities are becoming majority non-white very quickly. There are, consequently, increasing demands on the educational systems to provide appropriate services for the diverse needs represented.

In addition to the cultural differences presented by the increasing number of non-white students, public schools are also dealing more frequently with language differences. Baca and Cervantes (1989) found that in 1980, about 7.9 million school age children spoke languages other than English (a 40% increase from 5 years earlier). They also estimated that almost 1 million students had both a linguistic difference and a disability. Baca and Cervantes, as well as others, have suggested that by the year 2000, the general non-English speaking population will have grown to 40 million people.

MAJOR ISSUES

Many issues are involved in educating exceptional students from culturally diverse backgrounds. Only a selected number of them are addressed in this chapter, however. The major concerns discussed include (1) the disproportionate number of minority students who are in special classes, (2) the problems related to assessment of these students, and (3) the elements of an appropriate education for these students.

Disproportionate Numbers

As early as 1968, Dunn suggested that special education classes contained disproportionate numbers of ethnically different children. Other documentation (Killalea Associates, 1980; Mercer, 1973) supported this point of view. For example, Chinn and Kamp (1982), in reporting on data accumulated by the Office of Civil Rights, stated that "Blacks constituted 38 percent of the EMR (educable mentally retarded) students, which is over twice the percentage found in the general population (16 percent)" (p. 372).

Issues of over- or underrepresentation continue to be of concern. However, the categories have changed. For example, there appears to be less focus today on disproportionate representation in the area of mental retardation. In the latest report from the U.S. Department of Education (1993), it was noted that the number of students in the mental retardation category has declined. The report hypothesized that one of the reasons may be recent " . . . court rulings that stipulated that many minority group children had been inappropriately diagnosed as having mental retardation, because of discriminatory assessment and classification procedures . . ." (p. 8). There have also been concerns that non-English speaking students are overidentified with speech-language impairments or learning disabilities. However, as educators have become more knowledgeable about the issue of *difference v. disability,* there is some hope that students with language differences are less likely to be over represented in these two categories. In the area of serious emotional disturbance, there is a general feeling that students are under identified, although overrepresentation of African American students has sometimes been a focus in this group as well. In the area of gifted education, however, students from ethnically or linguistically different groups have traditionally been *under* represented.

It was during the early 1970s that concern regarding this unequal representation reached the point that advocacy groups and parents began to initiate litigation. Quite notable among the court cases were *Larry P. v. Riles, Diana v. State of California,* and *Lau v. Nichols. Larry P.* was a class action suit filed in federal district court in California on behalf of African American students who were allegedly placed inappropriately into classes for students with mental retardation. The case was decided in favor of the plaintiffs and upheld twice upon appeal. A major factor in this case was the use of discriminatory testing practices to identify African American students in this category. The *Diana* case, also filed in federal district court in California, involved virtually the same issues; however, this time the plaintiffs were Hispanic. This case, although settled out of court, resulted in acknowledgment that Hispanic students had been inappropriately placed. It also articulated guidelines for the future assessment and placement of other minority students. *Lau* was a case involving Chinese-speaking students in California. The Supreme Count unanimously decided that these students whose primary language was not English were being denied a meaningful education in a system where instruction was presented solely in the language of the majority (MacMillan, 1982).

It should be obvious that a primary cause of the disproportionate representation of minority students seems to be the methods by which we determine eligibility for special education. Furthermore, as illustrated by the arguments in *Lau v. Nichols,* a very limited range of appropriate and cost effective options seems to be available to school systems for educating minority students. Even though special education is conceptually based on the principle that teaching methodology and materials are geared to the individual needs of students who differ from their school age counterparts, it is not the best setting for students who are not disabled but rather culturally different. However, special education *may be* appropriate for those culturally different students who also have disabilities (see the conclusion of this chapter).

Assessment

Criticism has long been levied at the nature and practices of assessing culturally different students. Attention has primarily focused on the issue of bias. Both the standardized tests used in comprehensive assessments as well as the ways in which these tests are used have come under scrutiny. As early as 1977, research by Algozzine and others (Algozzine & Curran, 1978) found that issues influencing referral and identification included (1) the extent to which the student's behavior is disturbing to the teacher and (2) the perceived "teachability" of the student. The extent to which a student varies on these criteria from typical students in a given teacher's classroom, coupled with the teacher's ability to deal with student diversity, is critically related to whether a student is referred and labeled with a disability (McLeskey & Waldron, 1991). From this perspective, rather than relying on standardized tests, the teacher becomes the test for determining whether a student has a learning or behavior problem in his or her classroom. If, indeed, this teacher-as-test model reflects certain aspects of practice, then technical solutions to obtain more precise procedures for identifying students with learning disabilities are doomed to failure (McLeskey & Waldron, 1991).

The following are among the many problems found with most of the tests used for making educational decisions:

- Test information and questioning techniques are related to the majority culture (Nazarro, 1979).
- Tests demand linguistic styles that are similar to the majority culture (Bailey & Harbin, 1980).
- Norms are obtained from standardization samples that are mostly white and middle class (Bailey & Harbin, 1980).

Other problems, more specifically related to student performance variables, have also been cited:

- Minority students show a reluctance to participate in such a way as to maximize performance (Nazarro, 1979).
- Cognitive styles of minority students differ from the majority culture (Chinn & Kamp, 1982).

Cummins (1984) has highlighted some other problems associated with the assessment process. First, psychologists and teachers do not seem to be sensitive to the limitations of formal tests typically used with minority language children. For students being tested in a language not their own with items that sometimes reflect a culture not their own, the entire assessment process may be suspect. In addition, despite many recent efforts, we are still faced with a shortage of appropriate tests in languages other than English. Several publishers have begun to produce tests in Spanish, but they are limited in number and scope.

Second, there is a distinction between *surface language*, or the language used in basic interpersonal communication, and the higher level language *proficiency* needed to deal successfully with various cognitive/academic tasks. This distinction is particularly important when examining the skill levels of students whose primary language (L1) is not English (L2): Most individuals require at least 5 to 7 years to approach grade norms in L2 academic skills. However, because students may demonstrate peer-appropriate L2 conversational skills within about 2 years of arrival, teachers and appraisal personnel students often *seem* more proficient than they really are (Cummins, 1984). Formal measures such as the verbal scale of the *Weschler Intelligence Scale for Children,* when administered to NEP/LEP students, may be inappropriate because they require deeper metacognitive skills in the second language than the student has had an opportunity to master. Langdon (1983) has suggested that it may be unwise to subject students who have been in this country less than a year to the typical test batteries, unless there are circumstances requiring immediate attention.

It may be well worth taking a closer look at examples of test items that are very much culturally determined. Gouveia (n.d.) has developed an instrument entitled *The Hana-Butta Test*. He derived this test from Hawaiian plantation culture. A few examples from *The Hana-Butta Test* illustrate the nature of a culturally specific, or biased, test:

- A "puka" is a:
  a. fish
  b. star
  c. curve
  d. hole
  e. vine

- A woman who is "hapai" is:
  a. available
  b. married
  c. pregnant
  d. sexy
  e. a mother

- "Hana-butta" is known statewide as:
  a. high-fat butter made in Hana
  b. margarine from the Hana Dairy
  c. A famous peanut butter shake from Tutu's Snack Bar, Hana
  d. mucus running from the nose of a person with a bad cold
  e. a peanut butter sandwich

If you answered the above questions by choosing letters *d, c,* and *d,* respectively, you are correct. However, chances are that unless you have lived in Hawaii or have visited Hawaii and spent considerable time outside of Waikiki, you did not know the answers. It is obvious that cultural background can be very important when answering culturally specific questions. For many culturally different students, taking tests that have been based on white, middle-class experiences and values may prove just as difficult. Furthermore, poor performance on assessments may lead to identification and placement in special education programs, even though culture, *not* disability, is limiting a student's apparent mastery of critical information.

Suggestions have been offered to minimize the negative effects of bias inherent in traditional assessment practices. Chinn (1980) presented five ways in which the assessment of culturally different students can be improved:

1. Use culture-free tests.
2. Develop tests that are specific to one culture and thereby deemed as fair.
3. Use culture-fair tests (usually designed to minimize linguistic requirements).
4. Modify existing tests in order to create new norms and change the test sample.

5. Differentially weigh verbal and nonverbal portions of the present intelligence and achievement tests (p. 54).

Additional recommendations include:

1. Obtain pertinent school record information and information from parents/guardians (Langdon, 1983).
2. Collect data over longer periods of time—"longitudinal monitoring" (Cummins, 1984).
3. Delay eligibility assessment practices until students have had a chance to become language proficient.

One instrument that has been developed with cultural differences in mind is the *System of Multicultural Pluralistic Assessment (SOMPA)* (see Chinn and Kamp, 1982; or Mercer and Lewis, 1977). Cummins (1984) has stated that instruments such as the *Kaufmann Assessment Battery for Children* (Kaufman & Kaufman, 1983) and the *Learning Potential Assessment Device* (Feuerstein, 1979) may be more appropriate for use with culturally different students than the Weschler devices if in the hands of knowledgeable examiners.

The problems of bias in assessment are not only specific to the tests used and student characteristics. There is more to assessment than testing. Bailey and Harbin (1980) have suggested that bias can be found in other stages of the diagnostic and placement process:

> Decision making is a step-by-step process. For example, the steps in the diagnostic and placement process typically include (a) referral, (b) testing, (c) interpretation of results, (d) determination of eligibility, (e) recommendation for placement, and (f) actual placement. While much criticism has been aimed at the testing component of this process, each step has the potential for bias against certain individuals or groups of children (p.594).

Assuming that we can adequately identify and effectively place culturally diverse students with disabilities, we are now faced with the task of providing them with an appropriate education. This is not an easy objective to accomplish.

Appropriate Education

"It should be clear that cultural diversity requires no unusual special education" (Hilliard, 1980, p. 587). This statement is both true and false depending on the level of analysis. On a very general level, it can be argued that special education for minority students involves the same type of individualized programming to which all students with disabilities are entitled. On a more specific level, however, it becomes evident that in order to address the needs of some minority students, it may be necessary to undertake some major changes.

One type of programming alternative in some school districts is *bilingual special education*. Baca and Chinn (1982) have defined this approach as the "use of the home language and the home culture along with English in the individually designed program of special education for the student" (p. 42). Two types of bilingual programs include transitional and maintenance programs (ERIC, n.d.) and characterize variant philosophies. *Transitional programs* are designed with the primary goal of making linguistically different students competent in the use of English. *Maintenance programs* strive to develop competence in both languages (L1 and L2) and in both cultural environments. Although the maintenance type of program is attractive to many bilingual educators, the transitional is the most commonly found program. Relatively few maintenance type bilingual classes exist because few people who are professionally qualified as special education teachers are also bilingual. Moreover, some professionals who support a philosophy of cultural assimilation oppose bilingual education.

A program often confused with bilingual education is *English as a Second Language* (ESL) (Baca & Cervantes, 1989). The principal focus of ESL programs is to develop English proficiency, only one of the goals of bilingual education. As was pointed out earlier, bilingual education also attempts to develop students' native language and culture.

If the ultimate goal is appropriate education and if it is to be provided to culturally different students (whether disabled or not), the following areas should be addressed. *Teaching techniques* should be identified and implemented that take into account a student's linguistic background, cognitive and learning styles, and other learning-related characteristics. *Curriculum modifications* are necessary in order to acknowledge what Aragon (1974) called "the life style and heritage of all our students" (p. 28). Most of the curricular materials used in our schools still reflect a predominately Anglocentric perspective.

Almanza and Mosley (1980) have referred to traditional curriculum as having "a monolithic orientation relative to race, ethnicity, and culture" (p. 608). Instructional materials should be sensitive to cultural differences and encompass a wide range of cultural values and heritages. Moreover, classroom practices and methodology should be compatible with the culture of the students in a variety of ways that contribute to effective education. The majority culture has traditionally found its values and heritage reflected in teaching materials; why should it not be so for minority cultures as well? As educators, our goal must be to prepare competent citizens who demonstrate purpose and possess self-worth. Without cultural relevancy in school subjects:

> . . . the culturally different student who comes through our school system is bewildered and frustrated. By the time he finishes, he doesn't know what has "truth, beauty, or value"—whether it's those things he's learned and practiced at home (Aragon, 1974, p. 29).

Teacher Competencies

A corollary to this topic of appropriate education is the need for appropriately prepared teachers. Jones (1976) has reported that teacher attitudes and expectations toward minority students are negative in many instances. If this is true, then it may be prudent to provide pre-service and in-service teachers with accurate information on and techniques for working with various cultural groups. Suitable models for incorporating multicultural concepts into teacher training programs in special education have been developed (see Rodriguez, 1982). Researchers such as Banks and Banks, 1989; Bennett, 1990; and Sleeter and Grant, 1988, have recommended that the following requirements be included within the teacher education curriculum:

1. At least one course in multicultural education that takes into consideration the needs of all students
2. Information about the history and culture of students from a wide number of ethnic, racial, linguistic, and cultural backgrounds
3. Content about the contributions made by various groups
4. Information about first and second language acquisition and effective teaching practices for working with students from limited English proficient (LEP) backgrounds
5. Field experiences and student teaching opportunities with students from varying backgrounds (Coballes-Vega, 1992).

CONCLUSIONS

Earlier in this chapter, a statement was made that indicated that special education *may be* appropriate for students who are culturally different *and* disabled. The uncertainty of the *may be* stems from a number of *ifs:*

if we can effectively identify culturally diverse students who are disabled

if we can develop appropriate placements, suitable techniques, relevant materials, and individualized programs for teaching these students

if we can adequately prepare competent professionals

then and only then will we be able to provide an education that is *appropriate* and *special.*

Although progress is being made, it still remains "easier to identify the problems of educating culturally diverse exceptional children than it is to solve the problems" (Baca & Chinn, 1982, p. 41).

SUGGESTIONS FOR WORKING WITH PERSONS WHO ARE CULTURALLY DIFFERENT

The following competencies were originally developed by Bessant-Byrd (1981, pp. 94–103) for teachers who work with diverse populations of students:

1. Knowledge of the role of a value system and ability to evaluate its influence on behavior
2. Knowledge of the philosophy of various cultures and an interest in expanding that knowledge
3. Use of relevant information and materials characteristic of both traditional and contemporary lifestyles of various cultures
4. Understanding of different patterns of human growth and development within and between cultures
5. Recognition of potential cultural and linguistic biases in the composition, administration, and interpretation of existing assessment instruments
6. The ability to provide a flexible learning environment that meets individual needs of learners from various culture groups

When working with parents of students with cultural, ethnic, or linguistic differences, Walker (1993) has suggested some strategies to maximize overall academic progress:

1. Try to involve community resources, including churches and neighborhood organizations, in school activities.
2. Make home visits.

3. Allow flexible hours for conferences.

4. Question your own assumptions about human behavior, values, biases, personal limitations, etc.

5. Try to understand the world from the students' perspective.

6. Ask yourself questions about an individual student's behavior in light of cultural values, motivation, and world views, and how these relate to his/her learning experiences.

✦ PONDER THESE

1. *The* Peabody Individual Achievement Test (PIAT) *assesses general achievement. One subtest in this instrument is entitled "General Information." One of the test items asks, "What do we call the last car on a freight train?" Children from which of the following groups would be unable to answer this question—a failure more related to their cultural upbringing than to a lack of achievement?*

> *Southeast Asians*
>
> *Haitians*
>
> *Hawaiians*
>
> *Native Americans*

2. *List some of the problems and possible solutions for identifying gifted students who come from culturally different groups.*

3. *How are students from culturally diverse groups affected when the educational curriculum differs from their knowledge of their own cultural heritage? For example, how might a Native American child react when told that Christopher Columbus discovered their country?*

4. *Do you believe that discipline procedures should vary, depending on the student's background? What if parents use physical punishment to discipline their children and say that physical punishment is considered appropriate in their culture, yet you as a teacher do not condone this type of intervention?*

References

Algozzine, B. (1977). The emotionally disturbed child: Disturbed or disturbing? *Journal of Abnormal Child Psychology, 5,* 205–211.

Algozzine, B., & Curran, T. J. (1978). Teachers' predictions of children's school success as a function of their behavioral tolerances. *Journal of Educational Research, 72,* 344–347.

Almanza, H. P., & Mosley, W. J. (1980). Curriculum adaptations and modifications for culturally diverse handicapped children. *Exceptional Children, 46,* 608–613.

Aragon, J. (1974). Cultural conflict and cultural diversity in education. In L. A. Bransford, L. Baca, & K. Lane (Eds.), *Cultural diversity and the exceptional child,* (pp. 24–31). Reston, VA: The Council for Exceptional Children.

Baca, L. M., & Cervantes, H. T. (1989). *The bilingual special education interface* (2nd ed.). St. Louis, MO: Mosby.

Baca, L., & Chinn, P. C. (1982). Coming to grips with cultural diversity. *Exceptional Education Quarterly, 2*(4), 33–45.

Bailey, D. B., & Harbin, G. L. (1980). Nondiscriminatory evaluation. *Exceptional Children, 46,* 590–596.

Banks, J. A. (1994, May). Transforming the mainstream curriculum. *Educational Leadership,* 4–8.

Banks, J. A., & Banks, C. M. (1989). *Multicultural education: Issues and perspectives.* Needham Heights, MA: Simon & Schuster.

Bennett, C. (1990). *Comprehensive multicultural education.* Boston: Allyn & Bacon.

Bessant-Byrd, H. (1981). Competencies for educating culturally different exceptional children. In J. N. Nazarro (Ed.), *Culturally diverse exceptional children in school.* Reston, VA: ERIC Clearinghouse on Handicapped and Gifted Children.

Chinn, K. A. (1980). Assessment of culturally diverse children. *Viewpoints in Teaching and Learning, 56*(1), 50–63.

Chinn, P. C., & Kamp, S. H. (1982). Cultural diversity and exceptionality. In N. G. Haring (Ed.), *Exceptional children and youth* (3rd ed.) (pp. 371–390). Columbus, OH: Merrill.

Coballes-Vega, C. (1992, January). Considerations in teaching culturally diverse children. *ERIC Digest.*

Cummins, J. (1984). *Bilingualism and special education: Issues in assessment and pedagogy.* San Diego: College-Hill Press.

Dunn, L. M. (1968). Special education for the mildly retarded: Is much of it justifiable? *Exceptional Children, 35,* 5–22.

ERIC. (n.d.). *Bilingual education for exceptional children: Fact sheet*. Reston, VA: ERIC Clearinghouse on Handicapped and Gifted Children.

Fair, G. W., & Sullivan, A. R. (1980). Career opportunities for culturally diverse handicapped youth. *Exceptional Children, 46,* 626–631.

Feuerstein, R. (1979). *The dynamic assessment of retarded performance*. Baltimore: University Park.

Gonzalez, G. (1974). Language, culture, and exceptional children. In L. A. Bransford, L. Baca, & K. Lane (Eds.), *Cultural diversity and the exceptional child* (pp. 2–11). Reston, VA.: The Council for Exceptional Children.

Gouveia, W. (n.d.). *The Hana-Butta Test*. Maui, HI: Author.

Hilliard, A. G. (1980). Cultural diversity and special education. *Exceptional Children, 46,* 584–588.

Jones, R. L., & Wilderson, F. B. (1976). Mainstreaming and the minority child: An overview of issues and a perspective. In R. L. Jones (Ed.), *Mainstreaming and the minority child* (pp. 1–13). Reston, VA.: Council for Exceptional Children.

Kaufman, A., & Kaufman, N. (1983). *Kaufman Assessment Battery for Children*. Circle Pines, MN: American Guidance Service.

Killalea Associates. (1980). *State, regional, and national summaries of data from the 1978 civil rights survey of elementary and secondary schools. Prepared for the U.S. Office of Civil Rights*. Alexandria, VA: Author.

Langdon, H. W. (1983). Assessment and intervention strategies for the bilingual language-disordered student. *Exceptional Children, 50,* 37–46.

MacMillan, D. L. (1982). *Mental retardation in school and society* (2nd ed.). Boston: Little, Brown.

McLeskey, J., & Waldron, N. L. (1991). Identifying students with learning disabilities: The effect of implementing statewide guidelines. *Journal of Learning Disabilities, 24*(8), 501–506.

Mercer, J. R. (1973). *Labeling the mentally retarded*. Berkeley: University of California.

Mercer, J. R., & Lewis, J. F. (1977). *System of Multicultural Pluralistic Assessment: Technical manual*. New York: Psychological Corporation.

Nazarro, J. (1979). *Assessment of minority students* (Fact Sheet). Reston, VA: ERIC Clearinghouse on Handicapped and Gifted Children.

Rodriguez, F. (1982). Mainstreaming a multicultural concept into special education: Guidelines for teacher trainers. *Exceptional Children, 49,* 220–227.

Sleeter, C. E., & Grant, C. A. (1988). *Making choices for multicultural education: Five approaches to race, class, and gender*. Englewood Cliffs, NJ: Merrill/Prentice Hall.

U.S. Bureau of the Census. (1990). *Statistical abstract of the United States: 1990*. Washington, DC: U.S. Government Printing Office.

U.S. Department of Education. (1993). *To assure the free appropriate public education of all children with disabilities. Fifteenth annual report to Congress on the implementation of The Individuals with Disabilities Education Act*. Washington, DC: Author.

Walker, B. (1993, January). *Multicultural issues in education: An introduction*. Paper presented at Cypress-Fairbanks Independent School District In-Service, Cypress, Texas.

FOUR
EXCEPTIONAL
PERSPECTIVES

13
EARLY CHILDHOOD

Darrell was the kind of preschooler every teacher dreads having in the class—a 4-year-old public nuisance. Unable (or unwilling) to follow the simplest directions, he could usually be found poking an innocent classmate or doing his best in any number of ways to disrupt my Head Start class. But Darrell was not incapable of showing affection. I cannot easily forget the day he interrupted his finger painting to "lovingly" hug me and run his paint-covered fingers through my hair. I thought I caught a devilish gleam in his eye when he released his grip, but I quickly dismissed it. Darrell had long been tagged mentally retarded, and his misbehavior, we all knew, was due to his mental disability. Thus, Darrell was forgiven for this and other equally trying acts in the classroom.

It was George Washington's birthday, and I stood the class in a circle and put on a favorite record, "Chopping Down the Cherry Tree." The record was ideal for gross motor development. I instructed the children to swing their arms rhythmically to the "chop" of the music as if they were all little Georges chopping away at the proverbial cherry tree. The children loved it. Everyone swung his imaginary ax with the greatest enthusiasm, everyone of course except "dumb" Darrell, who just stood there with his arms straight out in front of him, hands clasped together making a huge fist. Patiently, I attempted to teach Darrell the act of chopping. But even after much demonstrating and coaxing, he stubbornly refused to change his original position and continued to stand motionless with his "ax" extended. Close to the end of my patience, I cried, "Darrell, why won't you chop with your ax like the rest of us?"

His reply shocked me into reassessing Darrell's mental retardation label: "I don't need to chop. Can't you see I have a power saw!"[1]

Richard was a blond, blue-eyed 6-year-old who had been living in a residential school for emotionally disturbed children for 3 years. On weekends he went home with his family. He was diagnosed as autistic and displayed many of the typical behaviors of children so labeled. Although he was quick to complain with high-pitched squeals, he never spoke and showed no emotion when people talked to him. He avoided eye contact with teachers, staff, or other children, preferring to isolate himself in a corner whenever he could. He liked to hold a toy truck upside down so that he could push its wheels and intently watch them spin. In the hope that some day Richard could learn to make letters and write his name, the staff had spent every school day reinforcing Richard for going to the table and making an approximation of a circle or a triangle, prerequisite skills for writing words. After so many days, weeks, and months of no improvement, the staff became discouraged and feared that Richard would never learn to make shapes, not to mention write his name. It was on one of these days that Richard left his corner, stepped up to the chalkboard, on which he had never written, and in perfect letters wrote, "PANTRY PRIDE." Never having written a letter before, he produced the name of the grocery store where his mother shopped. We were shocked and overjoyed, but our hearts sank when Richard returned to his corner and refused to produce another word. Yet Richard had stepped out of his usual behavior to show us his capacity for learning if only for a few minutes. We were then in a much better position to plan appropriate learning experiences.

Placed in a strange environment, the one thing that preschoolers are not is predictable. Thus, I prepared myself for the worst when I took my Head Start class of 30 inner-city 4-year-olds to the famous Bronx Zoo. How could I expect them to be orderly and restrained? Flashing through my mind were frightful fantasies of Freddy taking a bath with the walruses or Linda slipping through the bars to pet the leopards. To my great surprise, the children were

---

[1]This anecdote was contributed by Ms. Roxana G. Davison.

very well behaved despite their obvious excitement at viewing the many wild animals that had previously only been magazine pictures. My major problem in controlling the children occurred quite unexpectedly as we rounded a corner and faced a large square of lush green grass bearing several "Keep off the grass" signs. After having survived elephant pens and monkey cages, I was hardly concerned about a grassy plot of ground. I was, in fact, stunned when almost every child bolted from our orderly little procession and tumbled onto the grass screaming with delight. It took me several seconds to realize that these inner-city children were growing up playing on concrete sidewalks and black asphalt streets covered with broken glass. That simple plot of green grass gave them their greatest thrill of our entire zoo trip.

Craig was the precocious one of the group. I was continually in awe of his insight and his eagerness to solve the mysteries of his world. Of course, there were a few times when even Craig put two and two together and came up with five.

Craig's mother, a divorcee, was dating an obstetrician. Like so many preschoolers, Craig kept his teachers and classmates well informed about his mother's personal life by frequently making announcements such as, "My mother dates a doctor named Phil, and he delivers real babies."

One day as we were out for a drive, Craig shouted, "Oh, look! There's Dr. Phil's house!" Pointing to a van parked in front of the house, he said, "There's his truck too!"

Since I was acquainted with Dr. Phil and knew that he owned no truck, I said gently, "No, Craig, that truck doesn't belong to Dr. Phil."

Looking me squarely in the eyes, he impatiently retorted, "Well, I bet it is too his truck. He must have a truck because Mommy says he delivers babies!"

RATIONALE FOR EARLY CHILDHOOD EDUCATION

Early scholars such as Montessori, Froebel, and Hall first directed attention toward early childhood as important foundation years for learning. A widespread interest in early childhood education, however, did not develop until the 1960s when psychological research began to reveal that the early years are indeed most critical for a child's future development.

Research findings suggested that the rate of learning roughly parallels a child's physical growth. It appears that learning occurs quite rapidly in the first 2 years, slightly less rapidly for the next 4, and then begins to level off to a lower and gradually decreasing rate. In fact, some assert that 50% of a child's total intellectual capacity has been developed by age 4, and 80% by age 8. Skeels's (1966) classic study of orphanage children dramatically demonstrated that modifying the environment during the early formative years can greatly improve a child's capacity for intellectual and social development at a later age.

More recently, Schweinhart and Weikart (1985) reviewed seven longitudinal studies of the effects of early education on children living in poverty and found that every comparison of scholastic placement was favorable to the group that had received early childhood education. Moreover, avoiding later placement in special education programs emerged as one of the major financial benefits of preschool education (Peterson, 1987).

Today, a sound foundation during the early childhood years is considered essential for subsequent success in school. In fact, Burton White's (1975) research at Harvard University's Pre-School Project led him to conclude that the period that begins at 8 months and ends at 3 years is a period of primary importance to the development of human intelligence and social skill. White insists that "to begin to look at a child's educational development when he is 2 years of age is already much too late" (p. 4). The need for thoughtful and rich early stimulation is critical for all children, particularly for those children with physical, emotional, mental, or social handicaps (Hayden, 1979). McDaniels (1977) argues that we cannot wait until age 6, or even 3, to begin our interventions with young children. Programs for some young exceptional children should begin not long after birth.

This position entails the incorporation of the entire family into the intervention model. Indeed, the family as a system must become the focus of all intervention (Foster, Berger, & McClean, 1981; Turnbull & Turnbull, 1986; Winton & Turnbull, 1981). Such a perspective emphasizes not only the uniqueness of each individual child, but the uniqueness of each specific family. Turnbull, Summers, and Brotherson (1984) outline a framework for understanding the family as a system made up of (1) family resources, (2) family interactions, (3) family functions, and (4) family life cycle.

Nagera (1975) warns that poorly conceived school-based centers for infants and toddlers may do more harm than good. During the 1970s, educators learned that parents play a critical role in facilitating development. Today's educators recognize that well-conceived programs involve parents in the teaching of their young children (Anastasiow, 1981). In particular, home and center-based parent training can greatly change the young exceptional child's chances for developing to his or her full potential (Sandler, Coren, & Thurman, 1983; Shearer & Shearer, 1972; Sontag, 1977).

Legislative action, specifically Public Law 94–142, has mandated programs for all children with disabilities between the ages of 3 and 21. As a result of this significant law, the area of early childhood education has moved into the spotlight of attention. The guarantees of this law assure parental participation, protection of rights, written notification of any placement changes, teacher training efforts, and incentive funding to the states. Efforts to locate and identify preschool age children with disabilities (commonly referred to as *child find*) have been conducted nationwide. A U.S. Department of Education (1984) report to Congress argues that early intervention with children who have disabilities results in significant decreases in services required later. In those cases where early intervention eliminates or reduces the services otherwise needed when the child enters school, it results in notable cost savings.

Although the states were mandated under PL 94–142 to provide services to all students (aged 3 to 21 years) with disabilities, less than half of the states actually initiated services for the full 3- to 5-year-age range. This was due to the limited mandate of PL 94-142 with respect to early childhood special education. This legislation mandated early intervention for young children (under age 3 years) with disabilities only if such services existed for nondisabled children under 3 years.

DEFINITION OF EARLY CHILDHOOD EDUCATION

Early childhood education was traditionally conceived of as the group learning experiences provided for children from the ages of 3 to 8. Thus, programs for early childhood education encompassed nursery schools, kindergartens, and primary grades. The growing realization, however, that infancy and toddlerhood are critical years for later social and intellectual development has largely accounted for the current notion that early childhood education embraces programs for all children under 9 years of age. This notion has been reflected and put into application through PL 99–457 and its emphasis on families and children in the birth to 3 years of age range. Quite logically, a significant proportion of educational and psychological research is now focused on the infant and toddler years and on parental involvement.

Early childhood special education programs are, by necessity, noncategorical in nature. Only a small percentage of those children who eventually make up the special education population in the public schools have identifiable disabilities during the early stages of development. Indeed, it is often the demands of the traditional classroom that make a student's disability apparent. Therefore, professionals in early childhood special education must focus primarily on those factors that place an individual child "at risk" for developing a disability. As a result, students served by early childhood special education programs generally have no categorical label but are often identified as developmentally delayed.

Early childhood education relies on the continued execution of various important dimensions: (1) early identification, (2) continuous assessment, (3) appropriate curricula, (4) effective teaching procedures, (5) parental involvement, and (6) multidisciplinary interaction. The omission of any of these dimensions in any early childhood program is detrimental to the education of children with disabilities. The curriculum for a young child who is disabled is generally determined by the child's strengths and delays in seven areas of development: self-help skills, gross-motor development, fine-motor development, communication skills, perceptual development, conceptual development, and social-emotional development.

PREVALENCE OF YOUNG CHILDREN WITH DISABILITIES

Figures on the number of school age children who are disabled and who are receiving special education and related services are available, as the federal government maintains such data. Exact figures on the number of preschool age children with disabilities do not exist. In 1976, the National Advisory Committee on the Handicapped reported that in the United States, approximately 1,187,000 preschool children displayed physical, emotional, or mental disabilities. Haring and McCormick (1990) note that, of the approximately 3.4 million infants born in this country each year, about 7% have congenital abnormalities that will be identified prior to their becoming school age. To this group, other preschool children who are "at risk" for eventual school problems could be added. This group includes those children who are abused, malnourished, homeless, and/or live in poverty.

Of those children identifiable as needing special services, many are multiply disabled, having secondary deficits accompanying their major disability. Most of the young exceptional children do not fit neatly into the traditional special education categories. Many of the milder disabilities (e.g., mild retardation, learning disabilities) may not be evident until a child is of school age. Many of these children may be considered "at risk" for potential future school failure. They should be provided with services in various early intervention programs that do not specifically identify them as "disabled."

Some states have designated special categorical distinctions for preschool age children with disabilities. Terms such as *learning impaired* may be used with this population until these children reach school age. Then a reevaluation would be conducted and the children would be either declassified or reclassified. Unfortunately, some infants and preschoolers with disabilities are not receiving the educational experiences necessary to insure continued progress and later successful school adjustment.

ETIOLOGY

The causes of disabilities in young children can be divided into five major categories: (1) genetic, (2) prenatal, (3) perinatal, (4) postnatal, and (5) environmental. Although a child's difficulty often results from a complex interaction of two or more factors, most educators focus attention on remediation rather than search for causes. However, remediation can sometimes be facilitated when etiological, or causative, factors are understood.

Genetic difficulties include biochemical disorders, such as galactosemia and phenylketonuria (PKU), and such chromosomal abnormalities as Down syndrome. Today both PKU and galactosemia can be detected by urine tests, and, if found early enough, the harmful effects can be controlled by putting the infant on special diets. Some *prenatal* conditions frequently associated with childhood disabilities are (1) anoxia (i.e., premature separation of the placenta), severe anemia, or a heart condition of the mother; (2) Rh factor incompatibility; and (3) rubella contracted by the mother during the first trimester of pregnancy. Birth injuries, asphyxia, and prematurity are among the *perinatal* conditions that may affect the child during or immediately preceding birth. During infancy and early childhood, disabling conditions can result from malnutrition, accidental physical trauma (especially to the brain), child abuse/neglect, and diseases and infections such as encephalitis, meningitis, and chronic otitis media. Finally, it appears that a great proportion of the children suffering from school learning difficulties have simply not received the necessary experiential and cultural prerequisites such as social and educational stimulation.

Obviously, the early medical, nutritional, social, and educational needs of children must be satisfied in order to maximize their opportunities for healthy development. And it is equally true that the sooner an etiological factor is arrested or ameliorated, the less profound will be its debilitating effects. Unfortunately, early delivery of services, which may be of great importance to some young children and their families, is frequently difficult. Not only are funds and services limited but also the identification of children with less severe but potential disabling conditions is no easy task.

LANGUAGE DEVELOPMENT

That language and intellectual competence are closely intertwined is becoming increasingly obvious. Often accompanying immature language are such immature thought processes as delayed discrimination and reasoning skills. Indeed, severe language delay or inadequacy is the most significant single behavioral sign indicating a young child's need for special help in order to succeed in school.

Socialization depends upon experiences with language and communication. The ability to abstract the essence of experiences and the urge and power to express complex thoughts and feelings are uniquely human. Although animals may respond to symbols for specific things, such as a dog knowing he is going for a walk when he sees his leash, only people can generalize from their experiences and share an analysis and synthesis of their ideas with others. From infancy on, human learning is dependent upon the acquisition of the communication code of that culture.

The very young child faces the task of learning to understand the world's confusing happenings. Understanding is restricted to the immediate and concrete during early childhood. Concomitant with the development of language skills, the child gradually begins to deal with abstractions, and begins to use symbolization in more complex ways.

Unfortunately, as all educators know, the path leading from simple and concrete communication to the complex and abstract variety of understanding is a treacherous one that can be followed only if the child is afforded appropriate environmental experiences. A rich and stimulating language environment during the early childhood years is required to develop the verbal and intellectual skills essential for later school success (Horton, 1974; Vygotsky, 1978; White, 1975). Moreover, to develop intellect and expressive skills, a child must be provided with stimulating sensory and social experiences that involve the child emotionally and help create a need for communication. Clearly, insufficient and unsatisfying experiences with the social and physical worlds can hamper the drive to talk and question. They may eventually reduce the child's motivation and create language and thought patterns that cause school failure.

The language patterns of many children from lower socioeconomic levels are a source of considerable concern to linguists, psychologists, and educators. The language of lower-class children often differs significantly from the standard English spoken by middle-class children and expected by teachers within the public schools. Bereiter and Engelmann (1966) go so far as to equate cultural deprivation with language deprivation, insisting that for lower-class children to succeed in school, they must learn the middle-class language of the school system. Similarly, Bloom, Davis, and Hess (1965) treat the speech of lower-class children in terms of "language deficit." They maintain that the language and future learning of lower-class children are inhibited because their parents are less likely to provide the quantity and quality of verbal "corrective feedback" found in typical middle-class environments. Unfortunately, viewing a child from a language-deficit perspective suggests that the child is deprived of a structurally systematic and functionally adequate language. Further, it suggests that the lower-class child is generally deprived of culturalization when, in fact, the deprivation may relate only to middle-class culture. Hence, perceiving the lower-class child as having "language differences" rather than "language deficiencies" is preferable (Baratz, 1969).

Whether viewed as different or deficient, the language used by lower-class children in their homes frequently varies considerably from that used in school. Hess and Shipman (1967) conducted class related research that found language learning and intellectual growth to be by-products of the verbal interaction between mother and child. Their research revealed that middle-class mothers most often employed a democratic type of control, used expanded sentences, and provided labels for objects. Most lower-class mothers, on the other hand, used an imperative type of control, spoke in a restricted form of language, and failed to provide their children with labels for objects. Although language style does vary within lower socioeconomic groups, lower-class children typically develop a mode of communication, perhaps adequate at home, which nonetheless may not be sufficient for progress in school.

Language difficulties, however, are not unique to lower-class youngsters. Many middle- and upper-class parents fail to provide their children with a language environment conducive to later school success. Moreover, language disabilities result not only from faulty learning but often from emotional disturbance, hearing impairment, central nervous system dysfunction, and mental retardation, none of which knows social class distinctions.

EARLY INTERVENTION PROJECTS

Head Start

Because large numbers of children within the lower class have experienced school difficulties, the nation's first comprehensive effort to provide prerequisite educational opportunities focused on economically disadvantaged children. Within this population were found the highest incidence of language differences as well as all other types of disabilities. The first nationwide program specifically designed for children likely to experience later educational difficulties was Project Head Start. Head Start programs began with the hope of providing not only rich language environments but also a wide range of health, nutritional, and educational experiences for economically disadvantaged preschoolers.

The commencement of Project Head Start in the spring of 1965 engendered hope in some circles of one day significantly reducing personal failure and poverty in society. Born under the auspices of the Office of Economic Opportunity, Project Head Start authorized the organization and establishment of 6-week summer programs for children whose family income fell below the poverty level set by Congress. Geared to the early childhood years, the program attempted to provide whatever environmental supplements were needed to prevent failure in the elementary grades. Following the first summer's operation, Head Start programs for the full academic year were initiated. Although the personnel of early Head Start centers were left free to determine specific objectives and their means of achievement, greater levels of program specificity were gradually introduced. And because of abundant differences in beliefs among centers as to the needs of children, substantial variation in programs developed. The creators of some programs emphasized development of social skills while others concentrated on the development of good health and dietary habits. Many programs resembled a traditional nursery school, but others emphasized intensive directive instruction in language, reading-readiness skills, science, and math. Thus, Head Start was in effect many different programs with centers varying widely in terms of what and how they taught.

One of the most innovative and exciting aspects of Project Head Start was its concept of parent involvement. Active parents can add continuity to the child's home and school experiences while also encouraging at-home practice of the cognitive skills disadvantaged children may lack. In addition, a parent's active contribution to the child's education often engenders new feelings of adequacy and self-worth in the parent that, in turn, may enhance affectional relationships in the home (Evans, 1971). However, while federal Head Start officials encouraged parent participation, they failed to adequately specify how parents were to be involved; and there was substantial variation from center to center.

The nationwide interest in early childhood education and the exciting possibilities presented by Project Head Start appear in retrospect to have generated some unfortunate side effects. Amid the excitement, child development experts failed to caution the nation that a 6-week summer session or even a full-year program prior to school entrance would provide only a beginning in meeting the educational needs of young children. And specialists did not adequately inform the public that the scientific study of child development, in its infancy, could provide only a few clues about the necessary social and educational experiences required for optimal development of young children. Moreover, at the time, educators had not fully recognized the critical influence of the years from birth to age 3 and had not included infants and toddlers in the project. Thus, expectations of success for Head Start ran unrealistically high.

Although significant increases on cognitive measures were found, especially from those children from the southeastern geographical region and from large urban areas (Caldwell, 1972; Payne, Mercer, Payne, & Davison, 1973), the effects of the Head Start experience appeared to wash out as children entered school.

Some time after the initiation of Head Start, the nation's attitude toward early intervention became perceptibly more skeptical, and disillusionment displaced the former climate of optimism. Although Head Start had doubtlessly helped many young children overcome classroom difficulties, it failed to realize its promise of healing the nation's educational ills. Unfortunately, Head Start as initially conceived did not include many important aspects of educational planning more clearly understood by today's educators.

Educators now know that unless the content of a program is carefully defined, a preschool is just another place for a child to be (Schweinhart, Berrueta-Clement, Barnett, Epstein, & Weikart, 1985). Current Head Start programs have improved their content and are proving to have significant short- and long-term positive effects on low-income children (Schweinhart & Weikart, 1985). Today the federal government invests about a billion and a half dollars annually in such early childhood programs.

After the need for early educational experiences for children with disabilities received wide recognition in the late 1960s, Head Start legislation was amended to require that at least 10% of the enrollment opportunities in each state be made available to these children. Although the available spaces do not begin to equal the number of young children with disabilities, today many exceptional preschoolers are participating in this program.

Follow Through

In many primary schools throughout the nation, Project Follow Through has been implemented as a means of sustaining early gains produced by Head Start experiences. Authorized in 1968 under the Office of Economic Opportunity, the programs provide continued educational enrichment for primary-grade children formerly enrolled in Head Start classes. Clearly, all special services for young children have the greatest chance for lasting success when continued assistance is provided in the elementary grades.

Originally conceived as an extension of Head Start, Follow Through changed its focus as time progressed. The Office of Education altered it so that it was described as a "planned variation experiment." The major portion of a report conducted on this project was produced by Abt Associates, Inc. Their data analysis compared various features of thirteen of the early intervention models.

Although many conclusions could be drawn from the final report, there seemed to be two major findings: (1) the existence of substantial intersite variation across programs and (2) the superiority of the "basic skills" type of model. House, Glass, McLean, and Walker (1978) reviewed the evaluation, giving support to the first finding but seriously questioning the second. In their article, they present a number of arguments that challenge the second conclusion. House and his colleagues stress the very intricate dynamics of Project Follow Through and the lack of definitive answers:

> The truth about Follow Through is complex. No simple answer to
> the problem of educating disadvantaged students has been
> found. . . . Unique features of the local settings had more effect on
> test scores than did the models. This does not mean that federal
> programs are useless or inappropriate for pursuing national objec-
> tives; however, many of the most significant factors affecting educa-
> tional achievement lie outside the control of federal officials
> (p. 156).

Project RUN

Project RUN (Reach Us Now) is an early intervention program that focuses on the needs of children with disabilities (birth to 3 years of age) and their families. This program, which is funded and operated by the Mississippi Department of Mental Health, primarily serves children with severe to moderate disabilities. The program incorporates both the center-based and the home-based service delivery approaches, a parent training component, and multidisciplinary assessment/intervention. Project RUN emphasizes developmentally appropriate intervention, basic skill instruction, sensory stimulation, assistive technology, physical/occupational therapy, and facilitative parent-child interactions in its approach. The project serves persons in the 23 primarily rural counties of North Mississippi.

Project RUN also focuses on connecting parents and their children with disabilities with appropriate local services and assisting in the transition of the children into special education programs offered by their local school district. Approximately 83% of those students served by Project RUN make a successful transition to public school programs.

RECENT FEDERAL INITIATIVES SUPPORTING PRESCHOOL PROGRAMS

Four federal initiatives—Education for All Handicapped Children Act-B (EHA-B), the Preschool Incentive Grant Program, the State Implementation Grant Program, and the Handicapped Children's Early Education Program (HCEEP)—have played a critical role in encouraging preschool programs. The U.S. Department of Education (1984) reports that the number of states choosing to participate in these preschool programs has more than doubled since fiscal year 1978. They report that the accomplishments of the HCEEP, better known as the First Chance Network, are greater and more varied than those of any other documented education program.

In 1986, PL 99–457 was signed. This legislation was designed to amend and expand the mandate of PL 94–142, thus extending the rights and protections of PL 94–142 to all young children with disabilities who are 3 to 5 years of age. States applying for funds under PL 94–142 must provide assurances that all children with disabilities who are 3 through 5 years old are receiving a free, appropriate education at public expense. In addition, PL 99–457 provides for a state grant program addressing the needs of infants and toddlers (i.e., birth to 3 years of age) with disabilities through early intervention. Parent/family support, resource centers, and the development of individual family service plans (IFSPs), which are similar in concept to individual education plans (IEPs), are required under PL 99–457.

Furthermore, the law mandates interagency agreements to meet the needs of the target population. Social service agencies must now work cooperatively with educational agencies to serve children with disabilities and their families. A legal basis now exists for early intervention services to all young children who are disabled. States now have the opportunity to provide appropriate service delivery to persons with disabilities during the most critical stage of their development, birth through 5 years of age.

MAJOR ISSUES IN EARLY CHILDHOOD EDUCATION

Educational Strategies

Today, there are a variety of intervention strategies as evidenced by the variety of models in the Follow Through Project. The Follow Through Project classifies their various orientations into three main categories (Stebbins, St. Pierre, Proper, Anderson, & Cerva, 1977, pp. 131–132):

1. Basic Skills: These models focus first on the elementary skills of vocabulary, arithmetic computation, spelling, and language.
2. Cognitive-Conceptual: These models emphasize the more complex "learning-to-learn" and problem-solving skills.
3. Affective-Cognitive: These models focus primarily on self-concept and attitudes toward learning, and secondarily on "learning-to-learn" skills.

Underlying each of these orientations is a theoretical foundation derived from years of psychological research. Although a full discussion of these orientations currently in use is beyond the scope of this book, we can presently state that more research is needed before establishing the superiority of any specific orientation.

Parent Involvement

In past years the advice given to parents of exceptional children by physicians, teachers, and psychologists was often ill-founded: "Just wait and see what happens. He'll probably grow out of it." Instead, difficulties were compounded and the children fell further and further behind their nondisabled peers.

Clearly, the efforts to educate parents and to involve them in the total educational program of their child are warranted. The impact of parental (or primary caregiver) behavior is so profound that it not only greatly influences intelligence (Garber & Heber, 1973; White, 1975) but even affects the rate of neuromotor attainments such as sitting, crawling, and walking (Anastasiow, 1981; Kearsley, 1979). Furthermore, not only does the parent affect the child, but the presence of a child with a disability can have a powerful influence on parents. As Hayden (1978) points out: "Having a handicapped child can be a traumatic experience for parents, not only when they first learn of the child's disability but throughout the child's growing years" (p. 42).

Although some parents are quick to recognize when something is wrong with their child, some parents have difficulty accepting the reality of their child's disability. Such reality avoidance often prevents the child with a disability from receiving professional attention in the early years when remediation could be advantageous. And this unfortunate fact underscores the importance of the teacher's role in identifying disabilities.

The amendments to the Education for all Handicapped Children Act (PL 99–457) assure parental involvement and that efforts to get them involved through the development of individual family service plans (IFSPs) are underway. Although some disabling conditions are immediately obvious, others are more subtle and difficult to detect. Developmental lags or deviations in children are frequently overlooked because parents lack basic knowledge concerning child development and have little opportunity to compare their child's development with that of others (Allen, Rieke, Dmitriev, & Hayden, 1972). Moreover, even those few parents who can quickly detect minor disabilities in other children can be oblivious to their own child's slight limp, speech delay, or vision impairment. Understandably, many parents find it difficult to admit that their child is disabled.

Identification

Teachers should proceed with considerable caution, however, in their efforts to avail children with disabilities of needed services. Their job should be simply to observe the children carefully and alert parents that additional help *may* be needed. Teachers must remember that they are not in a position to render a definitive medical diagnosis of a disorder.

Before causing parents needless alarm, teachers should recognize that whether or not a particular developmental skill is appropriate may depend on the community in which the child lives. Personal judgments of disability may be subject to cultural or educational bias. Branding a child as disabled can have devastating effects on his or her self-esteem, and the label may well become a self-fulfilling prophecy. Stated differently, low expectations can encourage low performance.

Clearly, it is within the teacher's proper role to observe children carefully and to obtain professional assistance in interpreting behavioral signs. Appropriate parental warnings and referrals for further diagnosis should be made only after the teacher systematically records observations of the child's behavior. All early childhood teachers should familiarize themselves with developmental, age-appropriate behaviors and with potentially troublesome behaviors in young children. Teachers should keep in mind that even among "normal" children vast differences abound in the physical, social, and intellectual growth rates of individuals. Only those children who after careful observation appear well behind their peers in some basic facet of development will need to be referred for further diagnosis and special services. (For lists of specific behaviors indicative of potential problems, see Allen et al., 1972; and Wallace & Kauffman, 1986.)

In addition to the teacher's identification of students who need special services, there is now a trend toward the early identification of infants with disabilities. With our present knowledge, approximately 6.8% of children with disabilities can be identified at birth or very shortly thereafter. Pediatricians, then, are in the best position to identify infants and toddlers who are disabled, and, if appropriately trained, can communicate helpful suggestions to parents. Major efforts are currently being made to educate physicians in normal and exceptional child development (Guralnick, Richardson, & Heiser, 1982). Techniques for postnatal evaluation are presently available. To be useful, or perhaps justified, this early identification must be followed up with the appropriate commensurate services. Presently, only a few of these services are available to neonates with disabilities. However, along with increasing research in this area emphasizing the importance of the child's first 3 years of life, appropriate services are being developed as well.

Prevention

Early identification and intervention sometimes become a vehicle for preventing or inhibiting the further development of disabling conditions. If services for the child and the parents can be provided at a very early point in the infant's development, many major problems can be avoided at a later time. However, the prevention of severe problems also depends on the continued improvement of medical and health services and on the ability to improve environmental factors (e.g., proper nutrition, adequate medical care, and healthy living conditions).

CONCLUSION

Early childhood programs are here to stay. Research has clearly documented their importance. We have no substantial evidence, however, to indicate that any one teaching approach is superior in every situation and with every child. We do know that some exceptional children require positive reinforcement and direct instruction before they begin to manipulate and meaningfully interact with the physical environment. On the other hand, many young children clearly respond to directive teaching with greater enthusiasm and more correct responses if first given the opportunity to manipulate concrete objects. The likelihood is that the optimum development of the young child with disabilities is best fostered in an environment that provides ample opportunity for self-directed exploration supplemented by directive instruction in areas of the child's greatest need. Parent involvement can maximize training efforts.

The study of human behavior is still in its infancy. Seventy years ago, Freud and Watson were only beginning their studies on the nature of behavior and learning. The real impetus for early childhood education began as late as the 1960s, and the importance of the first 3 years is just beginning to be widely recognized.

We have learned much in a very short time. Yet, we are still falling far short in meeting the needs of our young children with disabilities. However, with continued progress in our commitment to educational programming and research, the future for young exceptional children is full of promise.

SUGGESTIONS FOR WORKING WITH YOUNG CHILDREN WITH DISABILITIES

1. Be familiar with milestones for normal development, and focus instructional activities around the delays of the child with disabilities. Help the child enjoy and appreciate his or her strengths.

2. Don't waste time teaching unnecessary skills. Focus on those skills that the child must have to succeed in school and in his or her social world.

3. Break down learning tasks so that the child proceeds one step at a time.

4. High expectations that the child can take the next developmental step are critical to his or her willingness to try.

5. Spend some time helping parents learn teaching principles such as goal setting, breaking down tasks, and so on. Parents can then support your educational program at home.

6. Ask parents about the most time-consuming and frustrating parts of their time with the child. Help parents set up at-home programs for the areas where they would like to see their child's behavior change. Frequent problem areas are bath taking, dressing, eating, discipline, bedtime routine, and success with neighborhood children.

7. Preschool children with disabilities need a good, sound educational program where time is not wasted on nonessential learning tasks. They also need a warm, loving connection with the teacher and an abundance of affirmation.

8. Low teacher-child ratios can enhance the progress toward learning goals.

✦ *PONDER THESE*

1. *Suppose you suspect that a child in your preschool group has a language deficiency. What would be the advantages and disadvantages of alerting the child's parents to this possible difficulty?*

2. *Read the following list of problem behaviors exhibited by a 6-year-old child with whom you work, and determine which of the behaviors you would work on first and why, and how you would go about changing these behaviors:*

   Antisocial behavior (kicking, hitting, scratching, spitting on others)

   Severe language and speech disorders (poor articulation, poverty of expression)

   Lack of independent play skills (cannot play alone with toys)

   Lack of appropriate self-help skills (cannot feed herself or himself without spilling or dress herself or himself without help)

3. *Consider what a "learning disability" is in a preschool youngster. How can it be manifested and identified?*

4. *Identify some specific concerns associated with the following areas that might put a preschool age child at risk for future school failure:*

   Medical factors

   Environmental factors

   Cultural factors

INFORMATION/RESOURCES

1. PEAL Software
    P.O. Box 8188
    Calabasas, CA 91372

2. UCLA/LAUSD Microcomputer Project
    UCLA Intervention Program
    1000 Veteran Avenue
    23-10 Rehabilitation
    Los Angeles, CA 90024

3. Optimum Resources, Inc.
    Weekly Reader Software
    10 Station Place
    Norfolk, CT 06058

References

Allen, K. E., Rieke, J., Dmitriev, V., & Hayden, A. H. (1972). Early warning: Observation as a tool for recognizing potential handicaps in young children. *Educational Horizons, 50,* 43–55.

Anastasiow, N. J. (1981). Early childhood education for the handicapped in the 1980's: Recommendations: *Exceptional Children, 47,* 276–282.

Baratz, J. (1969). Linguistic and cultural factors in teaching reading to ghetto children. *Elementary English, 46,* 199–203.

Bereiter, C., & Engelmann, S. (1966). *Teaching disadvantaged children in the preschool.* Englewood Cliffs, NJ: Merrill/Prentice-Hall.

Bloom, B., Davis, A., & Hess, R. (1965). *Compensatory education for cultural deprivation.* New York: Holt, Rinehart & Winston.

Caldwell, B. M. (1972). Consolidating our gains in early childhood. *Educational Horizons, 50,* 56–62.

Evans, E. D. (1971). *Contemporary influences in early childhood education.* New York: Holt, Rinehart & Winston.

Foster, M., Berger, M., & McClean, M. (1981). Rethinking a good idea: A reassessment of parent involvement. *Topics in Early Childhood Special Education, 1*(3), 55-56.

Garber, H., & Heber, R. (1973). *The Milwaukee Project: Early intervention as a technique to prevent mental retardation.* Storrs: The University of Connecticut Technical Paper.

Guralnick, M. J., Richardson, H. B., Jr., & Heiser, K. E. (1982). A curriculum in handicapping conditions for pediatric residents. *Exceptional Children, 48,* 338–346.

Haring, N. G., & McCormick, L. (1990). *Exceptional children and youth* (5th ed.). Englewood Cliffs, NJ: Merrill/Prentice Hall.

Hayden, A. H. (1978). Special education for young children. In N. G. Haring (Ed.), *Behavior of exceptional children* (2nd. ed., pp. 29–43). Englewood Cliffs, NJ: Merrill/Prentice Hall.

Hayden, A. H. (1979). Handicapped children, birth to age 3. *Exceptional Children, 45,* 510–516.

Hess, R. D., & Shipman, V. (1967). Cognitive elements in maternal behavior. *The craft of teaching and the schooling of teachers.* Denver: U.S. Office of Education, Tri-University Project, 57–85.

Horton, K. B. (1974). Infant intervention and language learning. In R. L. Schidfelbusch & L. L. Lloyd (Eds.), *Language perspectives—Acquisition, retardation and intervention* (pp. 469–491). Baltimore, MD: University Park.

House, E. R., Glass, G. V., McLean, L. D., & Walker, D. F. (1978). No simple answer: Critique of the Follow Through Evaluation. *Harvard Educational Review, 48,* 128–160.

Kearsley, R. B. (1979). Latrogenic retardation: A syndrome of learned incompetence. In R. B. Kearsley & I. E. Sigel (Eds.), *Infants at risk: Assessment of cognitive functioning.* Hillsdale, NJ: Lawrence Erlbaum Associates.

McDaniels, G. (1977). Successful programs for young handicapped children. *Educational Horizons, 56,* 26–33.

Nagera, H. (1975). Day-care centers: Red light, green light or amber light. *The International Review of Psycho-Analysis, 2*(1), 121–137.

National Advisory Committee on the Handicapped. (1976). *Annual report.* Washington, DC: U.S. Office of Education.

Payne, J. S., Mercer, C. D., Payne, R. A., & Davison, R. G. (1973). *Head Start: A tragicomedy with epilogue.* New York: Behavioral Publications.

Peterson, N. L. (1987). Early intervention for handicapped and at-risk children: An introduction to early childhood special education. Denver, CO: Love.

Sandler, A., Coren, A., & Thurman, S. K. (1983). A training program for parents of handicapped preschool children: Effects upon mother, father and child. *Exceptional Children, 49,* 355–358.

Schweinhart, L. J., Berrueta-Clement, J. R., Barnett, W. S., Epstein, A. S., & Weikart, D. P. (1985). The promise of early childhood education. *Phi Delta Kappan, 66,* 548–553.

Schweinhart, L. J., & Weikart, D. P. (1985). Evidence that good early childhood programs work. *Phi Delta Kappan, 66,* 545–551.

Shearer, M., & Shearer, D. (1972). The Portage project: A model for early childhood education. *Exceptional Children, 36,* 210–217.

Skeels, H. M. (1966). Adult status of children with contrasting early life experiences: A follow-up study. *Monographs of the Society for Research in Child Development, 31,* No. 3 (Whole No. 105), 1–68.

Sontag, E. (1977). Introductory speech to 1977 BEH Project Directors' Conference, Arlington, VA.

Stebbins, L. B., St. Pierre, R. G., Proper, E. C., Anderson, R. B., & Cerva, T. R. (1977). *Education as experimentation: A planned variation model, Volume IV—A, An evaluation of Follow Through.* Cambridge, MA: Abt Associates.

Turnbull, A. P., Summers, J. A., & Brotherson, M. J. (1984). *Working with families with disabled members: A family systems approach.* Lawrence, KS: The University of Kansas, University Affiliated Facility.

Turnbull, A. P., & Turnbull, M. R. (1986). *Families, professionals, and exceptionality: A special partnership.* Englewood Cliffs, NJ: Merrill/Prentice Hall.

U.S. Department of Education. (1984). *Sixth annual report to Congress on the implementation of Public Law 94–142: The Education for All Handicapped Children Act.* Washington, DC: Author.

Vygotsky, L. S. (1978). *Mind in society: The development of higher psychological processes.* Cambridge, MA: Harvard University.

Wallace, G., & Kauffman, J. M. (1986). *Teaching children with learning problems* (3rd. ed.). Englewood Cliffs, NJ: Merrill/Prentice Hall.

White, B. L. (1975). *The first three years.* Englewood Cliffs, NJ: Prentice-Hall.

Winton, P. J., & Turnbull, A. P. (1981). Parent involvement as viewed by parents of preschool handicapped children. *Topics in Early Childhood Special Education, 1*(3), 11-19.

14

Adolescence and Adulthood

Sometimes what seems like success may be just the opposite. For instance, Gary, a high school student, was involved in our "transition" project. This program attempts to help prepare students for various roles they must assume after formal schooling is over. At first glance, Gary looked like a success story. Not only did he complete high school but he also began taking courses at one of the local community colleges. Things were going so well for him that he qualified for and received financial aid from the school. Here was a textbook example of how the transition process can work successfully. Unfortunately, this story turns a bit sour. Although Gary was fortunate enough to get financial assistance, he did not know how to handle this monetary windfall. As soon as he received his check, he left school and has not been seen since. Is this a case of being successful too quickly?

A high school girl was seeking competitive employment. What happened to her during one particular interview illustrates that general job-seeking skills can be more important than highly refined vocational skills.

This girl went to interview at a local fish cannery. She had been trained very well in the specific vocational skills needed for this job, exceeding the skill level as determined by industry stan-dards. She was accompanied on this interview by one of her train-ers. However, she picked her nose during the entire interview. Of course, she didn't get the job. Her lack of personal hygiene negated any advantage she might have had over less qualified competitors. And when you think about it, it was good that she played her hand too soon, especially if you eat canned fish.

Phyllis has been a maid at the Ramada Inn since graduating from her high school program for persons with severe handicaps. In 5 years, she had never missed a day of work or been late. Her supervisor often said, "I wish I had 20 others just like her!" Once, during her first year of work, he happened to pass the break room just as it was time for the maids to return to work. Five or six of the maids had apparently decided to extend their 15-minute coffee break. However, Phyllis quickly told them, "Break's over. It's time to work." Her supervisor simply said, "She gives a good day's work for a fair wage. I wish everybody was like that."

Kevin, who is blind, went to the movies with a group of friends one evening. The person selling tickets became perplexed when Kevin stepped up to the window. The ticket person asked Kevin if he could see and the answer given was "No." As there was no recollec-tion of ever issuing a ticket to a blind person, the employee thought carefully about what to do. There was a long line, the ticketer was under pressure, and realized that a decision had to be made. With-out any further hesitation, he told Kevin that he would charge him half price as Kevin was only going to hear the movie. Kevin readily accepted this offer and later confided that he'd take this deal any-time.

With the original passage of PL 94–142, much attention was directed toward providing appropriate education to students in need of such. The thrust of these efforts was centered on the younger school age population even though this legislation mandated that concern be given to all individuals between the ages of 3 and 21. Parent groups were very concerned with this younger population as well. As a result, great changes were occurring in educating these children. Unfortu-nately, the needs of older students were overlooked to a great extent (Sherbenou & Holub, 1982).

More recently, increasing professional attention and action has been directed toward the needs of exceptional youth and adults. Some of this interest has been buttressed by the fact that the children to whom much attention was given over 20 years ago are now grown up. Additional motivation has been provided by the realization that many students with disabilities do not outgrow their problems. Years of frustration with a difficult and often unrewarding educational experience have taken their toll on far too many individuals.

As the termination of formal schooling approaches for youth with disabilities, there is much concern by parents, teachers, support personnel, administrators, school board members, and the community at large as to what lies ahead. The adult outcome data that has emerged over the last few years paints a less than optimistic picture for many individuals with disabilities.

What are the life choices for most exceptional youth as they prepare to exit lower education? The major options are presented below.

- Employment (full-time or part-time; supported or nonsupported)
- Further education or training (2- and 4-year colleges/universities, technical schools, trade schools, adult education, Job Training Partnership Act (JTPA) programs)
- Military service
- Volunteer work (community-based service, Peace Corps, etc.)
- "Domestic engineering" (househusband/wife)
- Absence of gainful employment or purposeful activity

This chapter will highlight many of the critical variables related to making a successful transition from adolescence to adulthood. Most of the discussion will focus on those exceptional adolescents and adults who are disabled; nevertheless, the issues and needs of gifted individuals will also be highlighted. We have also made an arbitrary distinction between individuals with milder forms of disability and those with more severe types of disability. This has been done for the sake of making the discussion clearer, as some specific issues for these two groups are significantly different.

ADOLESCENCE AND SECONDARY EDUCATION CONSIDERATIONS

Nature of Adolescence

Although trying to define adolescence in a universally accepted fashion is not easy, this stage of life is clearly very important. It is in itself a transitional phase of moving from childhood to adulthood. It is a difficult time for everyone and may even be more trying for youth who are disabled. Smith, Price, and Marsh (1986) have summarized the major tasks of adolescence documented in the literature:

- Creation of a sense of sexuality as part of a personal identity
- Development of confidence in social interactions
- Infusion of social values into a personal code of behavior
- Acceptance of biological changes
- Attainment of a sense of emotional independence
- Contemplation of vocational interests
- Identification of personal talents and interests
- Awareness of personal weaknesses and strengths
- Development of sexual interests with nonfamily members
- Development of peer relationships
- Completion of formal educational activities
- Preparation for marriage, parenting, and adult relationships (p. 212)

The relevance of some of these tasks for adolescents with disabilities will vary according to their level of functioning.

Special Concerns of Adolescence

In addition to the normal challenges the typical adolescent has to face, other at-risk conditions must also be considered. The exact relationship of these potential problem areas to exceptionality is not clearly understood; however, we do know that exceptional youth are just as susceptible to and may be more at risk. The statistics that correspond with these areas are staggering and sobering. Although we will simply list the areas of concern here, the reader is encouraged to examine them more closely. Professionals who work with adolescents must be familiar with these areas.

- Substance abuse (drugs and alcohol)
- Teenage pregnancy
- Teenage suicide
- Runaways/homelessness
- Dropping out of school
- Juvenile delinquency

These are problems to which teenagers are constantly being exposed and with which they must contend. These issues cannot be ignored as they will not go away. In today's society, we have to find ways to help adolescents deal with the complexities of life and to let them understand that others care about them.

Curricular Needs

Youth with mild disabilities.   Adolescents with mild disabilities include those individuals whose educational needs should allow them to be included in general education to a great degree. Categorically, this population often includes individuals with learning disabilities, mild behavior problems, and mild mental retardation. Some of the major issues affecting this population are described in the following paragraphs.

Caution must be exercised when presenting a list of general characteristics; however, it is instructive to provide a school-based perspective of the needs of this group of students. The following characteristics can be found in many students at the secondary level:

- Low achieving—typically demonstrated in reading, written expression, and math
- Plateau of basic skill development
- Deficiencies in the study skill area (e.g., note taking, test taking, time management, and using reference materials)
- Ineffective use of strategic behaviors necessary for academic success
- Social skills deficits
- At risk for dropping out

The last characteristic is worth exploring in more detail. The exit data for students who are mentally retarded or learning disabled, or who have severe emotional disturbance (the current terminology used in IDEA) are presented in Table 14.1 (U.S. Department of Education, 1994). These data, based on the 1991–92 school year, are cause for alarm, especially if one accepts the derived figures for what is likely to be the "real dropout" rate. The clear message sent by these data is that significant numbers of students are not finding the school experience to be worth staying around for.

For those students who are in school, some professionals argue that they are not being adequately prepared to deal with the demands of adulthood when one considers what those demands are and how many of them are addressed in school. All the demands of adult living

Table 14.1
Exit Data for Students Who Are Mentally Retarded, Learning Disabled, and Emotionally Disturbed, 1991-92

Source:From U.S. Department of Education, 1994, *Sixteenth Annual Report to Congress on the Implementation of the Individuals With Disabilities Education Act,* Washington, DC: Author.

Exit Basis	Select Groups		
	LD	ED	MR
diploma	49.7%	28.1%	36.1%
certificate	10.8	6.5	27.7
age-out	.5	1.0	6.0
dropout	21.3	35.0	19.6
unknown exit	17.7	29.4	10.5
"real" drop out	39.0	64.4	30.1

can be categorized into six arbitrary domains of adulthood, as illustrated in Figure 14.1. Even at this macro level, it is obvious that some important areas related to dealing with adulthood successfully are not directly taught to most students.

The dominant types of programming available to students with mild disabilities can be categorized into four major areas (Polloway & Patton, in press): academic content mastery (i.e., teaching general education content); remedial (basic skills, social skills training); maintenance (learning strategies, tutorial); and adult outcomes (vocational, life skills). To this day, much attention is still devoted to the remediation of basic skills, and too little attention is given to preparing students with mild disabilities for the realities of adult life. A balance between the academic needs and the life needs of students is lacking.

Many programs for students with mild disabilities still have a strong academic focus. This is due in part to the fact that some students are in diploma track programs. For certain students (e.g., those for whom postsecondary education is a possibility), a strong academic orientation is needed. Others who are less capable may benefit from continued efforts to develop basic skills and remediate deficiencies, as Polloway, Epstein, Polloway, Patton, and Ball (1986) have demonstrated. However, any focus on academics, whether developmental or remedial, should be integrated with life skills and vocational preparation as well.

Many professionals feel that a significant number of students who have mild disabilities exit formal school with insufficient preparation for "the life after." This fact becomes more poignant when one realizes that most secondary level students with disabilities do not pursue postsecondary education. There is a great need for comprehensive curricula for students with disabilities at the secondary level. Such curricula are sensitive to both the present and future needs of these students, with a strong emphasis on functionality.

Figure 14.1
Domains of Adulthood

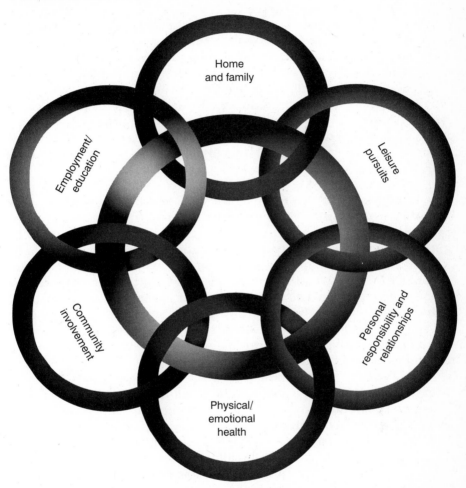

Source: From *Life Skills Instruction for All Students With Special Needs* by M. E. Cronin and J. R. Patton, 1993, Austin: Pro-Ed (p. 13).

Most secondary programs offer a combination of programmatic orientations, thus preparing students for a range of possibilities. Exemplary secondary programs can be identified by their attempts to realistically assess and match a student's interests, preferences, and abilities to the requisite demands of likely subsequent environments.

Youth with more severe disabilities.   The population referred to as more severely disabled can best be characterized as having "substantial functional limitations." Individuals in this group may have mental, physical, and/or other emotional/behavioral problems of such a degree and nature that they require extensive supports.

The most important curricular issue for this group is the need to teach basic daily living skills (e.g., self-care, communication, "functional" academics, socialization, leisure/recreational skills) and to provide appropriate vocational training. To be successful, practitioners need to (1) use a variety of training procedures, (2) provide instruction in community-based settings, (3) maintain skill acquisition by employing naturally occurring events, and (4) program for generalization of skills.

Low incidence conditions.   Youth with low incidence conditions include adolescents with vision, hearing, or certain types of physical/health problems. For this group, the major issues center on preparing them for postsecondary education and/or to function independently as adults. Specific training in the use of various assistive technology (both low and high tech) may be required. One of the most sensitive areas that needs careful attention is the acceptance of these individuals by others. We know how important peer acceptance is at this level of development, and for this reason, special effort might be required in ensuring that adolescents with vision, hearing, or physical disabilities are part of inclusive school settings.

Giftedness.   It is a tragic oversight to think that gifted adolescents do not have special needs in terms of intervention. It has been said that the needs of this group may be just as unique and important as those of adolescents with mental retardation. Students who excel in specified ways (see Chapter 11 for a breakdown of the different distinctions of giftedness) typically require unique forms of career development that match their diverse and accelerated needs. This group also requires programs that allow them to discover who they are (i.e., programs that emphasize self-examination) (Fleming, 1985). Gifted students can also benefit from well-designed and quality counseling services. The importance of this need is underscored by the amount of recent professional attention being given to this area.

TRANSITION FROM SCHOOL TO COMMUNITY LIVING

The need to better bridge the transition from school to community living has enjoyed a wave of interest and activity in recent years. In 1984 the Office of Special Education and Rehabilitative Services (OSERS) identified this topic as a national priority (Will, 1984) and funded a number of major transition projects. This early attention to the transition needs of students was initiated by concern about what was happening to students who had been served by special education during their school careers after they exited the school system. This need to better prepare young adults with disabilities for various subsequent environments and to assist them in being placed in such was also recognized by local education agency personnel and professionals in the field of special education, as well as by the parents of these youth.

The Individuals with Disabilities Education Act of 1990 provides a federal mandate for transition services that must be implemented for all students with disabilities reaching 16 years of age. It defines transition services as

> a coordinated set of activities for a student, designed within an outcome-oriented process, which promotes movement from school to post-school activities, including post-secondary education, vocational training, integrated employment (including supported employment), continuing and adult education, adult services, independent living, or community participation.
>
> The coordinated set of activities must be based on the individual student's needs, taking into account the student's preferences and interests; and include instruction, community experiences, the development of employment and other post-school objectives, and if appropriate, acquisition of daily living skills and functional vocational evaluation.

The concept of transition links the two themes of adolescence and adulthood and involves three distinct phases: assessment, planning, and action. It is an important part of the overall nature of preparing individuals for adulthood, as presented in Figure 14.2.

As pointed out in Figure 14.2, a person's quality of life is a function of being personally fulfilled, which comes from being able to deal with the demands of adulthood successfully. (This idea is a variation of the concept of quality of life proposed by Halpern [1993].) Those who deal successfully with the demands of adulthood typically possess usable knowledge and requisite skills and/or have necessary supports and services in place. This competence and support are achieved through exposure to appropriate transition education (i.e., comprehensive curricula— as defined earlier) and transition planning. It should be noted that families often contribute considerably to what is being referred to as transition education. The essence of the transition planning process is when school-based personnel, the family, and the student work together to determine transitional needs and a plan of action.

Figure 14.2
Preparing Students for Adulthood

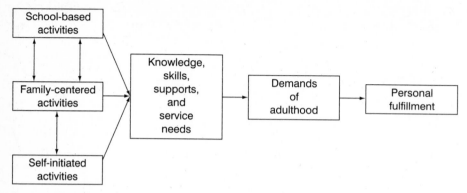

Source: From *Transition Planning Process: Recommended Practices* by J. R. Patton, Austin: Learning for Living, in press.

The prospect of youth with disabilities adjusting successfully to life after high school depends greatly on various personal factors (e.g., knowledge and skills) and other community supports (e.g., social workers, vocational rehabilitation counselors, postsecondary education staff, various adult service providers, and other community agencies). Certain students with disabilities may not need any specialized supports in adjusting to adult life; however, for those who do, school-based personnel must take the lead in assisting the student and the family in linking with needed services.

If transitional planning is to be effective, a number of concerns must be addressed within all phases of the process. We must assure that (1) transitional needs of students are addressed through curricula; (2) students' interests, preferences, and transitional needs are assessed adequately; (3) transition plans are comprehensive (i.e., not focused only on employment goals); and (4) linkage activities are continually enhanced. This whole process must be guided by the overriding goal of preparing young adults with disabilities to deal successfully with the complexities of adulthood that await them.

ADULTHOOD

In recent years, much effort has been directed towards the inclusion of all types of exceptional individuals into the mainstream of everyday life. For many, this has not been too difficult; for others—especially those who are more severely disabled—it has been a challenge.

The landmark legislation, the Americans with Disabilities Act (ADA), now provides civil rights protections to this group. The scope of the law applies to public or private employment, transportation, accommodations, and telecommunications. Fundamentally, it prohibits discrimination against persons with disabilities. Its intent is wonderful and welcomed; its actual implementation and effects await the test of time.

The demands placed on adults are many. As pointed out earlier in this chapter, a young adult needs to be competent in a number of skill areas to deal adequately with community living. However, certain demands change over time and individuals must be able to adapt to these changes. For this reason, it might be necessary to examine the experiences of exceptional adults throughout their life span.

Even though a model for conceptualizing successful community adjustment (see Figure 14.2) has been proposed, the concept remains elusive. Even within the current professional excitement related to "transition," no uniformity exists as to what successful outcomes actually are. Adjustment variables that are typically studied, and that imply what researchers think are important, relate to living environments, employment, monetary status and management, marriage and children, sexuality issues, infrequency of antisocial behaviors and use of leisure time. Although some consensus may be found to support the importance of most of these variables, we cannot help but be concerned about the value judgments implicit in some of them. For instance, people are no longer suspicious of any person or group that prefers a single lifestyle to being married and having children. Our responsibility is to help exceptional adults achieve to the best of their abilities and to accomplish what they want, not what we think that they want.

A cycle of frustration can arise for some individuals who are disabled, as described in the following scenario:

> Having a job, a sweetheart or spouse, a room or home of their own, and personal possessions have become the hallmark of normalcy for many . . . persons and their major goal. Yet, even when these have been acquired, individuals may still feel that they risk exposure through daily blunders or failures, and remain caught in a whirlwind of stress—coping with frustrations of what they are, struggling to be what they are not (Patton et al., 1990, p. 470).

Although we still lack precision in defining the specifics of community adjustment, we can refer back to Figure 14.2. This figure underscores the importance of (1) the knowledge and skills of the individual, (2) the supports and services that are needed, and (3) the demands placed upon the person to live and function adequately within the community setting—some of these demands are common to all adults while others are specific to a given person or setting.

For the purposes of this chapter, we will consider the term *exceptional adults* to apply to people with characteristics that make them uniquely different and with needs that usually require special attention. In general, adults with disabilities can be described as manifesting significant functional limitations interfering with major life activities. Many exceptional adolescents might not necessarily become exceptional adults.

Characteristics of Adults With Disabilities

As mentioned earlier, when discussing characteristics, there is always a danger of overgeneralization. Thus, do not think that each of the findings listed in the following paragraphs will apply to every adult who is disabled.

According to a recent census report (U.S. Department of Commerce, 1994), 48.9 million Americans (i.e., 19.4% of the total population) are disabled. Table 14.2 provides a number of analyses of these data. What is obvious is that a significant number of people with disabilities are not working.

Key Features of Community Living

Where do adults who are disabled work and live? What do they do with their time? How well do they get along in the community? To a great extent, the answers to these questions depend upon the abilities of the individual, the availability of appropriate individual supports and community services, and community attitudes/behaviors. This section of the chapter will describe some important dimensions related to living in the community.

Employment.   For those who are employed, there are a number of possible options. Many adults with disabilities are engaged in competitive employment and receive typical wages. Some people with disabilities have earned advanced graduate degrees and have become leaders in their fields. However, for most adults with disabilities who have been competitively employed, jobs are likely to be unskilled or semi-skilled. Another option is supported employment. This is a type of competitive employment where an individual acquires the essential vocational skills of a job while at the job site and under the supervision of a job coach/employment specialist. This particular employment

Table 14.2
Data on Disabled Adults

Who are the 48.9 Million Persons with Disabilities?		**What are the Leading Causes of Disability and Their Impact?**	
• under 15	6%	Over 27 million individuals age 15 and over reported having a limitation in a physical or daily living activity, causing a disability. Following are the leading causes	
• between age 15–64	60%		
• between age 21–64	56%		
• 65 and over	34%		
• men	22.9 million		
• women	26.0 million	• arthritis/rheumatism	7.2 million
• people with severe		• back spinal problems	5.7 million
disabilities	24.1 million	• heart trouble	4.6 million
• men	9.9 million	• lung/respiratory	
• women	14.2 million	trouble	2.8 million
		• high blood pressure	2.2 million
		• stiffness or deformity of the foot, leg, arm, or hand	2.0 million
Race and Ethnic Groups age 15–64		• diabetes	1.6 million
• Blacks	4.1 million		
• Asian and Pacific Islanders	515,000	**Those Individuals Age 15 and Over Reported the Following**	
• Persons of Hispanic origin	2.4 million	• used a wheelchair	1.5 million
		• women	919,000
• Whites not of Hispanic origin	22.6 million	• men	575,000
		• used a cane, walker, or crutches for six months or longer	4.0 million
• American Indian, Eskimo, or Aleut	285,000		
		• even when wearing corrective lenses, had difficulty seeing words or letters in ordinary newsprint	8.1 million
What is the Employment Status?		• even when wearing corrective lenses, could not see the words or letters in newsprint at all	1.6 million
Employed Persons Age 21 to 64			
• total	108.7 million		
• people with disabilities	14.3 million		
• men	7.9 million		
• women	6.4 million	• had difficulty hearing a normal conversation with another person	10.0 million
• of 14.3 million people with disabilities, those with severe disability	2.9 million		
• men	1.3 million	• could not hear what is said in a normal conversation	924,000
• women	1.6 million		

Source:From U.S. Department of Commerce, 1994.

option has been very successful and is being used throughout the country to gain employment for individuals with a wide range of abilities. A sheltered employment setting remains another employment option, although its attractiveness has waned dramatically over the course of the last few years with the advent of the supported employment model.

Living arrangements.   A great number of adults who are disabled live very much like anyone else—with their parents, relatives, nonrelated persons, or alone. As with all of us, living arrangements are determined to a great extent by income level and financial status. For many adults with disabilities, low levels of income limit the choices of where they can live. Consequently, we are reminded of the axiom that states: Where one lives greatly determines how one lives.

The continuum of living arrangements for adults who are more severely disabled includes the following:

1. Apartment programs: independent, residential, or cluster arrangements
2. Protected settings: care, boarding, or companion homes
3. Group homes: family-like setting within a residential neighborhood
4. ICF-MR programs (Intermediate Care Facilities for the Mentally Retarded): settings that provide 24-hour care (nursing, medical support, therapy, and training)
5. Institutions: residential facilities that tend to have individuals with the most severe handicaps

There has been a strong movement to establish living environments for all adults who are severely disabled in the community. Many arrangements involve the concept of supportive living. Although this trend is in evidence, the availability of community residences is limited in some locations, and the quality of services varies greatly.

Leisure and recreation.   As indicated in Figure 14.1, a major domain of adulthood is leisure pursuits. Adults who are disabled need leisure activities as much as anyone else to enhance their lives. Unfortunately, many remain outside the mainstream of community life with regard to recreational activities and leisure pursuits, due to the nature of their disabilities and/or the inaccessibility of various community programs. A lack of community funds, trained personnel, and community awareness of the needs of adults with disabilities have also contributed to this situation. However, therapeutic recreational programs designed for special populations do exist in many locales. And more attention has been given to the need to teach leisure skill activities while in school, as well as in continuing education.

Mobility.   Traveling about within one's environment provides the opportunities to develop awareness of other people and places, facilitates a sense of personal control over the environment, and is something most adults do. This aspect of community living is problematic for many adults with disabilities. In the past, public transportation systems have often been inaccessible or inefficient. With the passage of the Americans with Disabilities Act, these past oversights and discriminatory practices are now illegal.

Issues Related to Adulthood

For adults with various forms of disability, other issues are very important. Each of these issues influences their inclusion into society and their quality of life. These are issues that all persons must address in the course of their lives.

Continuing education.   As we all are finding these days, there is a real need to be lifelong learners. Adults who are disabled—perhaps more than nondisabled adults—require systematic efforts to assure their skills match the changing demands placed on them. As society gets technologically more complex, a great need for some form of continual updating is warranted.

Friendship.   As reflected in Figure 14.1, relationships are a very important part of adulthood. They provide a sense of belonging, a feeling of being accepted, and an attitude of personal worth. A significant number of adults with disabilities are often denied opportunities to form relationships, perhaps due to their isolation or lack of appropriate interpersonal skills.

Sexuality.   The areas of sexuality, marriage, and parenthood are of great concern for many adults with disabilities. These related topics can be controversial (e.g., persons who are mentally retarded as parents) or involve unique problems for individuals with physical disabilities. Nevertheless, there is a verifiable need to deal with the topic of sexuality.

Old age.   Far too little professional attention has been directed toward the needs of people with disabilities as they age. However, interest has developed concerning the needs of those who are elderly in general. We know that as people age, they naturally acquire various disabilities (e.g., visual, hearing, and other health problems). As a result, persons who were never considered disabled become so, thus having more in common with their long-term disabled peers.

FINAL THOUGHTS

It is clear that we must broaden our interests and professional efforts to take notice of older disabled populations. Although many persons with disabilities will not need any or require very few supports in adulthood, others may require more intensive and ongoing supports. If we want to maximize the probability of a successful transition from adolescence into adulthood or from school to community living, then we need to do a better job of preparing individuals with disabilities for such. To help accomplish this, we must recognize the major demands they will face as adults, appreciate the complex nature of these problems, and assure that they acquire the knowledge and skills to deal with these demands or be linked with supports and services to assist them in doing so.

SUGGESTIONS FOR WORKING WITH EXCEPTIONAL ADOLESCENTS AND ADULTS

Adolescents

1. Consider likely postsecondary settings when deciding what curricular orientation to follow.
2. Educators should be prepared to spend as much time counseling as teaching students.
3. Ensure that transitional planning occurs; involve parents as much as possible. Be sensitive to family values.
4. Know what postsecondary services and agencies exist and how they can be accessed.
5. Be perceptive of subtle "at risk" signs (e.g., depression) that can have tragic consequences.
6. Encourage young people with disabilities to get involved in extracurricular activities.

Adults

1. In general, be aware of the individual's life situation and personal preferences and interests.

2. Realize that exceptional persons need to be lifelong learners, and as a result, provide mechanisms for giving them the necessary skills and knowledge to deal with an ever-changing, complex society.
3. For adults with more severe disabilities, provide inclusive situations (e.g., living arrangements, work settings) where they are welcomed as contributing members.

✦ PONDER THESE

1. *What are the advantages and disadvantages of each of the following program orientations as the sole thrust of a secondary level special education curriculum?*

   Academic

   Functional/life skills

   Vocational

2. *What are some major life demands that are associated with the adult domains presented in Figure 14.1?*
3. *What are the advantages and disadvantages of technological advances for persons with disabilities?*
4. *How would you react if you found out that a group home for adults with mental retardation was going to be established next door to your house? What concerns would you have? Are they justified?*

References

Fleming, E. S. (1985). Career preparation. In R. H. Swassing (Ed.), *Teaching gifted children and adolescents* (pp. 340–374). Englewood Cliffs, NJ: Merrill/Prentice Hall.

Halpern, A. S. (1993). Quality of life as a conceptual framework for evaluating transition outcomes. *Exceptional Children, 59,* 486–498.

Patton, J. R., Beirne-Smith, M., Payne, J. S. (1990). *Mental retardation* (3rd ed.). Englewood Cliffs, NJ: Merrill/Prentice Hall.

Polloway, E. A., Epstein, M. H., Polloway, C. H., Patton, J. R., & Ball, D. W. (1986). Corrective Reading Program: An analysis of effectiveness with learning disabled and mildly retarded students. *Remedial and Special Education, 7*(4), 41–47.

Polloway, E. A., & Patton, J. R. (in press). *Strategies for teaching learners with special needs* (6th ed.). Englewood Cliffs, NJ: Merrill/Prentice Hall.

Sherbenou, R. J., & Holub, S. (1982). The learning disabled adolescent: Ages 12 to 15. *Topics in Learning and Learning Disabilities, 2*(3), 40–54.

Smith, T. E. C., Price, B. J., & Marsh, G. E. (1986). *Mildly handicapped children and adults*. St. Paul, MN: West.

Will, M. C. (1984). *OSERS programming for the transition of youth with disabilities: Bridge from school to working life*. Washington, DC: U.S. Department of Education.

15

YESTERDAY, TODAY, AND TOMORROW

The first children to catch the attention of special educators were the most severely disabled, the "hopeless," "bottom-of-the-barrel" cases. We are apt today to think that the needs of this group are just now being recognized for the first time in special education's history because of a recent reawakening of interest. But as the following descriptions show, the child with a severe disability was an object of concern in the early part of the nineteenth century as well as in the last half of the twentieth century.

The age of Charles Emile is fifteen: he was admitted to the school in June, 1843. He is described as being of a nervous and sanguine temperament and in an almost complete state of idiocy: the faculties which remain being in a state of extraordinary activity, and rendering him dangerous to himself and to others: but still idiotic in his inclinations, sentiments, perceptions, faculties of perception and understanding, and also of his senses, of which some were obtuse, and others too excitable. He was consequently unfit, to use the words of M. Voisin, "to harmonize with the world without." As regards his inclinations, he was signalized by a voracious, indiscriminate, gluttonous appetite, un érotisme hideux, *and a blind and terrible instinct of destruction. He was wholly an animal. He was without attachment; overturned everything in his way, but without*

*courage or intent; possessed no tact, intelligence, power of dissimu-
lation, or sense of propriety; and was awkward to excess. His moral
sentiments are described as null, except the love of approbation,
and a noisy instinctive gaiety, independent of the external world. As
to his senses, his eyes were never fixed, and seemed to act without
his will; his taste was depraved; his touch obtuse; his ear recognized
sounds, but was not attracted by any sound in particular; and he
scarcely seemed to be possessed of the sense of smell. Devouring
everything, however disgusting; brutally sensual; passionate—
breaking, tearing, and burning whatever he could lay his hand
upon; and if prevented from doing so, pinching, biting, scratching,
and tearing himself, until he was covered with blood. He had the
particularity of being so attracted by the eyes of his brothers, sisters,
and playfellows, as to make the most persevering efforts to push
them out with his fingers. He walked very imperfectly, and could
neither run, leap, nor exert the act of throwing; sometimes he sprang
like a leopard, and his delight was to strike one sonorous body
against another. When any attempt was made to associate him with
the other patients, he would start away with a sharp cry, and then
come back to them hastily.*

*M. Voisin's description concludes with these expressions: "All the
faculties of perception in this youth are in a rudimentary state; and
if I may venture so to express myself, it is incredibly difficult to draw
him out of his individuality, to place him before exterior objects, and
to make him take any notice of them. It would not be far from the
truth to say, that for him all nature is almost completely veiled"*
(American Journal of Insanity, *1845, 1, 335–336*).

---

*When I started teaching [children with mental retardation] in
Lexington, I had little information about my students—no confiden-
tial folders, only one psychological assessment (five years old and
showing that the child had a full-scale IQ of 93!), no educational
assessments, no minutes of staffing or eligibility meetings, no data
to tell me who had declared these children eligible for special education or why. After laborious digging through files I discovered that 10
of my 12 students had been retained in grade at least once. They
had all been behavior problems. One comment from a classroom
teacher was, "John is impotent in the classroom." I wondered if he
was potent outside the class, until it dawned on me that the teacher
had meant "impudent." IEPs hadn't been invented yet. Special education for persons with mental retardation was still a wastebasket
for all the misfits—ill-behaved and otherwise difficult children who*

were considered the garbage of the schools. No one expected you to teach them anything, just make them happy. Some of my colleagues of the 1970s were hired for special education because they were music or art teachers. You were expected to cut, paste, sing, but not teach reading or math skills. I thought these children deserved more. . . .

Probably the biggest changes [in special education] are those brought about by the law. I complain bitterly about the overwhelming paperwork involved in complying with PL 94–142. And sometimes I do not agree with the placement of a child. But I do at least know who was responsible for the placement and why the decision was made, and I know whether or not the parents agreed with the placement. Even more important, I know the procedures for having a child reevaluated and for considering a change in placement. I am relieved that children can no longer be placed in special education classes or removed from them by merely trading cumulative folders in the office file cabinet (P. L. Pullen, in Hallahan & Kauffman, 1986, pp. 68–69).

Many students now beginning their study of special education have difficulty understanding the changes that have taken place in the field just within the past two decades. Practices that we take for granted today were mandated by federal law only in the late 1970s. One of the reasons why professionals are not aware of historical events is that minimal attention is given to these topics in personnel preparation programs.

Many people also have the mistaken notion that special education is a discipline of twentieth century vintage. Actually, the profession dates back to the late eighteenth and early nineteenth centuries. Many people also think that the issues facing special education today are completely new. But if you read the historical literature you will see that today's issues and problems are remarkably similar to those of long ago. Issues, problems, and ideas arise, flower, go to seed, and reappear when the conditions are again right for their growth. Following are some examples.

Public Law 94–142, the Education of All Handicapped Children Act of 1975, reauthorized in 1990 as the Individuals with Disabilities Education Act, is hailed by many as a landmark piece of legislation. It is, but a lot of the ideas it puts forward are not really new. For instance, the law says that every child must have an IEP, an individual education program. However, individualization is not a new idea for special educators. It is an idea forcefully described by Dr. Edouard Seguin in 1866:

But before entering farther into the generalities of the training, the individuality of the children is to be secured: for respect of individuality is the first test of the fitness of a teacher. At first sight all children look much alike; at the second their countless differences appear like insurmountable obstacles; but better viewed, these differences resolve themselves into groups easily understood, and not unmanageable. We find congenital or acquired anomalies of function which need to be suppressed, or to be given a better employment; deficiencies to be supplied; feebleness to be strengthened; peculiarities to be watched; eccentricities to be guarded against; propensities needing a genial object; mental aptness, or organic fitness requiring specific openings. This much, at least, and more if possible, will secure the sanctity of true originality against the violent sameness of that most considerable part of education, the general training (Seguin, 1866, p. 33).

In 1968, Drs. Thomas, Chess, and Birch published a book entitled *Temperament and Behavior Disorders in Children.* They said that every child is born with a distinctive behavioral style and that the interaction of this behavioral style or temperament with how the child is managed determines whether or not the child will become disturbed. In their words:

Neither in theory nor in fact would we expect a one-to-one relation to exist between a specific pattern of temperament and the emergence of a behavior problem; temperament, in and of itself, does not produce a behavior disorder. We would anticipate that in any given group of children with a particular patterning of temperamental organization, certain of these children would develop behavior disorders and others would not. Hopefully, this variability in consequence could be identified as deriving from differences in the patterns of care and other environmental circumstances to which the children were exposed. However, we also would anticipate that given a uniform environment and set of stresses, certain patternings of temperament are more likely to result in behavior disorders than are others. We are therefore concerned with the identification of both the differential likelihoods for the development of disturbances that attach to different temperamental patterns, and the specific environmental factors that interact with each temperamental type to result in a pathologic consequence (p. 9).

In 1807, Dr. James Parkinson of London, in his book *Observations on the Excessive Indulgence of Children, Particularly Intended to Show its Injurious Effects on their Health, and the Difficulties it Occasions in their Treatment During Sickness,* made this point:

That children are born with various dispositions is undoubtedly true; but it is also true, that by due management, these may be so changed and meliorated by the attention of a parent, that not only little blemishes may be smoothed away, but even those circumstances which more offensively distinguish the child, may, by proper management become the characteristic ornaments of the man . . . On the treatment the child receives from his parents, during the infantine stage of his life, will, perhaps, depend much of the misery or happiness he may experience, not only in his passage through this, but through the other stages of his existence (Hunter & Macalpine, 1963, p. 616).

In the nineteenth century, professionals working with persons labeled insane (today called individuals with severe emotional disturbance) wanted only the highest calibre of attendants. They realized that attendants, who worked hour to hour and day to day with children and adults, were probably the most important staff members. In 1852, Dr. Issac Ray described the ideal attendants:

They must manifest patience under the most trying emergencies, control of temper under the strongest provocations, and a steady perseverance in the performance of duty, disagreeable and repulsive as it oftentimes is. They must be kind and considerate, ever ready to sacrifice their own comfort to the welfare of their charge, cleanly in all their ways, and unsaving of any pains necessary to render their charge so also. In all respects, their deportment and demeanor must be precisely such as refined and cultivated persons have indicated as most appropriate to the management of the insane. In short, they are expected to possess a combination of virtues which, in ordinary walks of life, would render their possessor one of the shining ornaments of the race (pp. 52–53).

In 1966, Dr. Nicholas Hobbs said that the ideal teacher-counselor, a person trained to work in residential institutions for children who are emotionally disturbed—could be described as follows:

But most of all a teacher-counselor is a decent adult; educated, well trained; able to give and receive affection, to live relaxed, and to be firm; a person with private resources for the nourishment and refreshment of his own life; not an itinerant worker but a professional through and through; a person with a sense of the significance of time, of the usefulness of today and the promise of tomorrow; a person of hope, quiet confidence, and joy; one who has committed himself to children and to the proposition that children who are emotionally disturbed can be helped by the process of re-education (pp. 1106–1107).

With these examples in mind, we hope you will read the rest of this chapter looking for the historical continuity of certain issues and concepts and the emergence of others while also trying to understand how sociopolitical forces are shaping the field of special education today.

Exceptional individuals have been found in every society and correspondingly, societies have always had covert and overt social attitudes toward these individuals. By studying the prevalent attitudes toward and treatment of exceptional people over the course of time, we can observe the historical development of the field of special education.

To study the history of exceptional individuals, we will focus on important events, notable individuals, and the sociopolitical factors of a given time. Our discussion of the development of the field of special education partitions history into two arbitrary periods: early developments and precursors of current practice. These time periods represent activity before or after 1950. Moreover, different societies show different attitudes. Our discussion here focuses on attitudes of Western societies, particularly those found in the United States.

Historically, the evolving attitudes toward exceptional individuals are represented by shifts in the way these individuals have been treated (see Figure 1.3). Intervention has evolved from one of providing services in segregated facilities to a much more inclusive notion of empowerment and self-advocacy. These themes will be evident in the discussion that follows.

THE EARLY DEVELOPMENT OF A FIELD

Societal recognition of exceptional individuals can be traced back to the ancient Greeks, Romans, and Chinese. Although most persons with mild disabilities probably went unnoticed, cases of exceptionality referred to within these societies must have been individuals with severe impairments. The ancient Greeks are recorded to have abandoned any deviant infant on a hillside to perish. Although this action is cold and inhumane by our standards, it was nonetheless a very direct intervention program. Often the Romans employed the deviant individual as a buffoon for entertainment purposes; Augustus Caesar maintained a personal "jester" named Gabba during part of his reign as emperor (Kanner, 1964). In China as early as 500 B.C., Confucius stressed a philosophy of responsibility toward other people that included a responsibility toward exceptional people (L'Abate & Curtis, 1975). As Christianity developed, spreading the idea that everyone is a "child of God," more humane treatment was displayed. As a result, exceptional individuals were likely to be cared for in monasteries and asylums.

Often, the explanation of such exceptional individuals was given to misinterpretation and superstition. Martin Luther (1483–1546) taught that certain persons with mental retardation were "possessed" by the devil, and the renowned Danish astronomer, Tycho Brahe (1546–1601), believed that his *imbecilic*[1] companion uttered divine revelations. In many uncivilized societies, the exceptional individual was considered an "infant of the good God," and, as a result, this person was granted certain privileges that allowed him to move about the society freely and undisturbed.

Prior to the eighteenth century, no documented programs providing the systematic education and training of exceptional individuals existed. At best, there might be facilities that would provide care for certain deviant people. In the middle of the eighteenth century, the first recorded attempts to work with exceptional individuals were initiated. Typically, throughout the historical development of the field of special education, persons who were deaf and/or blind were the first exceptionalities to receive attention.

A Field Emerging

Many historical documents attest to the fact that an age of optimism accompanied by effective education emerged in the first half of the nineteenth century. In an era of drastic world change, the French and American Revolutions of the eighteenth century gave credence to the tenets of egalitarianism. With this new spirit of humanism spreading throughout Europe and the United States, social conditions were opportune for new ways of thinking about exceptional individuals. By the late eighteenth century, events occurring in Europe gave birth to the field of special education.

Many historical reviews of special education choose Jean Marc Itard (1774–1838) and his systematic work between 1799 and 1804 with Victor, the "Wild Boy of Aveyron," as the benchmark for the beginning of the field. However, in the mid- to late eighteenth century, the individual efforts of Pedro Ponce de Leon and Jacob Periere with persons who were deaf and the work of Valentine Hauy with those who were blind are clearly significant. In addition to their achievements with the various exceptional individuals, these leaders contributed to the foundation of the field.

Jean Itard's work with Victor is significant because Itard, a physician, an authority on the diseases of the ear, and an educator of per-

---

[1]Many terms used in the past to describe disabled individuals (e.g., *imbecile, idiot, feebleminded, moron,* etc.) seem harsh and offensive today. Social attitudes and connotations of these terms have changed over the years. Terms in vogue today may have offensive connotations 50 years from now.

sons with deafness, shifted gears to tackle the challenge of educating and training a boy who was not deaf but rather lacked early stimulation and education. For the first time for which we have any records, an intensive program was initiated to educate an individual who was "retarded," deprived, and behaviorally disabled rather than deaf or blind. Itard believed that sensory stimulation was paramount to Victor's developmental progress and blamed the absence of this sensory input as instrumental in his retardation. Interestingly, after 5 years of intensive work with Victor, a dejected Itard terminated the educational program, claiming that his efforts with Victor were a failure. Although Itard personally felt that his work was less than noteworthy, the professional community at that time found his contributions laudable. More importantly for the field of special education, however, was the precedent set by Itard and his systematic work with Victor and the influence that he had on other key figures who were to follow.

Edouard Seguin (1812–1880), a student of Itard, based many of his ideas and activities on those of his mentor. Seguin was responsible for developing teaching methods related to the physiological and moral education of individuals with mental retardation, more commonly referred to during this period as *idiots*. In the late 1830s, Seguin while in Europe began focusing on their needs and education. In 1848 Seguin moved to the United States; he brought with him the experience of one of the true pioneers of a developing field. A great contribution to the field was his book, *Idiocy and Its Treatment by the Physiological Method,* published in 1866.

Equally significant to the continuing evolution of services for people with disabilities was the inauguration of residential settings that provided bona fide training and education to residents. Such an institution was the Abendberg, established in Switzerland by Johann Guggenbühl (1816–1863) in the 1840s. This institution was important because of the influence it had on the many prominent visitors it attracted. Although later forced to close due to deteriorating conditions, the Abendberg was, nonetheless, the precursor of formal institutional care and training of individuals with mental retardation. By this time in both Europe and the United States, institutions dedicated to the education and training of persons who were deaf and/or blind had already been established.

While the birth of formal special education programs occurred in Europe, systematic efforts in the United States were soon to follow the European example. In colonial times, individuals with mild to moderate disabilities blended into society. Often these persons passed as normal because society made few demands that they could not meet. That is, a premium was put on physical abilities rather than on mental or academic abilities. Thus, persons who were mildly disabled coped until society began to demand more complex skills or looked at them more closely in school settings. Because the industrial revolution, which began in England in the late eighteenth century, accelerated the need for better educated citizens, it was not long before there was a more identifiable group of exceptional individuals. The recognition of more children with mild learning problems was further increased by legislative action mandating compulsory education. Regardless of these changes, the lives of those with more severe limitations were basically unaffected because these new changes did not necessarily increase the noticeability of individuals who had always been visibly different.

In the United States, an individual who became very concerned with the conditions of exceptional people was Samuel Gridley Howe (1801–1876). Howe, a physician initially concerned with the problems of persons who were blind, was instrumental in the founding of the Perkins School for the Blind located in Watertown, Massachusetts. In 1848, Howe extended his interests and work to individuals with mental retardation by establishing the first school for "idiotic" and "feeble-minded" youth in Massachusetts.

Prior to Howe's accomplishments, two other familiar names were already at work in their respective fields. In 1817, the Reverend T. H. Gallaudet (1787–1851) founded the first American residential school for persons who were deaf, the American Asylum for the Deaf and Dumb, in Hartford, Connecticut. In the following year, a small number of individuals who were mentally retarded also received services at this institution. In 1829, Louis Braille (1809–1852) introduced his raised dot system (braille), which allowed persons who were blind to read and write.

From the pioneering work of Howe, Gallaudet, and other early professionals, an interest in providing services to exceptional people in the United States was definitely emerging. In addition, during the 1840s, a crusade for better treatment of the insane, championed by the zealous Dorothea Dix, gained much attention. Similar notice was attained by Samuel Howe's vociferous confrontation with the governor of Massachusetts over a threatened veto of funds designated for exceptional persons. There was a hope and optimism that individuals with more severe disabilities could be removed from society, educated, and then reintegrated into the community. During this time, many promises were made concerning the ability of people with disabilities to learn and the possibility that they would eventually assume productive roles in the community. The optimistic spirit created by the early achievement of individuals such as Itard, Seguin, Guggenbühl, and Howe was soon to give way to sharp criticism that would drastically affect the treatment of persons with special needs for many years.

Disillusionment and Backlash

By the late nineteenth century, unfulfilled promises made by the enthusiastic pioneers in the field drew strong criticism. While these professionals sincerely believed that many individuals who were severely involved cognitively and/or physically could regain a normal status in society through appropriate education and training in residential facilities, their critics were stressing that no "curing" had occurred as promised. Although the notion that these individuals could be "cured" was false, it was, nonetheless, an important factor in the growing criticism levied at training programs for people with disabilities.

The general attitude toward integrating exceptional individuals into society was changing to one of segregation. Residential institutions now began to function as protecting agents for society by isolating individuals with disabilities within their walls. Under a custodial philosophy, these institutions gave little attention to the education and training of their charges. The custodial care of the late nineteenth century was different from the care afforded people who were disabled in the earlier era of the monastic asylum (pre-1700s). Naivete could not now explain the failure to provide services as it could prior to the eighteenth century. There is a difference between the benign acceptance that existed before 1700 due to the lack of adequate knowledge and the termination of educational services in the late 1800s due to skepticism.

Certain characteristics that mark the opening of the twentieth century were also beginning to evolve at this time. Because the social attitude in the late 1800s associated feeblemindedness with criminal behavior, poverty, incorrigibility, and disease, the efforts to segregate those so labeled from society were enhanced. In 1869, Sir Francis Galton published a book entitled *Hereditary Genius* that extended the evolutionary ideas of his cousin, Charles Darwin, to include mental characteristics. The eugenics movement, whose aim was to control hereditary qualities through selective breeding, was to mature in the early 1900s and would utilize many of Galton's ideas.

Prior to the Civil War in the 1860s, American society was largely agrarian, but, after the war, urbanization commenced at a rapid pace. The complications of urbanization were exacerbated by the influx of immigrants from Europe and the continuing consequences of the industrial revolution. These factors were significant in establishing compulsory education laws. This began, for the first time, a period when school-based issues related to students with special needs came to the forefront of public notice.

During this time of skepticism, a number of events related to special education occurred. In 1869, the first day class for students who were blind was established in Boston, Massachusetts, and the first day class for persons with mental retardation was founded in Providence, Rhode Island. And in 1871, the first ungraded class for children with behavioral problems was initiated in New Haven, Connecticut.

By the latter part of the nineteenth century, the earlier feeling of optimism and enthusiasm had metamorphosed into one of criticism and skepticism, which finally culminated in a state of alarm by the early part of the twentieth century. Although services were continuing for individuals who were deaf and blind, they were regressing for those who were mentally retarded. Provoked by a few events that began in the late 1800s, a period of alarm began in the early 1900s.

The early 1900s were paradoxical when one considers that, despite legislative advances made on behalf of exceptional individuals, an attitude of paranoia was developing. This state of concern flourished at the height of the eugenics scare, which was fueled even more by the discovery of Gregor Mendel's laws of inheritance and the advent of intelligence testing.

The eugenics movement, finding strong support in Mendel's work, espoused the idea that not only were the "feebleminded" a direct threat to this and future societies, but also that this disability could be inherited. In 1912, H. H. Goddard put fuel on the fire when he published his study of the Kallikak family in which he ostensibly documented the genetic transmission of feeblemindedness through five generations. Smith (1985) has reexamined this work in detail and found major flaws in the research and resultant findings, thus illuminating a social myth that had a profound impact on the lives of many people over the course of many decades.

In 1905, Alfred Binet and Theodore Simon provided French schools with an instrument that would have significant worldwide implications throughout this century. The mental scale or intelligence test that Binet and Simon developed would now identify many individuals with learning-related disabilities who previously had gone unnoticed. And this development gave the eugenics faction within the emerging social sciences a means of furthering their philosophy. A few years later in 1916, Louis Terman and his colleagues developed Binet's instrument into a workable scale for use in the United States.

It did not take long for the effects of the eugenics movement to be felt throughout the United States. In 1907, Indiana passed the first sterilization law in this country. And by 1930, 30 states had enacted similar legislation—evidence that the eugenics proponents were being heard. For persons with mental retardation, the social attitudes toward them before the turn of the century had evolved from optimism to caution. Now they were being considered as burdens to society rather than contributing citizens.

Signs of Change

In spite of the alarmist atmosphere during the second decade of the twentieth century, the United States passed legislation that increased services to children with disabilities. New Jersey mandated education for individuals with disabilities on a statewide basis in 1911. Ohio passed similar legislation in 1919. By 1918 children were required to attend school as a result of compulsory education laws. However, those children who were severely disabled were not included in this mandate. Some students with mild learning-related disabilities were beginning to be recognized.

World War I affected the treatment of people with disabilities in a number of ways. National attention was certainly focused on events transpiring in Europe, and, as a result, the alarmist period decelerated. The war itself resulted in changing social attitudes to some degree. Even though World War I was more a killing than a maiming war, the need for federal assistance to disabled veterans was answered in the form of the Federal Civilian Rehabilitation Act of 1920. The fear of individuals with severe disabilities prevalent in the early 1900s subsided, perhaps influenced by the many disabled husbands and sons now returning from the ravages of war. The period following the war ameliorated the eugenics scare.

Some laudable events affecting individuals with exceptional needs occurred during the 1920s. In 1921, the National Society for Crippled Children was established. A year later, the Council for Exceptional Children (CEC), a national organization for professionals concerned with the education of students who are disabled, was established in New York, with Elizabeth Farrell chosen as the first president. Although not immediately apparent, the establishment of CEC was quite significant because, for the first time, organization was brought to a field that did not previously have any unifying structure.

Because of the compulsory education laws and the increasing use of mental tests, public educators were becoming acutely aware of the need for special educational services. Also at this time, many new psychological and social concepts were being hypothesized, a trend that can be exemplified by J. B. Watson's book *Behaviorism* published in 1919. Although the 1920s did not encourage a general optimism in the United States, worse yet was the stock market crash of 1929 that brought widespread financial catastrophe to the nation. Consequently, economic constraints were now operating nationwide.

Individuals with special needs benefitted from a few prominent events that occurred during the 1930s. Herbert Hoover brought national attention to the needs of persons with disabilities in a White House conference on youth and children that he sponsored in 1930.

In 1942, Kurt Goldstein published his work resulting from his efforts with brain injured soldiers of World War I. Many authorities consider Goldstein's endeavors to be some of the critical events leading to the eventual creation of the area of learning disabilities.

In the latter part of the 1930s, the treatment of persons with disabilities in the United States was greatly enhanced by many talented individuals who fled to the United States when the Nazis gained control of Germany. Marianne Frostig, Alfred Strauss, and Heinz Werner all immigrated to this country, established various programs for exceptional individuals, and had a powerful influence on other professionals interested in the characteristics and needs of special populations.

During the 1940s, notable advancement was observed in certain activities that involved children with behavior disorders. Intervention efforts were reflected by programs such as Bruno Bettelheim's Orthogenic School (founded in Chicago in 1944) and New York City's "600" schools for children with behavior disorders (begun in 1946).

World War II and the Korean conflict provided more human reminders of disability. The national attitude became even more favorable and supportive of rehabilitation programs because many families experienced the cruelties of war. As a result, a more progressive social attitude toward individuals with disabilities was also extended to other forms of exceptionality and induced a new interest in the exceptional person.

PRECURSORS TO CURRENT PRACTICE

While the latter part of the 1940s was devoted to recovering from another world war, a new social attitude and the culmination of years of work by various professionals inspired further developments. In 1947, Alfred Strauss and Laura Lehtinen published their book *Psychopathology and Education of the Brain-Injured Child*, based on many years of work at the Wayne County Training School in Northville, Michigan. While at this school, Alfred Strauss, Heinz Werner, and their associates were responsible for directly influencing many future leaders such as Newell Kephart, William Cruickshank, and Samuel Kirk. Much of the work accomplished at Wayne County Training School formed the basis for the later development in the area of special education we now call learning disabilities.

State level legislative advancements continued so that, by 1948, 41 of the 48 states required local school systems to provide special education for at least one exceptionality. Although there was still much room for improvement, this was certainly progress in the right direction. In 1954, federal legislation created a foundation for cooperative research in education; however, this action was not funded until 1958 with the enactment of the Cooperative Research Act. Thus, a provision for financial backing of special education was established through the efforts of advocacy groups and, later, the influence of political leaders such as John Kennedy and Hubert Humphrey, who had relatives with disabilities.

Although the United States was involved in Korea in the early 1950s, it was not as economically demanding as the two world wars, and the development of special education services was not stymied. The decade of the fifties witnessed the emergence of perhaps two of the most important forces responsible for the current state of services to persons with special needs: parent organizations and litigation.

In 1950, the National Association for Retarded Children (NARC), a parent group that espoused the needs of children with mental retardation, was created. The importance of this parent group rested in the collective nature of its efforts. The establishment of similar parent groups for the other disability areas followed. According to Hallahan and Kauffman (1991), parent organizations serve an important role by

> (1) providing an informal group for parents who understand one another's problems and needs and help one another deal with anxieties and frustrations; (2) providing information regarding services and potential resources; and (3) providing the structure for obtaining needed services for their children (p. 22).

In 1954, the landmark *Brown v. Board of Education* decision handed down by the Supreme Court declared that racial segregation was unconstitutional. The implications of this decision for exceptional individuals would arrive years later, as a legal precedent guaranteeing certain rights had been set. Eventually, the rights of exceptional individuals would be affirmed through other legal decisions in the early 1970s.

The field of learning disabilities, still in utero, came closer to parturition in 1957 when William Cruickshank published his research on children with cerebral palsy. This research was important because Cruickshank had extended the early work done with brain injured children who were mentally retarded to children with neurological damage who also displayed normal intelligence.

A Field in the Limelight

By the end of the 1950s, the field of special education was ready for the exponential growth that was soon to follow in the 1960s. This predisposition was shaped by a rekindled interest in exceptional individuals and by the need for technological advancement due to the Sputnik scare of 1957. It did not take long for a virtual renaissance to occur in the services for exceptional individuals.

Not since the optimism of the first half of the nineteenth century had there been such enthusiasm for the education and training of special people as existed in the 1960s. This activism was engendered by the Kennedy administration. In 1962, President Kennedy established a presidential panel on mental retardation that was commissioned to construct a plan to combat mental retardation in the next decade.

One method of gauging the extent of services during this time is inspection of the quantity and quality of the legislation that was passed. During the 1960s a number of significant laws were enacted, reflecting the country's willingness to address the needs of special populations. Passage of the Elementary and Secondary Education Act in 1965 provided services to individuals who were disabled (Title I of this Act). Two amendments to this Act, PL 89–313 and PL 89–750, extended the coverage of the original act to include exceptional individuals. In 1965, PL 89–313 assured that exceptional children in state operated schools or hospitals would be provided with federally supported educational services. The effects of PL 89–750, passed in 1966, were threefold: (1) to provide a prototype program for the education of persons with disabilities; (2) to furnish a grant program that would benefit individuals with disabilities; and (3) to create the Bureau of Education for the Handicapped (BEH)—later to become the Office of Special Education Programs.

Programs for people with disabilities were greatly expanded during this period. A closely related project, started in 1965, was the Head Start program. This program emerged from research studies concerning early intervention and from President Johnson's War on Poverty. Head Start also went through the familiar cycle of optimism, skepticism, and refinement. At the core of many special education endeavors, the basic philosophy of early intervention remains a fundamental concept.

During the early 1960s, the field of learning disabilities became an identifiable part of special education. In 1963, Samuel Kirk launched the field in an address at a meeting of parents held in Chicago. The Learning Disabilities Association of America (LDA), at the time known as the Association for Children with Learning Disabilities (ACLD)—the parent organization specifically concerned with the problems of children with learning disabilities—was formed during this same time. The early work of Goldstein, Strauss, and Werner and the later work of Kephart, Cruickshank, and Kirk are considered to be responsible for the evolution of learning disabilities as a distinct field. Two books that served as guides for teachers of special education in the 1960s were Kephart's *The Slow Learner in the Classroom* (1960) and Cruickshank et al. *A Teaching Method for Brain-Injured and Hyperactive Children* (1961). The development of the *Illinois Test of Psycholinguistic Abilities* (Kirk & McCarthy, 1961) must also be considered to have had a major impact on the field of learning disabilities.

The 1960s also witnessed many developments in the area of childhood behavioral and emotional problems (Kauffman, 1993). Nicholas Hobbs and his associates began their ecologically based Project Re-ED in Tennessee and North Carolina in 1961. The concept of an engineered classroom was introduced by Frank Hewett in his book *The Emotionally Disturbed Child in the Classroom* (1968).

Although the field of special education was generally in a controlled, euphoric state with regard to its own status during the latter part of the sixties, certain key questions were beginning to be asked. In 1968, Lloyd Dunn published an article challenging the efficacy of placing children in self-contained special education classes. Other concerned people were becoming alarmed at the number of children from minority and lower socioeconomic groups who were placed in special classes. Professionals in the area of mental retardation were similarly shocked at the inordinate number of individuals who were mildly retarded residing in institutions.

A detectable change of attitude seemed to be occurring in professional circles. While many people maintained their enthusiasm into the seventies, other dedicated individuals were starting to reappraise various aspects of special education. This ambiance of reexamination has endured to this day and is evidenced in many issues related to the needs of exceptional populations.

Today it is wishful thinking to conclude that we have the available techniques to change children as we'd like, regardless of the disabilities they have. Although advances have been made, there is still a long way to go. For example, in dealing with children with severe disabilities, the work of Lovaas and his colleagues has been remarkably effective. Using behavior modification techniques, he and his coworkers have vastly improved the condition of numerous children who are autistic, schizophrenic, and retarded. But are his techniques always successful? In every child he's worked with, his research reports document how he has produced some improvement. In some cases, the improvement has been extreme—the child who was formerly psychotic now appears very normal (Lovaas, 1982). In other cases the improvement has been painfully slow. The case of Jose highlights the reality that progress may come in small increments and much time may be needed to reach important goals.

Jose was 4 years old at the start of treatment. His extreme negativism was reflected in tantrums, biting, and extreme stubborn-
ness. He did not play with peers. He did not respond to his name
or any commands. He had no speech, could not dress himself, was
not toilet-trained, nor did he have any other self-help behaviors.
Appropriate play was essentially absent. He was found to be
untestable on intelligence tests. He had a social quotient of 59. In
short, he was extremely behaviorally retarded.

He was treated as an inpatient at the UCLA Neuropsychiatric
Institute for one year. His mother was given some limited training
in how to continue therapy with him as described above. His treatment was primarily designed to overcome his negativism and to
build some basic language skills. The latter included simple labeling, color discrimination, response to simple commands, and form
discriminations. Some work was also done on the reinforcement of
spontaneous babbling.

We probably made slower progress with Jose than with any of
the other children. At discharge, his gains in language were minimal. He would obey some commands; his vocabulary included a
number of common nouns, some names, and a few verbs. He
would use these words to label objects or express a desire for
something, but never for commenting. He would attempt to imitate
new words spontaneously on occasion. His greatest improvements
were social. His social quotient of 74 reflected increases in smiling,
laughing, and self-help skills. He was partially toilet trained. He
was testable on the Stanford Binet Intelligence Scale (IQ–47).

At present, Jose uses only a few words spontaneously (e.g.,
"car," "go to school," etc.), and what he has retained of his speech
training is negligible. He can take care of himself at dinner, and is
fully toilet trained. His greatest gains at home have been in his play,
which has become elaborate and creative, enabling him to entertain
himself (Lovaas, Koegel, Simmons, & Long, 1973, p. 158).

Litigative and Legislative Impact

Various controversial issues raised in the 1960s continued to be the
concern of professionals during the 1970s. Issues such as intelligence
testing, labeling, placement, prevention, fundamental rights, mainstreaming, and deinstitutionalization came under the discussion of
competent, intelligent individuals who actively support their own position in these controversies. Consequently, we found ourselves in an era
when professionals in the field were reevaluating their efforts as well
as the efforts of others. For example, programs favoring perceptual-
motor and process training to improve academic performance (e.g.,
reading) were called into question because there were a paucity of
sound studies that validate the effectiveness of such programs to

achieve these ends. In order to expedite resolution of these and other questions, we needed to develop rigorous research projects, encourage replication of previous research, and perhaps most importantly, cultivate creative thinking.

Growth and change have often been accomplished primarily through legal and legislative action. Actually, our national attitude has been reflected by the actions of each branch of our government. Events such as Hoover's White House Conference, Kennedy's activism, and Johnson's War on Poverty definitely exemplify the executive branch's efforts. Before 1970, legislative accomplishments established laws mandating compulsory education, rehabilitative services, and variable services for persons with disabilities. Only recently, however, has the judicial branch become an active, integral part of the treatment of persons with special needs.

During the early 1970s, four major legal decisions helped shape the current state of special education services. The right to education for individuals who are mentally retarded, regardless of the degree of impairment, was guaranteed in 1972 as part of a consent decree in a case filed by the Pennsylvania Association for Retarded Children (PARC) (*PARC v. Commonwealth of Pennsylvania*). Also in that year, the same right was extended to all exceptional children (*Mills v. Board of Education of the District of Columbia*). In 1971 the right to treatment for institutionalized persons with mental retardation was argued in an Alabama court of law (*Wyatt v. Stickney*). And in 1970 the issue of misplacement was contested in a California suit (*Diana v. State Board of Education*). Although settled out of court, this legal battle was responsible for issuing mandates regarding placement that were to be followed in the future. Even though these and other court cases have had an impact on special education services, the mandates issued in the rulings have not always been followed because of the difficulty in implementing them.

Significant legislative events also occurred during the 1970s that provided a legal basis for many services to individuals with disabilities. Late in 1973, President Nixon signed into law, after two previous vetoes, the revised amendments to the Vocational Rehabilitation Act (PL 93–112). Section 504 of this law has been considered the "Bill of Rights for the Disabled."

In November of 1975, President Ford signed into law the Education for All Handicapped Children Act (EHA) (PL 94–142), which remains to this day one of the landmark events in the history of the treatment of persons with disabilities. As the culmination of years of previous legislative and legal activity, this Act, which has no expiration date, authorized substantial increases in aid to special education through federal funding to states. Unfortunately, the federal government never funded the law to the extent originally envisioned, thus creating some debate about whether it is prudent to continue to authorize legislation that has mandates the federal government cannot meet.

The funding issue aside, the Act guaranteed the legal rights of exceptional students related to education. Never before has federal legislative action had the singular impact of PL 94–142 on special education. The law provided regulations that addressed six major principles related to practice: zero reject (i.e., all students are to benefit); testing, classification, and placement; individualized and appropriate education; least restrictive appropriate educational placement; procedural due process; and parent participation and shared decision making (Turnbull, 1993).

Public Law 94-142 has been amended three times (1983, 1986, 1990) since its original passage. Table 15.1 provides a summary of these amendments and the public law number associated with each amendment. Each time the law has been reauthorized and amended, new pieces have been added. Certain changes have had a significant impact on the delivery of services and are discussed below.

The 1983 amendments (PL 98-199) initiated what can be called the formalized transition movement. This action resulted from the efforts of the Office of Special Education and Rehabilitative Services to focus attention on what happens to students after they leave formal schooling. Funding was targeted to develop model transition programs throughout the country. Many of the funded programs have influenced the way transition services are implemented nationally.

In 1986, PL 99–457 was signed into law. This legislation was designed to address certain shortcomings of the original law and its regulations. One of the most important components of these amendments was the mandate to provide services to children with disabilities (ages 3 to 5 years) and the creation of incentives to the states through early intervention grant programs to provide services to infants and toddlers (birth through 2 years of age).

The early intervention component focused on not only young children with disabilities but their families as well. The law required the development of an Individual Family Service Plan (IFSP) similar in concept to the Individual Education Plan (IEP) and focused on the family's strengths and needs relating to the enhancement of the child's development. Training for parents of children with disabilities was also a priority. PL 99–457 also mandated interagency agreements for providing service to any of those individuals addressed under the law.

The 1990 amendments (PL 101-476) created more change. The name of the law became the "Individuals with Disabilities Education Act" (IDEA) to reflect a sensitivity to preferred terminology. As Table 15.1 shows, two new categories of disability were added. In addition, certain aspects of transition were further specified.

Table 15.1
Chronology of PL 94–142

Year	Activity	Public Law No.	Key Features
1975	Enactment of original law	94–142	• Free appropriate public education • Least restrictive environment • Nondiscriminatory evaluation • Individualized education program • Procedural safeguards • Parental participation
1983	Amendments	98–199	• Funding for transition initiatives
1986	Amendments	99–457	• Services mandated for ages 3–5 • Financial incentives for the development of infant and toddler programs
1990	Amendments	101–476	• Change in name of law • Language change—use of term *disability* in place of *handicap* • Two new categories: autism and traumatic brain injury • Statement of transition services requires in IEP for students no later than age 16 • States could be sued

Although both PL 94–142 and its amendments have collectively brought about drastic changes in the education of persons with disabilities, many legal, philosophical, procedural, and practical issues remain problematic. There is serious interest to reduce the administrative complexities required by the law and to give back to the states more responsibility for implementation of the law. The manner in which we answer the questions surrounding these issues will determine the nature and quality of services for persons with disabilities in the future.

Another extremely significant piece of legislation enacted in 1990 was the Americans with Disability Act (ADA) (PL 101-336). It has been referred to as the most important action related to civil rights since the Civil Rights Act of 1964 (Hardman, Drew, & Egan, 1996). Its intent is to provide "clear, strong, consistent, and enforceable standards prohibiting discrimination against individuals with disabilities, without respect to their age, nature of disability, or extent of disability" (Turnbull, 1993, p. 23). As an outcome of these protections, the law affords individuals opportunities to participate and strive for quality of life.

The law applies to both public and private settings and affects employment, public services, transportation, public accommodations (e.g., restaurants, shopping centers), and telecommunications. Even though there is some discussion about whether the law has had as much of an impact on the lives of persons with disabilities as was intended, it nevertheless has served notice that the disabled population is entitled to the same rights and opportunities as anyone else.

As discussed in Chapter 1, the movement to empower individuals to be in control of their lives has been mirrored by the movement to have persons with disabilities included as contributing members of school and/or community. Although many segregating practices (e.g., self-contained classes, sheltered employment) remain, an inclusionary attitude is taking hold in the United States. Although strong debate wages on the topic of "full inclusion," the idea of having people with disabilities learning, working, and living alongside of their nondisabled peers is attractive and necessary. However, it is important to reiterate that mere physical placement is not equivalent to the intent of being included that suggests a sense of belonging and acceptance.

THOUGHTS ABOUT TOMORROW

Unquestionably, we live in times characterized by terms such as *austerity, budget cuts, fiscal restraint*—terms that can be threatening to people who require various social services. We can also be intimidated by the pace of change associated with living in a time of paradigmatic shift as we enter into the information age. Times like these require that we all take action, as suggested in the following admonition directed toward professionals working in the area of mental retardation.

> We can influence the future in many ways by what we do or, at the very least, try to do today. We can no longer remain passive observers, but must become active participants in the problems and needs of persons who are mentally retarded. Our attention should focus not only on individuals with retardation but also on the public, because the key to the future rests there. Without positive public sentiment toward those who are mentally retarded, which must be nurtured by what happens today and reflected in financial support for our efforts, the outlook for this group is not

favorable. Our highest priorities should be social acceptance of people who are mentally retarded, active participation on the behalf of all advocates, and the continued search for new knowledge (Beirne-Smith, Patton, & Ittenbach, 1994, p. 555).

Without doubt we also live in times when the *possibilities* for helping exceptional individuals reach their fullest potential are more exciting than ever. Advances in medicine, multimedia, and assistive technology are revolutionizing our thinking about how to provide services. Reconstructive surgery, implants, prostheses, and microcomputer programs for controlling devices that allow individuals with disabilities to communicate or move more effectively are becoming more readily available each year.

We tend to think of technology as something very cold, perhaps even frightening. But the application of technology to the solution of everyday problems of individuals with disabilities typically calls forth very warm and touching human responses. Consider, for example, the case of Lois, a 50-year-old woman who is severely physically disabled by cerebral palsy. She had never been able to communicate with anyone through words until Howard F. Batie demonstrated his computerized communication system. What was her first response when she could finally send a verbal message to another human being? "Thanks," repeated over and over. And what was her first connected sentence in 50 years, addressed to her mother? "Dear Mother: Thank you for all the patient love I have received all my life" (Myers, 1982, p. 39).

The technological revolution in this information age is well under way and gaining speed. In school settings, teachers of students with disabilities will need to be armed with knowledge of instructional technology and the technological advances most pertinent to the types of children they teach. In the workplace, technological competence is expected. In the community, common everyday activities are requiring technological proficiency as well.

FINAL THOUGHTS

To understand the history of services to exceptional individuals, we must ultimately look behind the laws, the lawsuits, and the programs. We must realize that the advances made are indices of the prevailing social climate. Unless an acceptable social atmosphere exists to support the recent legal and legislative actions, these achievements will only masquerade as being effective and will eventually collapse under the pressure of criticism. Without the proper social attitude, court decisions and legislation can become little more than political displays.

Over a century and a half ago, the field of special education emerged through the early efforts of a few devoted individuals. Since that time, the people of the United States have witnessed changes in their attitude toward exceptionality. Many issues that were debated in the past continue to be argued today. We can see this recycling phenomenon in issues such as individualized instruction, mainstreaming/inclusion, and various teaching philosophies. Commensurate with the changes in national attitude and the reemergence of certain issues over time, the concept of exceptionality has changed too. The attitude of society emphasizes the specific concerns predicated by the various social dynamics of a given time period.

Through the perspective of historical study, we can improve our understanding of how we got where we are today to plan accordingly for the future. Having a perspective on the development of a field, we might possibly avoid some of the pitfalls of the past.

✦ *PONDER THESE*

1. *Should individual teachers be held legally responsible when their students fail to learn?*

2. *Technological advances make it possible for us to do a better job of early detection and prevention of handicapping conditions. What handicapping conditions should we be most concerned about reducing or preventing? Is prevention always justified? For example, would we be justified in not allowing parents whose babies carry a very high risk of defects to have children? Can abortion of handicapped fetuses be justified?*

3. *Many technological advances find their way into our everyday lives, but our society does not seem to have enough money to provide them for persons with disabilities. For example, many grocery stores now have computers that read the prices on items by laser scanner and tell you the price of the item, the total due, and the amount of your change using highly realistic voice synthesizers. But voice synthesizers of this quality are seldom available for people with disabilities who could use them for communication. How can our society make sure that its best technology is accessible to its citizens with disabilities?*

4. *As a final word, it seems appropriate for the reader to ponder the following prophetic words of the National Advisory Committee on the Disabled (1976) in their annual report:*

> *The crucial central issue goes far beyond optimum pedagogical practices or research or funding or the mechanics of moving youngsters into different settings. The overriding issue in this and all other provisions affecting the disabled is the matter of attitudes.*
>
> *The progress of the past 200 years, and the last ten in particular, will in fact remain essentially meaningless until disabled people win their appropriate place not just in "regular" classrooms but in the "regular society," there to be judged not on the basis of their disabilities but on the basis of their worth as human beings (p. 3).*

References

Beirne-Smith, M., Patton, J. R., & Ittenbach, R. (1994). *Mental retardation* (4th ed.). Englewood Cliffs, NJ: Merrill/Prentice Hall.

Cruickshank, W., Bentzen, F., Ratzburg, F., & Tannhauser, M. (1961). *A teaching method for brain-injured and hyperactive children.* Syracuse, NY: Syracuse University Press.

Galton, F. (1969). *Hereditary genius.* London: Macmillan.

Goldstein, K. (1942). *After-effect of brain injuries in war.* New York: Grune & Stratton.

Hallahan, D. P., & Kauffman, J. M. (1991). *Exceptional children: Introduction to special education* (4th ed.). Englewood Cliffs, NJ: Merrill/Prentice-Hall.

Hardman, M. L., Drew, C. J., & Egan, M. W. (1996). *Human exceptionality: Society, school, and family* (5th ed.). Boston: Allyn & Bacon.

Hewett, F. (1968). *The emotionally disturbed child in the classroom.* Boston: Allyn & Bacon.

Hobbs, N. (1966). Helping the disturbed child: Psychological and ecological strategies. *American Psychologist, 21,* 1105–1115.

Hunter, R., & Macalpine, I. (Eds.). (1963). *Three hundred years of psychiatry, 1535–1860: A history in selected English texts.* London: Oxford University Press.

Kanner, L. (1964). *A history of the care and study of the mentally retarded.* Springfield, IL: Charles C. Thomas.

Kauffman, J. M. (1993) *Characteristics of children's behavior disorders* (4th ed.). Englewood Cliffs, NJ: Merrill/Prentice Hall.

Kephart, N. (1960). *The slow learner in the classroom.* Columbus, OH: Charles E. Merrill.

Kirk, S., & McCarthy, J. (1961). The Illinois Test of Psycholinguistic Abilities— An approach to differential diagnosis. *American Journal of Mental Deficiency, 66,* 399–412.

L'Abate, L., & Curtis, L. T. (1975). *Teaching the exceptional child.* Philadelphia: Saunders.

Lovaas, O. I. (1982, September). *An overview of the Young Autism Project.* Paper presented at the annual convention of the American Psychological Association, Washington, DC.

Lovaas, O. I., Koegel, R. L., Simmons, J. O., & Long, J. S. (1973). Some generalization and follow-up measures on autistic children in behavior therapy. *Journal of Applied Behavior Analysis, 6,* 131–165.

Myers, W. (1982). Personal computers aid the disabled. *IEEE Micro, 2*(1), 26–40. National Advisory Committee on the Handicapped. (1976). *Annual report.* Washington, DC: U.S. Office of Education.

Parkinson, J. (1963). Observations on the excessive indulgence of children, particularly intended to show its injurious effects on their health, and the difficulties it occasions in their treatment during sickness. London: Symonds et al., 1807. In R. Hunter & I. Macalpine (Eds.), *Three hundred years of psychiatry, 1535–1860.* London: Oxford University Press.

Ray, I. (1852). On the best methods of saving our hospitals for the insane from the odium and scandal to which such institutions are liable, and maintaining their place in the popular estimation; including the consideration of the question, how far is the community to be allowed access to such hospitals? Paper presented at a meeting of the Association of Medical Superintendents of American Institutions for the Insane, New York, May 18, 1852. (Reprinted in *American Journal of Insanity, 9,* 36–65.)

Seguin, E. (1866). *Idiocy and its treatment by the physiological method.* New York: Lea & Blanchard.

Smith, J. D. (1985). *Minds made feeble: The myth and legacy of the Kallikaks.* Rockville, MD: Aspen.

Strauss, A., & Lehtinen, L. (1947). *Psychopathology and education of the brain-injured child.* New York: Grune & Stratton.

Thomas, A., Chess, S., & Birch, H. G. (1968). *Temperament and behavior disorders in children.* New York: New York University.

Turnbull, H. R. (1993). *Free appropriate public education: The law and children with disabilities* (4th ed.). Denver: Love.

Watson, J. B. (1930). *Behaviorism* (rev. ed.). Chicago: University of Chicago Press.

Index

cultural *Pluralistic Assessment*), 251
Special education. *See also* Exceptionality
early development of, 308–315
in early twentieth century, 313–315
in eighteenth century, 309–310, 312
future trends in, 323–324
history of, 303–323
legislation on, 14–18, 319–323
in mid-twentieth century, 315–319
in nineteenth century, 310–313
vignettes on, 303–305
Specialized audiometric tests, 183
Speech audiometry, 183
Speech flow disorders, 203–204
Speech impairment, 202–204. *See also* Communication disorders
Speech/language intervention, 207
Speech-language therapists, 206–207
Speechreading, 184, 188
Spina bifida, 143–144
Stapedial reflex testing, 183
State Implementation Grant Program, 273
Stereotyping, 11
Strabismus, 167
Stuttering, 203–204, 208
Supported employment, 12
Supported living, 12
Surface language, 249
Symptomatic epilepsy, 147
System of Multicultural Pluralistic Assessment (SOMPA), 251

TASH (Association for Persons with Severe Handicaps), 115

TBI (traumatic brain injury), 136, 137–140
TDDs (telecommunication devices for the deaf), 188
Teaching Method for Brain-Injured and Hyperactive Children, A (Cruickshank), 318
Technology, 122, 152–153, 169, 188, 324
Telecommunication devices for the deaf (TDDs), 188
Temperament and Behavior Disorders in Children (Thomas, Chess, Birch), 306
Testing
and cultural diversity, 248–251
of hearing impairments, 182–183
Timothy W. v. Rochester (NH) Public Schools, 114
Total communication, 185
Trace Research and Development Center, University of Wisconsin/Madison, 209
Transitional bilingual programs, 252
Transition services, 127, 290–292, 293
Transportation, 121–122
Traumatic brain injury (TBI), 136, 137–140, 141, 154
Tympanometry, 183

UCLA/LAUSD Microcomputer Project, 279
University of Illinois at Chicago Circle, 40
University of Kansas, 40, 44
University of Minnesota, 40
University of Virginia, 40
University of Wisconsin/Madison, 209

Vertical enrichment, 229
Visual acuity, 163–164
Visual impairments
characteristics of people with, 167–169
definition of, 162–165
educational concerns and, 169–171, 172
etiology of, 165–167
everyday living concerns and, 171
information/resources on, 173
placement considerations for, 170–171
prevalence of, 9, 164
suggestions for working with persons with, 171–172
types of, 166–167
vignettes on, 159–162
Visual periphery, 163–164
Vocational Act Amendments of 1992 (PL 102-569), 14
Vocational Rehabilitation Act, Section 504 (PL 93-112), 14, 16–17, 77, 78, 320
Voice disorders, 202–203

Weschler Intelligence Scale for Children, 249
Wheelchair-bound persons, 154. *See also* Physical and health impairments
Wild Boy of Aveyron, 96–97, 309–310
Wild Boy of Aveyron, The, 96
Wyatt v. Stickney, 114, 320